Absolute Beginner's Guide to C,
2nd Edition

Absolute Beginner's Guide to C, 2nd Edition

Greg Perry

SAMS
PUBLISHING

A Division of Prentice Hall Computer Publishing
201 West 103rd Street, Indianapolis, Indiana 46290

For Chris Fellers: Your help with my first book led to more than 25 more.
Thanks for the encouragement when I needed it.

Trademarks

Publisher
Richard K. Swadley

Associate Publisher
Jordan Gold

Acquisitions Manager
Stacy Hiquet

Managing Editor
Cindy Morrow

Acquisitions Editor
Stacy Hiquet

Development Editor
Dean Miller

Production Editor
Mary Inderstrodt

Copy Editor
Matt Usher

**Editorial and Graphics
Coordinator**
Bill Whitmer

Editorial Assistants
Carol Ackerman
Sharon Cox
Lynette Quinn

Technical Reviewer
Gary Farrar

Marketing Manager
Gregg Bushyeager

Cover Designer
Tim Amrhein

Inside Illustrator
Gary Varvel

**Director of Production and
Manufacturing**
Jeff Valler

Imprint Manager
Juli Cook

Manufacturing Coordinator
Paul Gilchrist

Book Designer
Michele Laseau

Production Analyst
Mary Beth Wakefield

Proofreading Coordinator
Joelynn Gifford

Indexing Coordinator
Johnna Van Hoose

Graphics Image Specialists
Tim Montgomery
Dennis Sheehan
Sue VandeWalle

Production
Juli Cook
Terri Edwards
Rich Evers
Greg Kemp
Jamie Milazzo
Shelly Palma
Chad Poore
Casey Price
Ryan Rader
Kris Simmons
Tonya R. Simpson
Ann Sippel
S.A. Springer
Bobbi Sutterfield
Dennis Wesner

Overview

Contents

Part 5 Form Follows Functions

Acknowledgments

My thanks go to all my friends at Sams Publishing. Most writers would refer to them as *editors;* to me they are *friends.* The acquisitions editor for the majority of my books, Stacy Hiquet, specializes in kindness and patience. Mary Inderstrodt and Matt Usher turn my questionable work into award-winning copy. Dean Miller and Gary Farrar helped developed this manuscript into something for everyone, and they managed to maintain accuracy where I failed miserably. Last but not least, Richard Swadley, the big chief who gives all the grief, deserves the final credit for the success of every book from Sams. Richard's initial direction for every book seems to hit the bull's-eye, and he knows exactly what the audience needs and wants.

I want all my readers to understand this: The people at Sams Publishing care about you most of all. The things they do result from their concern for your knowledge and enjoyment.

On a more personal note, my beautiful bride Jayne, my proud parents Glen and Bettye Perry, and my friends, who wonder how I find the time to write, all deserve credit for supporting my need to write.

About the Author

Greg Perry is a speaker and writer in both the programming and applications sides of computing. He is known for bringing programming topics down to the beginner's level. Perry has been a programmer and trainer for the past 16 years. He received his first degree in computer science, and then he received a Master's degree in corporate finance. Besides writing, he consults and lectures across the country, including at the acclaimed Software Development programming conferences. Perry is the author of more than 25 other computer books, including *Absolute Beginner's Guide to Programming, Turbo C++ Programming 101, Moving from C to C++, QBasic Programming 101, Teach Yourself Object-Oriented Programming with Turbo C++,* and *Teach Yourself Object-Oriented Programming with Visual C++* (all published by Sams Publishing). In addition, he has published articles in several publications such as *Software Development, Access Advisor, PC World, Data Training,* and *Inside First Publisher.* In his spare time, he gives lectures on traveling in Italy, his second-favorite place to be.

Introduction

Are you tired of seeing your friends get C programming jobs while you're left out in the cold? Would you like to learn C but just don't have the energy? Is your old, worn-out computer in need of a hot programming language to spice up its circuits? This book is just what the doctor ordered!

Absolute Beginner's Guide to C breaks the commonality of computer books by talking to you at your level without talking down to you. This book is like your best friend sitting next to you teaching C. *Absolute Beginner's Guide to C* attempts to *express* without *impressing*. It talks to you in plain language, not in "computerese." The short chapters, line drawings, and occasionally humorous straight talk guide you through the maze of C programming faster, friendlier, and easier than any other book available today.

Who's This Book For?

This is a beginner's book. If you have never programmed before, this book is for you. No knowledge of any programming concept is assumed. If you can't even spell C, you can learn to program in C with this book.

The phrase *absolute beginner* has different meanings at different times. Maybe you've tried to learn C before but gave up. Many books and classes make C much more technical than it is. You might have programmed in other languages but are a beginner in C. If so, read on, o faithful one, because in 32 quick chapters, you'll know C.

What Makes This Book Different?

This book doesn't cloud issues with internal technical stuff that beginners in C don't need. The author (me) is of the firm belief that introductory principles have to be taught well and slowly. Once you tackle the basics, the "harder" parts never seem hard. This book teaches you the real C that you need to get started.

C can be an extremely cryptic and difficult language. Many people try to learn C more than once. The problem is simply this: Any subject, whether it be brain surgery, mail sorting, or C programming, is easy if it's explained properly. Nobody can teach you anything, because you have to teach yourself; but if the instructor, book, or video doing the teaching doesn't make the subject simple and *fun,* you won't *want* to learn the subject.

I challenge you to find a more straightforward approach to C than is offered in *Absolute Beginner's Guide to C.* If you can, call me because I'd like to read it. (You thought maybe I'd offer you your money back?) Seriously, I've tried to provide you with a different kind of help from that which you find in most other places.

The biggest advantage that this book offers is that the author (still me) really *likes* to write C programs and likes to teach C even more. I believe that you will learn to like C, too.

This Book's Design Elements

Like many computer books, this book contains lots of helpful hints, tips, warnings, and so on. You will run across many *icons* (little pictures) that bring these specific items to your attention. A glance at the icon gives you an idea of the purpose of the text next to the icon. Here are descriptions of this book's icons:

> **WARNING**
>
> This icon points out potential problems you could face with the particular topic being discussed. Often the icon indicates a warning you should heed, or it provides a way to fix a problem that can occur.

Clue: Many of this book's hints and clues (and there are lots of them) are highlighted by this icon. When a really neat feature or code trick coincides with the topic you're reading about, this icon pinpoints just what you can do to take advantage of the added bonus.

> **NOTE**
>
> Throughout the C language, certain subjects provide a deeper level of understanding than others. This icon tells you about something you might not have thought about before, such as a new use for the topic being discussed.

> **SKIP THIS, IT'S TECHNICAL**
>
> If you don't want anything more than the beginning essentials of C, don't read the material in this box. Actually, you probably will enjoy this material, but you can safely skip it without losing your understanding of the chapter.

Occasionally you will see a **Fun Fact** in the margin. These Fun Facts convey interesting information about computers, programming, and the C language.

Each chapter ends by reviewing the key points you should remember from that chapter. The items under the **Rewards** and **Pitfalls** headings list things you should and shouldn't do. One of the key features that ties everything together is the **In Review** section. This chapter summary states the chapter's primary goal, lists a code example that highlights the concepts taught, and provides a code analysis that offers an explanation of that code example. You'll find these chapter summaries, which begin in Chapter 2, to be a welcome wrap-up of the chapter's main points.

This book uses the following typographic conventions:

- Code lines, variables, and any text you see on-screen appears in `monospace`.
- Placeholders on format lines appear in *`italic monospace`*.
- Parts of program output that the user typed appear in **`bold monospace`**.
- New terms appear in *italic*.
- Optional parameters in syntax explanations are enclosed in flat brackets ([ ]). You do *not* type the brackets when you include these parameters.

How Can I Have Fun with C?

Appendix B contains a complete, working Blackjack program. The program was kept as short as possible without sacrificing readable code and game-playing functionality. The game also had to be kept generic in order to work on all C compilers. Therefore, you won't find fancy graphics, but once you learn C, you'll easily be able to access your compiler's specific graphics, sound, and data-entry routines to improve the program.

The program uses as much of this book's contents as possible. Almost every topic taught in this book appears in the Blackjack game. Too many books offer nothing more than snippets of code. The Blackjack game gives you the chance to see the "big picture." As you progress through this book, you'll understand more and more of the game.

What Do I Do Now?

Turn the page and learn the C language.

Contents

Part 1

First Steps with C

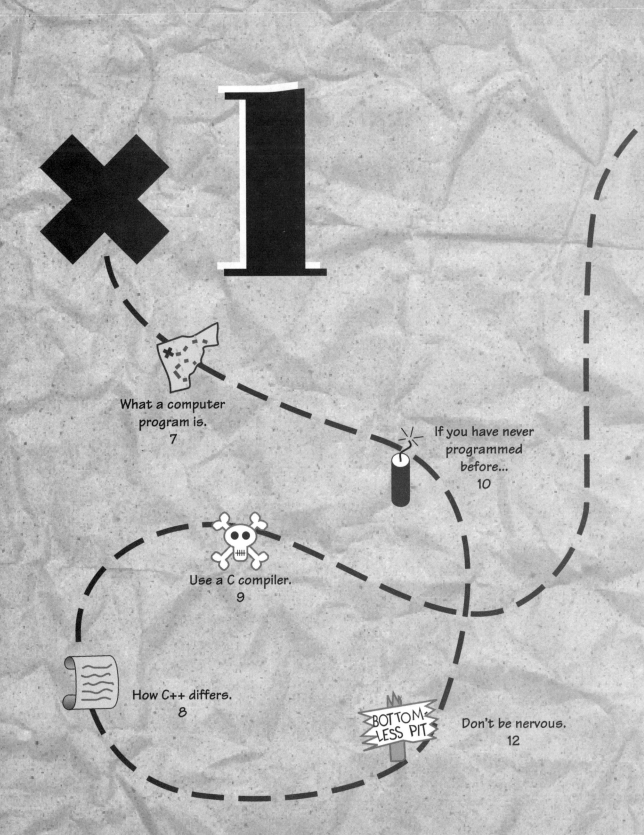

1

What a computer
program is.
7

If you have never
programmed
before...
10

Use a C compiler.
9

How C++ differs.
8

BOTTOM-
LESS PIT

Don't be nervous.
12

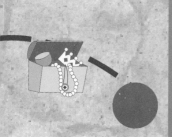

What Is C Programming?

Rewarding and Fun

Fun Fact

The Bell Labs developed the C language.

Although some people consider C to be difficult to learn and use, you'll soon see that they are wrong. C is touted as being a cryptic programming language, and it can be; but a well-written C program is just as easy to follow as a program written in any other programming language. The demand for C programmers today is high, and there is no end in sight to that demand.

If you've never written a program in your life, this chapter begins at the beginning, teaching you introductory programming concepts, explaining what a program is, and providing a short history of the C language. Get ready to be excited! C is a programming language rich in its capabilities.

What Is a Program?

A computer isn't smart. On your worst days, you are light-years ahead of your computer in intelligence. The computer's only advantage is that it obeys your instructions. Your computer will sit for days, processing the data you supply, without getting bored and without wanting overtime pay.

The computer can't decide what to do on its own. Computers can't think for themselves so *programmers* (people who tell computers what to do) must give computers extremely detailed instructions. Without instructions, a computer is useless. A computer can no more process your payroll without detailed instructions than an automobile can start by itself and drive around the block by itself. The collection of detailed instructions that you supply when you want your computer to perform a specific task is known as a *program*.

NOTE

Word processors, computer payroll systems, computer games, and electronic spreadsheets are nothing more than computer programs. Without such programs, the computer would just sit there, not knowing what to do next. A word processing program contains a list of detailed instructions, written in a computer language such as C, that tells the computer exactly how to be a word processor. When you program, you are telling the computer to follow the instructions in the program you have supplied.

There are thousands of programs you can buy for your computer, but when a business wants a computer to perform a specific task, that business hires programmers to write programs that follow the specifications needed by the business. You can make your computer do many things, but you might not be able to find a program that does exactly what you want. This book rescues you from that dilemma. After you learn C, you will be able to write programs that contain instructions that tell the computer how to behave.

Clue: A computer program tells your computer how to do what you want. Just as a chef needs a recipe to make a dish, a program needs instructions to produce results. (See Figure 1.1.) A recipe is nothing more than a set of detailed instructions that, if properly written, describes the proper sequence and contents of the steps needed to prepare a certain dish. That's exactly what a computer program is to your computer.

Programs produce *output* when you *run* or *execute* them. The prepared dish is a recipe's output, and the payroll or word processor is the output produced by a running program.

FIGURE 1.1.
Just as a chef needs a recipe to cook, your computer needs a program to know what to do next.

What You Need to Write C Programs

Before you can write and execute a C program on your computer, you need a *C compiler*. A C compiler takes the C program you write and *compiles* it (which is a technical term for making the program computer-readable), enabling you to run the compiled program when you're ready to look at the results. Today's C compilers are much more advanced than the language compilers of a few years ago. They offer full-screen editing, pull-down menus, and online help to provide more assistance to the beginning programmer.

It is hard to find a C compiler these days. Most of the time, C compilers come *bundled* (techie-speak for *included with*) an advanced version of C, known as *C++*. Therefore, when you shop for a C compiler, you will almost always find a C and a C++ compiler combined in the same box. Buy the combined C++/C package, you will have C now and C++ when you're ready to learn it.

> **NOTE**
> The last chapter of this book briefly describes how C++ differs from and improves upon C.

The most popular C compilers today are *Turbo C++* and *Borland C++*, both made by Borland International, Inc. *Borland C++* is basically Turbo C++ along with many additional programs that help advanced C and C++ programmers.

Microsoft Corporation offers a powerful version of C++ and C called *Visual C++*. As with Borland C++, Visual C++ provides you with advanced DOS, Windows, and Windows NT programming. You can write Windows programs with Turbo C++ as well, but Turbo C++ does not include as many add-on Windows programming tools as Borland C++ and Visual C++.

By the way, it is *very* difficult to write Windows programs, especially for people who are new to programming. Don't be in a hurry to bite off more than you can chew. First learn to write simple DOS-based C programs (and this book is all you need for that!) and then you can gradually migrate over to the more difficult areas of C++ and Windows programming.

There are other C compiler vendors on the market, but Borland and Microsoft lead the pack in sheer numbers of C programming customers.

WARNING

The C program you write is called *source code*. A compiler takes C source code and translates that code into *machine language*. Computers are made up of nothing more than thousands of electrical switches that are either *on* or *off*. Therefore, computers must ultimately be given instructions in *binary*. The prefix *bi* means *two,* and the two states of electricity are called *binary states*. It's much easier to use a C compiler to convert your C programs into 1s and 0s that represent internal on and off switch settings than for you to do it yourself.

The Programming Process

Most people follow these basic steps when writing a program:

1. Decide exactly what the program is to do.

2. Use an *editor* to write and save your programming language instructions. An editor is a lot like a word processor (although not usually as fancy) that lets you create and edit text. All the popular C compilers include an integrated editor along with the programming language compiler. All C program filenames end in the .C file extension.

3. Compile the program.

4. Check for program errors. If there are any, fix them and go back to step 3.

5. Execute the program.

NOTE

An error in a computer program is called a *bug*. Getting rid of errors is called *debugging* a program.

Today's C compilers, such as Turbo C++, let you perform these five steps easily, all from within the same environment. For instance, if you have Turbo C++, you can use Turbo C++'s editor, compile your program, view any errors, fix the errors, run the program, and look at the results, all from within the same screen and using a uniform set of menus.

SKIP THIS, IT'S TECHNICAL

If you have never programmed before, this all might seem confusing. Relax. Most of today's C compilers come with a handy tutorial you can use to learn the basics of the compiler's editor and compiling commands.

In a nutshell, most C compilers require only this of you when you write C programs: Start the compiler, type your program, and then select **R**un from the menu. Turbo C++ includes the shortcut keystroke Alt+R (press and hold the Alt key, press the R key, and then let up on both) followed by Enter to compile and run your program. The compiler takes care of compiling and executing the program and informing you of any errors.

Clue: Many times, your C compiler can find bugs in your programs. If you spell a command incorrectly, for instance, your C compiler informs you when you compile the program.

Just in case you still don't fully understand the need for a compiler, your source code is like the raw materials that your computer needs. The compiler is like a machine that converts those raw materials to a final product, a compiled program, that the computer can understand.

Using C

Fun Fact

In 1983, ANSI (American National Standards Institute) created the X3J11 committee to set a standard version of C. This became known as ANSI C.

C is one of the most popular programming languages in use today. Because of the many possible versions of C, a committee known as the *ANSI* committee developed a set of rules (known as *ANSI C*) for all versions of C. As long as you run programs using an ANSI C compiler, you can be assured that you can compile your C programs on almost any computer that has an ANSI C compiler. By choosing the appropriate setting, you can make most compilers, including Borland's and Microsoft's, ANSI C compatible. (See your compiler manual for details.)

Clue: As soon as you compile a C program, you can run the compiled program on any computer that is compatible with yours, whether or not the computer has an ANSI C compiler.

C is more efficient than most programming languages. It is also a relatively small programming language. In other words, you don't have to learn many *commands* in C. Throughout this book, you will learn about C commands and other elements of the C language, such as operators, functions, and preprocessor directives.

> **WARNING**
>
> Put on your thinking cap and set your phaser on C because the next chapter takes you on a journey through your first C program.

Rewards

✖ Get a C compiler and install it on your computer. Most compilers come with a quick tutorial that helps you load the compiler onto your computer's hard disk.

✖ Learn the C programming language. This book takes care of that! As you learn more about C, try to stay with ANSI C commands instead of using compiler-specific C functions that might not be available in other compilers you use later.

Pitfalls

✖ Don't be nervous, because C programs can be easy to write. C compilers often have many more features than you will ever have to learn.

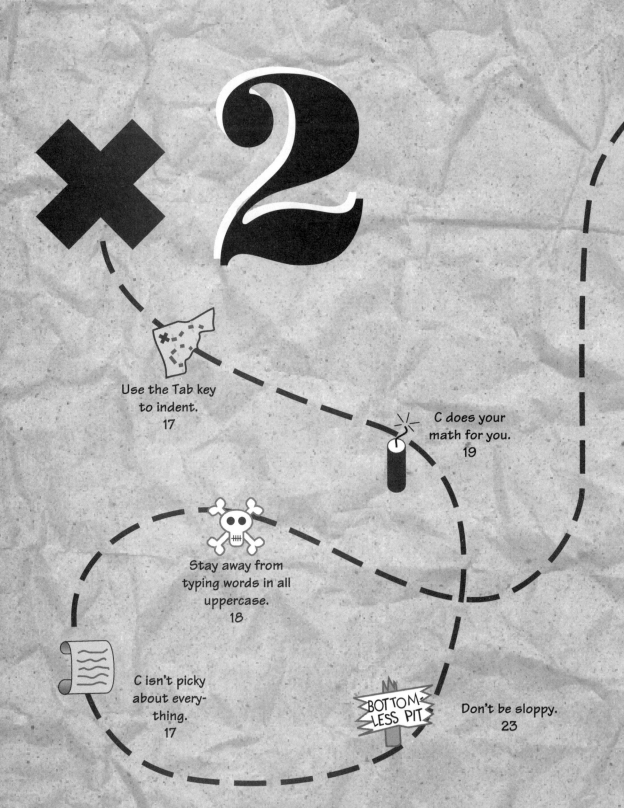

2

Use the Tab key to indent.
17

C does your math for you.
19

Stay away from typing words in all uppercase.
18

C isn't picky about everything.
17

BOTTOM-LESS PIT

Don't be sloppy.
23

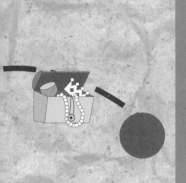

How Do I Get Started in C?

With the *main()* Function

You get to see your first C program in this chapter! Please don't try to understand *every* character of the C programs discussed here. Relax and just get familiar with the look and feel of C. After a while you will begin to recognize elements common to all C programs.

Getting a Glimpse

This section shows you a short but complete C program and discusses another program that appears in Appendix B. Both programs contain common and different elements. The first program is extremely simple. Here it is:

```c
/* Prints a message on the screen */
#include <stdio.h>
main()
{
  printf("This C stuff is easy!\n");
  return 0;
}
```

If you were to type this program using your C compiler's editor, compile the program, and run it, you would see this message appear on the screen:

```
This C stuff is easy!
```

NOTE

It took a lot of work to produce that one-line message! Actually, of the seven lines in the program, only one—the one that starts with printf—does the work that produces the output. The other lines provide "housekeeping chores" common to most C programs.

Clue: To see a really long program, glance at Appendix B. Although the Blackjack game there spans several pages, it contains elements common to the shorter program you just saw.

Look through both the programs just discussed and notice any similarities. One of the first things you might notice is the use of braces ({}), parentheses (()), and backslashes (\). Be careful when typing C programs into your C compiler. C gets picky, for instance, if you accidentally type a square bracket ([) when you should type a brace.

> **NOTE**
>
> C isn't picky about everything. For instance, most of the spacing you see in C programs serves to make the programs clearer to people, not to C. As you program, add blank lines and indent sections of code that go together to help the appearance of the program and to make it easier for you to find what you are looking for.

Clue: Use the Tab key to indent instead of typing a bunch of spaces. Most C editors let you adjust the *tab spacing* (the number of spaces that appear when you press Tab). Some C program lines get long, so a tab setting of three provides ample indention without making lines too long.

C requires that you use lowercase letters for all commands and predefined functions. (You'll learn what a function is in the next section.) About the only time you use uppercase letters is on a line with `#define` and inside the printed messages you write.

The *main()* Function

The most important part of a C program is its `main()` function. Both of the programs discussed earlier have `main()` functions. Although at this point the distinction is not critical, `main()` is a C *function,* not a C command. A function is a routine that comes with C or that you write. A function is nothing more than a routine that performs some task. C programs are made up of one or more functions. Each program must *always* include a `main()` function. A function is distinguished from a command by the parentheses that follow the function name. These are functions:

```
main()    calcIt()    printf()    strlen()
```

and these are commands:

```
return    while    int    if    float
```

When you read other C programming books and manuals, the author might decide to omit the parenthesis from the end of function names. For example, you might read about the `printf` function instead of `printf()`. You'll learn to recognize function names soon enough so such differences won't matter a lot to you. Most of the time, authors want to clarify the differences between functions and non-functions as much as possible so you'll more often see the parenthesis than not.

> **WARNING**
>
> One of the functions just listed, `calcIt()`, contains an uppercase letter. However, the preceding section said you should stay *away* from uppercase. If a name has multiple parts, such as `doReportPrint()`, it's common practice to use uppercase letters to begin the separate words to increase readability. (Spaces aren't allowed in function names.) Stay away from typing words in *all* uppercase. An uppercase letter for clarity once in a while is okay.

Clue: The required `main()` function and all of C's supplied function names must contain lowercase letters. You can use uppercase for the functions that you write, but most C programmers stay with the lowercase function name convention.

Just as Chapter 1 marks the beginning place to read in a book, `main()` is always the first place the computer begins when running your program. If `main()` is not the first function listed in your program, `main()` still determines the beginning of the program's execution. Therefore, make `main()` the first function in every program you write. The programs in the next several chapters have only one `main()` function. As you improve your C skills, you'll learn why adding additional functions after `main()` improves your programming power even more.

After the word `main()`, you always see an opening brace (`{`). When you find a matching closing brace (`}`), `main()` is finished. There might be additional pairs of braces within a `main()` function as well. For practice, look again at the long program in Appendix B. `main()` is the first function with code, and several other functions follow—each with braces and code.

> **NOTE**
>
> The statement `#include <stdio.h>` is needed in almost every C program. It helps with printing and getting data. For now, always put this statement somewhere before `main()`. You will understand why the `#include` is important in Chapter 7, "What Do `#include` and `#define` Mean?"

Kinds of Data

Your C programs must use data made up of numbers, words, and characters; programs process that data into meaningful information. Although there are many different kinds of data, the following three data types are by far the most common used in C programming:

- ✖ Characters
- ✖ Integers
- ✖ Floating-points (also called *real numbers*)

> **SKIP THIS, IT'S TECHNICAL**
>
> "How much math am I going to have to learn?! I didn't think that was part of the bargain!" you yell. Well, you can relax, because C does your math for you; you don't have to be able to add 2 and 2 to write C programs. You do, however, have to understand data types so that you will know how to choose the correct type when your program needs it.

Fun Fact

The American National Standards Institute (ANSI), which developed ANSI C, also developed the code for the ASCII chart.

C's Characters

A C *character* is any single character that your computer can represent. Your computer knows 256 different characters. Each of them is found in something called the *ASCII table,* located in Appendix C. (ASCII is pronounced *ask-ee.* If you don't *know-ee,* you can just *ask-ee.*) Anything your computer can represent can be a character. Any or all of the following can be considered characters:

```
A     a     4     %     Q     !     +     =     ]
```

Clue: Even the spacebar produces a character. Just as C needs to keep track of the letters of the alphabet, digits, and all the other characters, it has to keep track of any blanks your program needs.

As you can see, every letter, number, and space is a character to C. Sure, a 4 looks like a number, and it sometimes is, but it is also a character. If you indicate that a particular 4 is a character, you can't do math with it. If you indicate that another 4 is to be a number, you can do math with that 4. The same holds for the special symbols. The plus sign (+) is a character, but the plus sign also performs addition. (There I go, bringing math back into the conversation!)

All of C's character data is enclosed in *apostrophes* ('). Some people call apostrophes *single quotation marks.* Apostrophes differentiate character data from other kinds of data, such as numbers and math symbols. For example, in a C program, all of the following are character data:

```
'A'     'a'     '4'     '%'     ' '     '-'
```

None of the following can be character data because they have no apostrophes around them:

```
A     a     4     %     -
```

Clue: None of the following are valid characters. Only single characters, not multiple characters, can go inside apostrophes.

```
'C is fun'  'C is hard'  'I should be sailing!'
```

The first program in this chapter contains the character '\n'. At first, you might not think that \n is a single character, but it's one of the few two-character combinations that C interprets as a single character. This will make more sense later.

If you need to specify more than one character (except for the special characters that you'll learn, like the \n just described), enclose the characters in *quotation marks* (" "). A group of multiple characters is called a *string*. The following is a C string:

"C is fun to learn."

> **NOTE**
>
> That's really all you need to know about characters and strings for now. Later in this book you'll learn how to use them in programs. When you see how to store characters in variables, you'll see why the apostrophe and quotation marks are important.

Numbers in C

Although you might not have thought about it before now, numbers take on many different sizes and shapes. Your C program must have a way to store numbers, no matter what the numbers look like. You must store numbers in numeric variables. Before you look at variables, a review of the kinds of numbers will help.

Whole numbers are called *integers*. Integers have no decimal points. (Remember this rule: Like most members of Congress, integers have no point whatsoever.) Any number without a decimal point is an integer. All of the following are integers:

10   54   0   -121   -68   752

WARNING

Never begin an integer with a leading 0 (unless the number *is* zero), or C will think you typed the number in *hexadecimal* or *octal*. Hexadecimal and octal, sometimes called *base-16* and *base-8*, respectively, are weird ways of representing numbers. 053 is an octal number, and 0x45 is a hexadecimal number. If you don't know what all that means, just remember for now that C puts a *hex* on you if you mess around with leading zeroes before integers.

Numbers with decimal points are called *floating-point numbers*. All of the following are floating-point numbers:

```
547.43      0.0      0.44384      9.1923      -168.470      .22
```

Clue: As you can see, leading zeroes are okay in front of floating-point numbers.

The choice of using integers or floating-point numbers depends on the data your programs are working with. Some values (such as ages and quantities) make great integers, while other values (such as money amounts) make great floating-point numbers. Internally, C stores integers differently from floating-point values. As you can see from Figure 2.1, a floating-point value usually takes twice as much memory as an integer. Therefore, if you can get away with using integers, do so and save floating-points for values that need the decimal point.

NOTE

Figure 2.1 shows you that integers generally take less memory than floating-point values, no matter how large or small the values stored there are. On any given day, a large post office box might get much less mail than a smaller one. The contents of the box don't affect what the box happens to hold. The size of C's number storage is affected not by the value of the number, but by the type of the number.

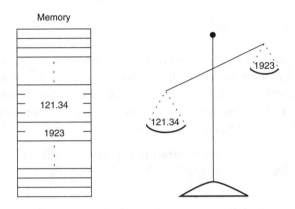

FIGURE 2.1.
It often takes more memory to store floating-point values than integers.

Different C compilers use different amounts of storage for integers and floating-point values. As you will learn later, there are ways of finding out exactly how much memory your C compiler uses for each type of data.

Rewards

✖ Keep the Caps Lock key off! Most C commands and functions require lowercase letters.

✖ Put lots of extra spacing in your C programs to make them more readable.

✖ A C function must have parentheses following its name. A C program consists of one or more functions. The main() function is always required. C executes main() before any other function.

✖ If you use a character, enclose it in single quotes. Strings go inside quotation marks. Integers are whole numbers without decimal points. Floating-point numbers have decimal points.

Pitfalls

✖ Don't be sloppy about your typing. When C needs a certain special character such as a brace, a square bracket will not do.

✖ Don't put leading zeroes before integers unless the integer *is* zero.

In Review

This chapter's goal was to familiarize you with the "look and feel" of a C program, primarily the main() function that includes executable C statements. As you saw, C is a free-form language that isn't picky about spacing. C is, however, picky about lowercase letters. C requires lowercase spellings of all its commands and functions, such as printf().

At this point, don't worry about the specifics of the code you see in this chapter. The rest of the book explains all the details.

Code Example

```
/* Prints a character and some numbers */
#include <stdio.h>
main()
{
  printf("A letter grade of %c\n", 'B');
  printf("A test score of %d\n", 87);
  printf("A class average of %.1f\n", 85.9);
  return 0;
}
```

Code Analysis

This short program does nothing more than print three messages on-screen. Each message includes one of the three data types mentioned in this chapter, namely a character (B), an integer (87), and a floating-point number (85.9).

The main() function is the only function in the program written by the programmer. The left and right braces ({ and }) always enclose main()'s code as well as any other function's code that you might add to your programs. You'll see another function, printf(), that is a built-in C function that produces output. Here is the program's output:

```
A letter grade of B
A test score of 87
A class average of 85.9
```

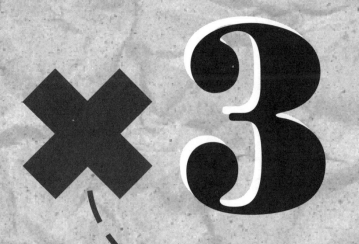

×3

Add comments as
you write your
program.
28

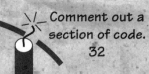

Comment out a
section of code.
32

Redundant
comments are a
waste of time.
30

You need
comments.
28

Don't nest one
comment inside
another.
34

How Do I Know What's Happening?

Through Comments

Your computer must be able to understand your programs. Because the computer is a dumb machine, you must be careful to spell C commands exactly right and type them in the same order you want them executed. However, people also read your programs. You will change your programs often, and if you write programs for a company, the company's needs will change over time. You must ensure that your programs are understandable to *people* as well as to computers. Therefore, you should document your programs by explaining what they do.

Commenting on Your Code

Throughout a C program, you should add *comments*. Comments are messages scattered throughout your programs that explain what's going on. If you write a program to calculate payroll, the program's comments explain the gross pay calculations, state tax calculations, federal tax calculations, social security calculations, and all the other calculations that are going on.

> **NOTE**
>
> If you write the program and only you will use it, you don't really need comments, right? Well, not exactly. C is a cryptic programming language. Even if *you* write the program, you aren't always able to follow it later.

Clue: Add comments as you write your programs. Get in the habit now, because programmers rarely go back and add comments later. When they must make a change later, programmers often lament about their program's lack of comments.

There is another advantage to commenting as you write the program instead of waiting until after you finish. While writing programs, you often refer back to statements you wrote earlier in the process. Instead of reinterpreting C code you've already written, you can scan through your comments, finding sections of code that you need faster. If you didn't comment, you would have to decipher your C code every time you looked through a piece of it.

Program *maintenance* is the process of changing a program, over time, to fix hidden bugs and to adapt the program to a changing environment. If you write a payroll, program for a company, that company could eventually change the way it does payroll, and you (or another programmer) will have to modify the payroll, program to conform to the company's new payroll procedures. Commenting speeds program maintenance. With comments, you or another programmer can quickly scan through a program listing finding the areas that need changing.

Comments are *not* C commands. C ignores every comment in your program. Comments are for people, and the programming statements residing between the comments are for the computer. (See Figure 3.1.)

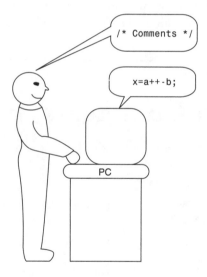

FIGURE 3.1.
Comments are for people, and C programming statements are for the computer.

Consider the following C statement:

```
return ((s1 < s2) ? s1 : s2);
```

You don't know C yet, but even if you did, this statement takes some study to figure out. Isn't this better:

```
return ((s1 < s2) ? s1 : s2); /* Gets the smaller of 2 values */
```

The next section explains the syntax of comments, but for now, you can see that the message between the /* and the */ is a comment.

The closer a comment is to spoken language and the further a comment is from C code, the better the comment is. Don't write a comment just for the sake of commenting. The following statement's comment is useless:

```
printf("Payroll");  /* Prints the word "Payroll" */
```

WARNING

You don't know C yet, and you *still* don't need the preceding line's comment! Redundant comments are a waste of your time, and they don't add anything to programs. Add comments to explain what is going on to people (including yourself) who might need to read your program.

Specifying Comments

C comments begin with /* and end with */. Comments can span several lines in a program, and they can go just about anywhere in a program. All of the following lines contain C comments:

```
/* This is a comment that happens to span two lines
before coming to an end */

/* This is a single-line comment */

for (i = 0; i < 25; i++)  /* Counts from 0 to 25 */
```

NOTE

Notice that comments can go on lines by themselves or before or after programming statements. The choice of placement depends on the length of the comment and the amount of code the comment describes.

The Blackjack program in Appendix B contains all kinds of comments. By reading through the comments in that program, you can get an idea of what the program does without ever looking at the C code itself.

Don't comment every line. Usually only every few lines need comments. Many programmers like to place a multiline comment before a section of code and then insert a few smaller comments on lines that need them. Here is a complete program with different kinds of comments:

```c
/* Written by: Perilous Perry, finished on April 9, 1492 */
/* Filename: AVG.C */
/* Computes the average of three class grades */
#include <stdio.h>
main()
{
  float gr1, gr2, gr3;  /* Variables to hold grades */
  float avg;            /* Variable to hold average */
  /* Asks for each student's grade */
  printf("What grade did the first student get? ");
  scanf(" %f", &gr1);
  printf("What grade did the second student get? ");
  scanf(" %f", &gr2);
  printf("What grade did the third student get? ");
  scanf(" %f", &gr3);

  avg = (gr1 + gr2 + gr3) / 3.0;  /* Computes average */
  printf("\nThe student average is %.2f", avg);
  return 0;  /* Goes back to DOS */
}
```

Many companies require that their programmers embed their own names in comments at the top of programs they write. If changes need to be made to the program later, the original programmer can be found to help out. It's also a good idea to include the filename that you use to save the program on disk at the beginning of a program so that you can find a program on disk when you run across a printed listing.

NOTE

This book might comment too much in some places, especially in the beginning chapters. You are so unfamiliar with C that every little bit of explanation helps.

SKIP THIS, IT'S TECHNICAL

For testing purposes, you might find it useful to *comment out* a section of code by putting a /* and */ around it. By doing this, you cause C to ignore that section of code, and you can concentrate on the piece of code you're working on. Do not, however, comment out a section of code that already contains comments because you cannot embed one comment within another. The first */ that C runs across triggers the end of the comment you started. When C finds the next */ without a beginning /*, you get an error.

White Space

White space is the collection of spaces and blank lines you find in many programs. In a way, white space is just as important in making your programs more readable than comments are. People need white space when looking through C programs instead of a program that runs together too much. Consider the following program:

```
#include <stdio.h>
main(){float s,t;printf("How much do you make? ");scanf(" %f",
&s);t=.33*s;printf("You owe %.2f in taxes.",t);return 0;}
```

This program is a perfectly good C program—to a C compiler, but not to a person looking at the program. Although the code is simple and it doesn't take a lot of effort to figure out what is going on, the following program, even though it has no comments, is *much* easier to decipher:

```
#include <stdio.h>
main()
  {
    float s, t;

    printf("How much do you make? ");
    scanf(" %f", &s);

    t = .33 * s;
    printf("You owe %.2f in taxes.", t);
    return 0;
  }
```

This program listing is identical to the previous program except that this one includes comments whereas the previous one did not. The physical length of a program does not determine readability; the amount of whitespace does. (Of course, a few comments would improve this program too, but the purpose of this exercise is to show you the difference between no white space and good white space.)

NOTE

You might be wondering why the first line of the squeezed program, the one with the #include, did not contain code after the closing angle brace. After all, it would seem that the point of unreadable code would be made even more strongly if the #include contained trailing code. The author (that's me) tried to do just that! Many, if not all, C compilers refuse to allow code after a #include (or any other statement that begins with a pound sign (#)). Some C compilers even refuse to allow comments at the end of such lines, although many of today's C compilers do let you put comments there.

The Future of Comments

Many of today's C compilers support another kind of comment that was originally developed for C++ programs. This new kind of comment is not approved for use by ANSI C, but might be someday soon because it's so popular. The new style of comment begins with two slashes (//) and ends only at the end of the line.

Here is an example of the new style of comment:

```
// Short program!
#include <stdio.h>
main()
{
  printf("Looking good!");  // A message
  return 0;
}
```

Because the new style of comment isn't sanctioned by the ANSI C committee, this book doesn't use it again. However, you should become familiar with this style because it's easier to use than /* and */, and many C programmers are beginning to use it.

Rewards

✖ The three rules of programming are comment, comment, comment. Use comments abundantly.

✖ When you want to comment, begin with /*. End the comment with */.

✖ If you want to use the new style of comment, begin the comment with //. This kind of comment, however, isn't yet approved by ANSI C.

Pitfalls

✖ Don't use redundant comments. Worthless comments aren't helpful, and they waste valuable programming time.

✖ Don't nest one comment inside another. If you want to comment out a section of your program, you must make sure that the section doesn't contain other comments.

✖ Don't write programs that have little white space. Put as much indention and as many extra lines throughout a program as needed to group lines that go together. As you learn more about the C language, you'll learn where white space adds to a program's readability.

In Review

You must add comments to your programs, not for computers, but for people. Although C programs can be cryptic, comments eliminate lots of confusion. A comment is just a message that describes what's going on in the C code. Anything between the /* and */ is a C comment. C ignores all comments because it knows that comments are for people.

In addition to comments, add lots of white space to your programs to make your programs more readable. If a program is crunched together without blank lines and helpful indention, you'll feel as if you're reading an entire book with one long paragraph when you go back and study and modify the code later. Easing program maintenance through comments and ample white space saves you time and energy if you change the program later.

Code Example

Here are two lines without comments:

```
scanf(" %d", &a);
yrs = (a >= 21) ? 0 : 21 - a;
```

Here are the same two lines with comments:

```
scanf(" %d", &a);  /* Gets the user's age */
yrs = (a >= 21) ? 0 : 21 - a;  /* Calculates the number of */
                               /* years until adulthood */
```

Code Analysis

As you can see from these lines, it's not always obvious what goes on in C programs. Comments explain in plain, spoken language exactly what's going on with the code. Not every line in every C program needs a comment, but many do to clarify what's happening.

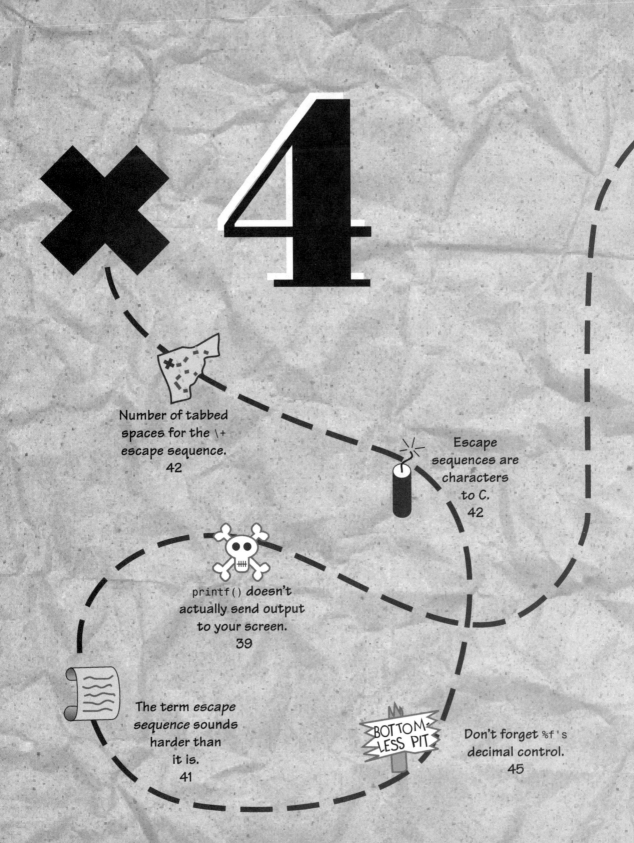

4

Number of tabbed spaces for the \+ escape sequence.
42

Escape sequences are characters to C.
42

printf() doesn't actually send output to your screen.
39

The term *escape sequence* sounds harder than it is.
41

BOTTOM-LESS PIT

Don't forget %f's decimal control.
45

Can I See Results?

With *printf()*

If neither you nor anybody else could see your program's output, there would be little use for your program! Ultimately, you have to be able to view the results of a program. C's primary means for output is the `printf()` function. There is no actual command that performs output, but the `printf()` function is a part of every C compiler and one of the most-used features of the language.

What *printf()* Does

In a nutshell, `printf()` produces output on your screen. As Figure 4.1 shows, `printf()` sends characters, numbers, and words to the screen. There is a lot to `printf()`, but you don't have to be an expert in all the `printf()` options (very few C programmers are) to use `printf()` for all your program's screen output.

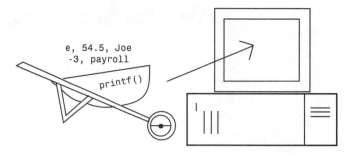

FIGURE 4.1.
`printf()` *sends characters, numbers, and words to the screen.*

The Format of *printf()*

`printf()` takes many forms, but once you get used to its format, `printf()` is easy to use. Here is the general format of `printf()`:

`printf(`*controlString* `[, `*data*`]);`

This book often shows the format of commands and functions when you first see them. The format is the general look of the statement. If something in a format appears in brackets, such as , *data* just shown, that part of the statement is optional. You almost never type the brackets themselves. If brackets are required in the command, that is made clear in the text following the format. `printf()` requires a *controlString*, but the *data* following the *controlString* is optional.

WARNING

`printf()` doesn't actually send output to your screen, but does send it to your computer's *standard output device*. Most operating systems, including MS-DOS, route the standard output to your screen unless you know enough about MS-DOS to route the output elsewhere. Most of the time you can ignore this standard output device stuff because you'll almost always want output to go to the screen. Other C functions you will learn about later route output to your printer and disk drives.

WARNING

You might be wondering why some of the words in the format appear in italics. It's because they're *placeholders*. A placeholder is a name, symbol, or formula that you supply. Placeholders are italicized in the format of functions and commands to let you know that you should substitute something at that place in the command.

Here is an example of a `printf()`:

```
printf("I am %d", 16);  /* Prints I am 16 */
```

Because every string in C must be enclosed in quotation marks (as mentioned in Chapter 2), the controlString must be in quotation marks. Anything following the controlString is optional and is determined by the values you want printed.

 (margin note: Placeholders)

 (margin note: control string must be in quotation marks "............." control string)

 (margin note: "I am %d," control string; "I am %d" control string)

Fun Fact

The designers of C borrowed formatting control strings from the FORTRAN language.

command & function need ;

> **NOTE**
>
> Every C command and function needs a semicolon (;) after it to let C know that the line is finished. Braces and the first lines of functions don't need semicolons because nothing is executing on those lines. All statements with `printf()` should end in a semicolon. You won't see semicolons after `main()`, however, because you don't explicitly tell C to execute `main()`; you do, however, tell C to execute `print()` and many other functions. As you learn more about C, you'll learn more about semicolon placement.

Printing Strings

String messages are the easiest type of data to print with `printf()`. You only have to enclose the string in quotation marks. The following `printf()` prints a message on the screen:

```
printf("Read a lot");
```

When the computer executes this statement, the message `Read a lot` appears on-screen.

> **NOTE**
>
> The string `Read a lot` is the *controlString* in this `printf()`. There is little *control* going on here, just output.

The following two `printf()` statements:

```
printf("Read a lot");  \n .
printf("Keep learning");
```

might not produce the output you expect. Here is what the two `printf()`s produce:

```
Read a lotKeep learning
```

An escape sequence should be used eg \n

Clue: C does not automatically move the cursor down to the next line when a `printf()` executes. You must insert an *escape sequence* in the `controlString` if you want C to go to the next line after a `printf()`.

Escape Sequences

C contains a lot of *escape sequences,* and you'll use some of them in almost every program you write. Table 4.1 contains a list of some of the more popular escape sequences.

Table 4.1. Escape sequences.

Code	Description
\n	Newline
\a	Alarm (the computer's bell)
\t	Tab
\\	Backslash
\"	Quotation mark

NOTE

The term *escape sequence* sounds harder than it really is. An escape sequence is stored as a single character in C and produces the effect described in Table 4.1. When C sends `'\a'` to the screen, for example, the computer's bell is sounded instead of the characters \ and a actually being printed.

You will see a lot of escape sequences in `printf()` functions. Anytime you want to "move down" to the next line when printing lines of text, you must type \n so that C produces a *newline*, which moves the blinking cursor down to the next line on the screen. The following `printf()` statements print their messages on separate lines because of the `\n` at the end of the first one:

```
printf("Read a lot\n");
printf("Keep learning");
```

SKIP THIS, IT'S TECHNICAL

The \n could have been placed at the beginning of the second line and the same output would have occurred. Because escape sequences are characters to C, you must enclose them in quotation marks so that C knows that the escape sequences are part of the string being printed. The following *also* produces two lines of output:

```
printf("Read a lot\nKeep learning");
```

Because a quotation mark ends a string and because a backslash signals the start of an escape sequence, they have their own escape sequences. `\a` rings your computer's bell, and `\t` causes the output to appear moved over a few spaces. Be sure to check your compiler's manual for other escape sequences your version of C supports. Although Table 4.1's escape sequences are almost universal (and ANSI C compatible), not all ANSI C compilers support the escape sequences in every compiler mode. (Visual C++ does not let you use `\a` when you compiler in the *QuickWin* mode, for example.)

The following `printf()` statements produce the output shown in their comments:

```
printf("Ready\tSet\tGo!\n");      /* Ready     Set      Go! */
printf("Ring my charm!\a\n");     /* Ring my charm! <BEEP> */
printf("I said, \"No way.\"\n");  /* I said, "No way." */
printf("\\ means escape\n");      /* \ means escape */
```

Clue: Different C compilers might produce a different number of tabbed spaces for the `\t` escape sequence.

Conversion Characters

When you print numbers and characters, you must tell C exactly how to print them. You indicate the format of numbers with *conversion characters.* Table 4.2 lists a few of C's most-used conversion characters.

Table 4.2. Conversion characters.

Conversion Character	Description
%d	Integer
%f	Floating-point
%c	Character
%s	String

what is a value?
eg int, floating point
char

When you want to print a value inside a string, insert the appropriate conversion characters in the `controlString`. Then, to the right of the `controlString,` list the value you want to be printed. Figure 4.2 is an example of how a `printf()` can print three numbers—an integer, a floating-point value, and another integer.

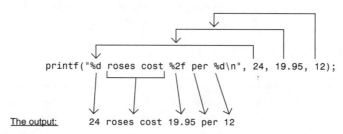

```
printf("%d roses cost %2f per %d\n", 24, 19.95, 12);
```

The output: 24 roses cost 19.95 per 12

FIGURE 4.2.
printf() *conversion characters determine how and where numbers print.*

Strings and characters have their own conversion characters as well. Although you don't need %s to print strings by themselves, you might need %s when printing strings combined with other data. The next `printf()` prints a different type of data value using each of the conversion characters:

```
printf("%s %d %f %c\n", "Sam", 14, -8.76, 'X');
```

This printf() produces this output:

```
Sam 14 -8.760000 X
```

> **NOTE**
>
> The string Sam needs quotation marks, as do all strings, and the character X needs single quotation marks, as do all characters.

> **WARNING**
>
> C is crazy when it comes to floating-point numbers. Even though the -8.76 has only two decimal places, C insists on printing six decimal places.

You can control how C prints floating-point values by placing a . between the % and the f of the floating-point conversion character. (Figure 4.2 used this decimal control.) The following printf() produces four different-looking numbers even though the same floating-point number is given:

```
printf("%f %.3f %.2f  %.1f", 4.5678, 4.5678, 4.5678, 4.5678);
```
2 spaces

C rounds the floating-point numbers to the number of decimal places specified in the %.f conversion character and produces this output:

```
4.567800 4.568  4.57  4.6
```
2 spaces

Clue: Just wait! The conversion characters will mean a lot more when you learn about variables in the next chapter.

One last thing: The printf() *controlString* controls *exactly* how your output will appear. The only reason two spaces appear between the numbers is that the *controlString* has two spaces between the %fs.

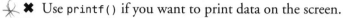
Use printf, to put data on the screen

Reward

- ✖ Use printf() if you want to print data on the screen.
- ✖ Every printf() requires a control string that determines how your data will look when printed.
- ✖ Strings are easy to print. They need no special format codes or conversion characters.
- ✖ Use escape sequences to print newlines, tabs, quotes, and backslashes, and to ring the bell.
- ✖ Use conversion characters to control how numbers will look.

Pitfalls

- ✖ Don't expect C to know how to format your data automatically. You must use conversion characters.
- ✖ Don't forget %f's decimal control unless you want C to print six decimal places with all floating-point values.

✗ Very Important

In Review

printf() sends data to the screen. A program that can't write to the screen is rarely useful. The programs you write must be able to communicate with the user sitting at the keyboard.

printf() requires a *controlString* that describes the format of the data that follows. With the *controlString* you can specify exactly how you want your numbers and character data printed. You also can print escape sequences, which is a fancy name for special output controls that you sometimes need, such as a newline at the end of lines of output.

Code Example

Consider the following partial program listing:

```
printf("%c %s %d %f %.2f\n", 'Q', "Hello!", 14, 64.21, 64.21);
printf("%c\n", 'Q');
printf("%s\n", "Hello!");
printf("%d\n", 14);
printf("%f\n", 64.21);
printf("%.2f", 64.21);
```

Code Analysis

The first printf() statement prints five data values—a character, a character string, an integer, a floating-point number, and another floating-point number. The subsequent five lines then print those values one at a time. The last floating-point value's decimal places are specified in the last printf() to limit the number of decimal positions printed. Here is the code's output:

```
Q Hello! 14 64.210000 64.21
Q
Hello!
14
64.210000
64.21
```

The equals sign
tells C...
54

Most C vari-
ables are
defined after
an opening
brace.
53

There is a way to
store strings in
variables.
51

Your C
program's
variables vary
in size.
50

Don't mix data types
and variable types.
56

How Do I Store Stuff?

Using Variables

No doubt you've heard that computers process data. Somehow, you've got to have a way to store that data. In C, as in most programming languages, you store data in *variables*. A variable is nothing more than a box in your computer's memory that holds a number or a character. Chapter 2 explained the different types of data: characters, strings, integers, and floating-points. This chapter explains how to store those types of data inside your programs.

Kinds of Variables

There are several different kinds of variables in C because there are several different kinds of data. Not just any variable will hold just any piece of data. Only integers can hold integer data, only floating-point variables can hold floating-point data, and so on.

> **NOTE**
>
> Throughout this chapter, think of variables inside your computer as acting like post office boxes in a post office. Post office boxes vary in size and have unique numbers that label each one. Your C program's variables vary in size, depending on the kind of data they hold, and each variable has a unique name that differentiates it from other variables.

The data you learned about in Chapter 2 was called *literal data* (or sometimes, *constant data*). Specific numbers and letters don't change. The number 2 and the character 'x' are always 2 and a character 'x'. Lots of data you work with changes. Data such as age, salary, and weight all changes. If you were writing a payroll program, you would need a way to store changing pieces of data. Variables come to the rescue. Variables are little more than boxes in memory that hold values that can change over time.

There are many types of variables. Table 5.1 lists some of the more common types. Notice that many of the variables have data types (character, integer, and floating-point) similar to that of literal data. After all, you must have a place to store integers, and you do so in an integer variable.

Table 5.1. Several types of C variables.

Name	Description
char	Holds character data such as 'x' and '*'.
int	Holds integer data such as 1, 32, and -459. Stores data between -32768 and 32767.
long int	Holds integer data greater than 32767 and less than -32768.
float	Holds floating-point data such as 0.0003, -121.34, and 43323.4.
double	Holds extremely large and small floating-point data. (float can hold only values from -3.4 x 10^{38} to +3.4 x 10^{38}—that's 3.4 times 10 with 38 zeroes after the 10.)

WARNING

You might notice that there are no string variables, although there *are* character string literals. C is one of the few programming languages that has no string variables, but as you'll see in Chapter 6, "Can C Store Words?" there is a way to store strings in variables.

The *Name* column in Table 5.1 lists the keyword needed when you create variables for programs. In other words, if you want an integer, you need to use the int keyword. Before completing your study of variables, you need to know one more thing: how to name them.

Naming Variables

All variables have names, and because you are responsible for naming them, you must learn the naming rules. All variable names must be different. You can't have two variables in the same program with the same name.

A variable can have from 1 to 32 characters in its name. Your program's variables must begin with a letter of the alphabet, but after that letter, variable names can have other letters, numbers, or an underscore in any combination. All of the following are valid variable names:

```
myData    pay94    age_limit    amount    QtlyIncome
```

Clue: C lets you begin a variable name with an underscore, but you shouldn't do so. Because some of C's built-in variables begin with an underscore, there's a chance you'll overlap one of those if you name your variables starting with underscores.

These variable names are *not* valid:

```
94Pay     my Age     rate*pay
```

You ought to be able to figure out why these variable names are not valid. The first one, `94Pay`, begins with a number, the second variable name, `my Age`, contains a space, and the third variable name, `rate*pay`, contains a special character (`*`).

WARNING

Don't name a variable with the same name as a function or a command. If you give a variable the same name as a command, your program won't run; if you give a variable the same name as a function, you can't use that same function name later in your program without causing an error.

Defining Variables

Declaring or

Before you use a variable, you have to *define* it. Variable definition (sometimes called *variable declaration*) is nothing more than letting C know you'll need some variable space so it can reserve some for you. To define a variable, you only need to state its type, followed by a variable name. Here are the first few lines of a program that defines some variables:

```
main()
{   Type   name/ declare
  char initial;
  int age;
  float amount;
  /* Rest of program would follow */
```

declare

The sample code just presented has three variables—`initial`, `age`, and `amount`. They can hold three different types of data—character data, integer data, and floating-point data. If the program didn't define these variables, it wouldn't be able to store data in the variables.

You can define more than one variable of the same data type on the same line. For example, if you wanted to define two character variables instead of just one, you could do so like this:

```
main()
{
  char initial1, initial2;   /* Defines 2 characters */
  int age;
  float amount;
  /* Rest of program would follow */
```

or like this:

```
main()
{
  char initial1;
  char initial2;   /* Defines a second */
  int age;
  float amount;
  /* Rest of program would follow */
```

SKIP THIS, IT'S TECHNICAL

Most C variables are defined after an opening brace, such as the opening brace that follows a function name. These variables are called *local variables.* C also lets you create *global* variables by defining the variables before a function name, such as before `main()`. Local variables are almost always preferable to global variables. Chapter 30 addresses the differences between local and global variables, but for now, all programs will stick with local variables.

Storing Data in Variables

The *assignment operator* puts values in variables. It's a lot easier to use than it sounds. The assignment operator is simply the equals sign (=). The format of putting data in variables looks like this:

```
variable = data;
```

The `variable` is the variable name that you want to store data in. You must have defined the variable previously, as the preceding section explained. The `data` can be a number, character, or mathematical expression that results in a number. Here are examples of three assignment statements that assign values to the variables defined in the preceding section:

```
initial = 'G';   /* Assigns values to three variables */
age = 31;
amount = 2983.43;
```

You also can store answers to expressions in variables:

```
sales = 4432.67 / 1.20;   /* Divides to get value */
```

and even use other variables in the expression:

```
newSales = sales + 2167.65;   /* Uses value from
                                 another variable */
```

Figure 5.1 gives you an idea of what C does when you use an assignment statement.

Clue: The equals sign tells C this: Take whatever is on the right and stick it into the variable on the left. The equals sign kind of acts like a left-pointing arrow that says "That-a-way!" Oh, and never use commas in numbers, no matter how big the numbers are!

Suppose you were getting paid lots of money to write a payroll calculation program for a small business. You would have to define some floating-point variables to hold the rate being paid per hour, the number of hours worked, the tax rate, and so on. The Blackjack program in Appendix B must keep track of lots of things, and many variables are used there. At the start of most of the program's functions, you'll see a place where variables are being defined.

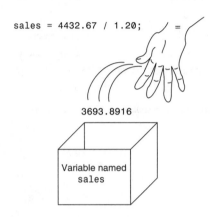

sales = 4432.67 / 1.20;

3693.8916

Variable named sales

FIGURE 5.1.
The assignment operator (=) puts values into variables.

like putting sugar into coffee to make it drinkable

int income = 1278 × 6

Clue: You can define variables and give them initial values at the same time. The following code defines three variables and gives initial values to two of them, val and numSold:

```
int numSold = 25, numBought;
float val = 436.54;
```

3; numSold, numBought, val

2; val, numSold

Rewards

✖ Learn how to name variables, because you'll have to use them in your programs.

✖ Always define variables before using them.

✖ You can define more than one variable on the same line.

✖ The equals sign is called the assignment operator. The assignment operator helps you store values in variables.

Pitfalls

✖ Don't mix data types and variable types. Refrain from storing values of one data type in variables of another data type. The results might confuse you if you mix data types.

✖ Don't define variables before a function begins even though you can. Such variables, called global variables, can cause problems if you're not careful. Instead, define variables after an opening brace of a function. These local variables are safer for you to use for now.

✖ Don't put commas in numbers. Enter the value thirty thousand as `30000`, not as `30,000`.

Wrong → int cloth
better   char cloth.

Wrong char income (if not used for calculation)
better int income

In Review

This chapter taught you a lot about the different types of variables in C. Because there are different kinds of data, we must have different kinds of variables to hold that data. The choice of data types is up to you, the programmer. Choose a variable's data type carefully to ensure that the data type matches any value you will store in that variable.

Don't use a larger data type for a variable when a smaller one is ample to hold the data. Using a long int when a regular int will suffice is not efficient and results in a slower and larger program.

Code Example

```
main()
{
    /* Defines a different variable for each data type */
    char priceCode = 'J';
    int quantity = 100;
    long int wholeSaleQuant = 45000;
    float price = 13.54;
    double yrlySales = 9845543.23;
```

Code Analysis

The statements in the preceding program section both reserve variable storage and assign initial values to those variables. You don't always have to assign initial values to variables. Many times you don't know the value that a variable will hold because the value will come from the user at the keyboard or from a disk file or a calculation. Whether you know the initial value or not, you still must reserve storage for all your variables before you use them in the program.

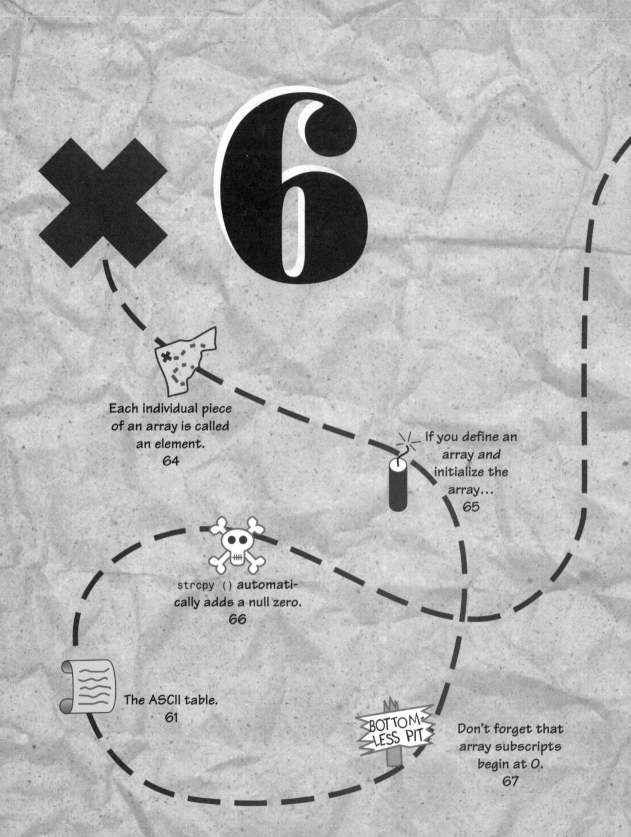

6

Each individual piece of an array is called an element.
64

If you define an array and initialize the array...
65

strcpy () automatically adds a null zero.
66

The ASCII table.
61

BOTTOM-LESS PIT

Don't forget that array subscripts begin at 0.
67

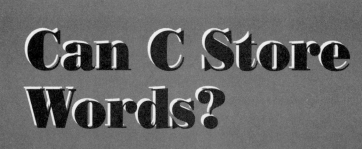

Can C Store Words?

In Character Arrays

Although C doesn't have string variables, there is a way to store string data. This chapter explains how. You already know that string data must be enclosed in quotation marks. Even a single character enclosed in quotation marks is a string. You also know how to print strings with `printf()`.

The only task left is to see how to use a special type of character variable to hold string data so that your program can input, process, and output that string data.

"I Am the String Terminator!"

C does the strangest thing to strings: It adds a zero to the end of every string. The zero at the end of strings has several names. Here are some of them:

✖ Null zero

✖ Binary zero

✖ String terminator

✖ ASCII 0

✖ \0

> **WARNING**
>
> About the only thing you *don't* call the string-terminating zero is *zero!* C programmers use the special names for the string-terminating zero so that you'll know that a regular numeric zero or a character `'0'` is not being used at the end of the string; only the special *null zero* appears at the end of a string.

C marks the end of all strings with the string-terminating zero. You never have to do anything special when entering a string literal such as `"My name is Julie."` C automatically adds the null zero. You'll never see the null zero, but it is there. In memory, C knows when it gets to the end of a string only when it finds the null zero.

NOTE

If you look at Appendix C, you'll find the ASCII table (discussed in Chapter 2). The very first entry is labeled *null,* and the ASCII number for null is 0. Look further down at ASCII 48, and you'll see a 0. ASCII 48 is the character '0', whereas the first ASCII value is the *null zero.* C puts the null zero at the end of strings. Even the string "I am 20" ends in an ASCII 0 directly after the character 0 in 20.

Clue: The string terminator is sometimes called \0 (*backslash zero*) because you can represent the null zero by enclosing \0 in single quotes. Therefore, '0' is the character zero, and '\0' is the string terminator.

Figure 6.1 shows how the string "Crazy" is stored in memory. As you can see, it takes 6 bytes (a *byte* is a single memory location) to store the string, even though the string has only five letters. The null zero that is part of the string "Crazy" takes one of those six memory locations.

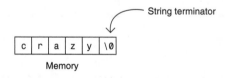

FIGURE 6.1.
A string always ends with a null zero in memory.

The Length of Strings

The *length* of a string is always the number of characters up to, but not including, the null zero. There will be times when you need to find the length of a string. The null zero is never counted when determining the length of a string. Even though the null zero must terminate the string (so C knows where the string ends), the null zero is not part of the string length.

Given the definition of the string length, the following strings both have lengths of nine characters:

August 10

and

Batter up

> **WARNING**
>
> The first string's length doesn't end at the 0 in 10 because the 0 in 10 isn't a null zero; it's a character zero.

Clue: All single characters of data have a length of one. Therefore, both 'X' and "X" have lengths of one, but the "X" consumes two characters of memory because of its null zero. Any time you see a string literal enclosed in quotation marks (as they all must be), picture in your mind that terminating null zero at the end of that string in memory.

Character Arrays: Lists of Characters

Character arrays hold strings in memory. An *array* is a special type of variable that you'll hear much more about in upcoming chapters. All the data types—int, float, char, and the rest—have corresponding array types. An array is nothing more than a list of variables of the same data type.

Before you use a character array to hold a string, you must tell C that you need a character array in the same place you would tell C that you need any other kind of variable. Use brackets ([and]) after the array name, along with a number indicating the maximum number of characters the string will hold.

An example is worth a thousand words. If you needed a place to hold month names, you could define a character array called `month` like this:

Fun Fact

You can use C to create your own computer languages.

```
char month[10];  /* Defines a character array */
```

Clue: Array definitions are easy. Take away the `10` and the brackets, and you have a regular character variable. Adding the brackets with the `10` tells C that you need 10 character variables, each following the other in a list named `month`.

The reason 10 was used when defining the array is that the longest month name, `September`, has nine characters. The tenth character is for—you guessed it—the null zero.

Clue: You *always* have to reserve enough character array space to hold the longest string you will need to hold, plus the string terminator. You can define more array characters than needed, but not fewer than you need.

If you want, you can store a string value in the array at the same time you define the array:

```
char month[10] = "January";  /* Defines a character array */
```

Figure 6.2 shows you what this array looks like. Because nothing was put in the last two places of the array (January takes only seven characters plus an eighth place for the null zero), you don't know what's in the last two places. (Some compilers, however, fill the unused elements with zeroes to kind of *empty* the rest of the string.)

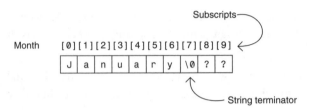

FIGURE 6.2.

Defining and initializing an array named month *that holds string data.*

Clue: Each individual piece of an array is called an *element*. The month array has 10 elements. You can distinguish between them with *subscripts*. Subscripts are numbers that you specify inside brackets that refer to each of the array elements.

All array subscripts begin with 0. As Figure 6.2 shows, the first element in the month array is called month[0]. The last is called month[9] because there are 10 elements altogether, and when you begin at 0, the last will be 9.

Each of the elements in a character array is a character. The combination of characters—the array or *list* of characters—holds the entire string. If you wanted to, you could change the contents of the array from January to March one element at a time, like this:

```
month[0] = 'M';
month[1] = 'a';
month[2] = 'r';
month[3] = 'c';
month[4] = 'h';
month[5] = '\0';   /* Very important */
```

It is vital that you insert the null zero at the end of the string. If you don't, the month array would still have a null zero three places later at month[7]; when you attempt to print the string, you would get this:

```
Marchry
```

Clue: Printing strings in arrays is easy. You can use the `%s` conversion character:

```
printf("The month is %s", month);
```

SKIP THIS, IT'S TECHNICAL

If you define an array *and* initialize the array at the same time, you don't have to put the number in brackets. Both of the following do exactly the same thing:

```
char month[8] = "January";
```

and

```
char month[] = "January";
```

In the second example, C counts the number of characters in January and adds one for the null zero. You won't be able to store a string larger than eight characters later, however. If you want to define a string's character array and initialize it but leave extra padding for a longer string later, you could do this:

```
char month[25] = "January";  /* Leaves room for
                                 longer strings */
```

Initializing Strings

You won't want to initialize a string one character at a time as done in the preceding section. However, unlike with regular non-array variables, you can't assign a new string to the array like this:

```
month = "April";  /* NOT allowed */
```

You can only assign a string to a month with the equals sign *at the time you define the string*. If later in the program you want to put a new string into the array, you must either assign it one character at a time or use C's strcpy() (*string copy*) function that comes with your C compiler. The following statement assigns a new string to the month:

```
strcpy(month, "April");  /* Puts new string in month array */
```

Clue: In your programs that use strcpy(), you must put this line after the #include <stdio.h>:

```
#include <string.h>
```

WARNING

Don't worry. strcpy() automatically adds a null zero to the end of the string it creates.

NOTE

The Blackjack game in Appendix B uses a character array to hold the player's first name. See if you can spot which function uses the character array. (It's not called main().)

Rewards

✖ Store strings in character arrays.

✖ Reserve enough array elements to hold the longest string you'll ever store in the character array.

✖ You can initialize a character array at the time you define the array, assign one element at a time, or use strcpy().

✖ Be sure to include STRCPY.H if you use strcpy().

Pitfalls

✖ Don't put a string into a character array unless the character array contains enough elements to hold the string.

✖ Don't forget that array subscripts begin at 0, not 1 (as they do in some programming languages).

✖ Don't count wrong! If you don't reserve enough elements for the terminating zero, C won't be able to process your character arrays properly.

In Review

Besides storing the numeric data types you read about in Chapter 5, C supplies a way to store character strings also. Unlike single character variables, character strings can hold many characters, such as words, addresses, and paragraphs of text.

C doesn't support a string variable data type. Despite the efficiency obtained by not supporting string variables, programmers can't give up being able to store character string data. Therefore, C offers character arrays that hold several characters of data in string-like form.

Code Example

```
/* Stores the days of the week in seven
different character arrays */
char day1[7] = "Sunday";
char day2[7] = "Monday";
char day3[8] = "Tuesday";
char day4[10] = "Wednesday";
char day5[] = "Thursday";
char day6[] = "Friday";
char day7[] = "Saturday";
char myName[6];
strcpy(myName, "Julie");
```

Code Analysis

When you want to store string data, define character arrays as shown here. You must add brackets after the variable names or C will think you're defining single-character variables. Always reserve enough for the null zero that terminates every string. If you assign a string to the array when you define the array, you don't have to count the number of characters and add one for the null zero. The last three day variables do not include the total number of characters because C is able to count the number needed to hold the data being assigned.

Be sure to note that seven array names shown here happen to have numbers in their names but those numbers have nothing to do with subscripts. day4[] has 10 elements becuase the initial defining subscript was 10. The 4 in day4 simply differentiates the name from the other day name arrays.

If you want to define an array without assigning data, as done in the myName array, you must include the maximum number of elements when you define the array. You then can use strcpy() to assign a string value to the array.

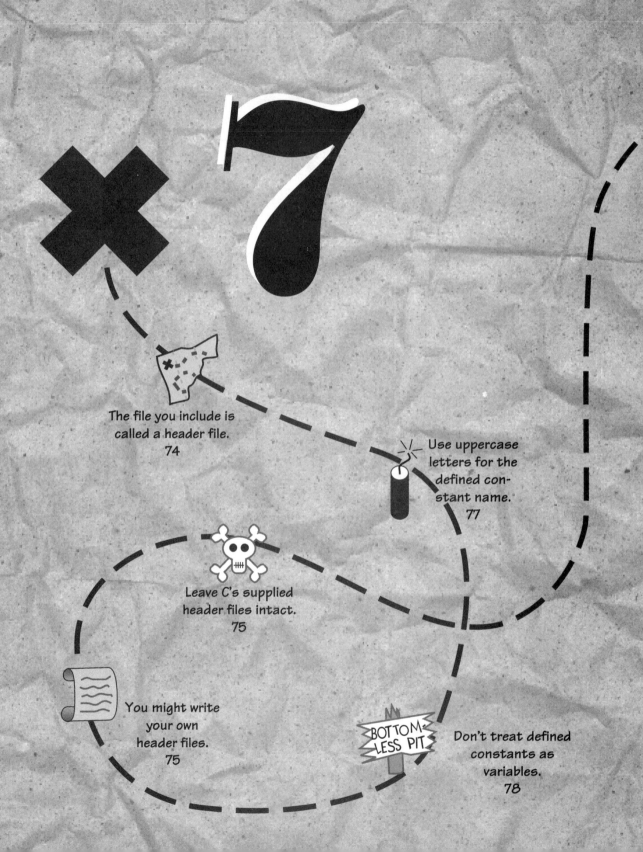

×7

The file you include is
called a header file.
74

Use uppercase
letters for the
defined con-
stant name.
77

Leave C's supplied
header files intact.
75

You might write
your own
header files.
75

BOTTOM-
LESS PIT

Don't treat defined
constants as
variables.
78

What Do #include and #define Mean?

They're Preprocessor Directives

Two types of lines you see in many C programs are not C commands at all. They are *preprocessor directives*. A preprocessor directive always begins with a pound sign (#). Preprocessor directives don't cause anything to happen at runtime (when you run your program). Instead, they do work during the compiling of your program.

The most often-used preprocessor directives are

✖ `#include`

✖ `#define`

In earlier chapters, you saw examples that used `#include`. This chapter finally takes the secret out of that mysterious preprocessor directive.

Including Files

`#include` has two formats, which are almost identical:

`#include <filename>`

and

`#include "filename"`

Figure 7.1 shows what `#include` does. It's nothing more than a *file merge* command. Right before your program is compiled, the `#include` statement is replaced with the contents of the filename specified after `#include`. The filename can be stated in either uppercase or lowercase letters as long as your operating system allows for either in filenames. For example, MS-DOS does not distinguish between uppercase and lowercase letters in filenames, but UNIX does. If your file is named `myFile.txt`, MS-DOS lets you use any of the following `#include` directives:

```
#include <MYFILE.TXT>
#include <myfile.txt>
#include <myFile.txt>
```

but UNIX allows only this:

```
#include <myFile.txt>
```

Clue: If you've used a word processor before, you've probably used an #include type of command. You might have merged a file stored on disk into the middle of the file you were editing.

Here's what you wrote:

Your source file:

```
        :
/* Part of a C program */
age = 31;
printf("I am %d years old" , age);
#include "addr.h"
printf("That's my address");
/*Rest of program follows */
        :
```

The file named addr.h:

```
printf("\n6104 E. Oak\n");
printf("St. Paul, MN\n");
printf("       54245\n");
```

BEFORE

Here's what the compiler sees:

```
        :
/* Part of a C program */
age = 31;
printf("I am %d years old" , age);
printf("\n6104 E. Oak\n");
printf("St. Paul, MN\n");
printf("       54245\n");
printf("That's my address");
/*Rest of program follows */
        :
```

AFTER

FIGURE 7.1.

#include inserts a disk file into the middle of another file.

When you install your compiler, the installation program sets up a separate location on your disk (in a *directory*) for various #include files that come with your compiler. When you want to use one of these built-in #include files, use the #include format with the angled brackets, < and >.

WARNING

"How do I know when to use a built-in #include file?" you ask. Good question! All built-in functions, such as printf(), have corresponding #include files. When this book describes a built-in function, it also tells you exactly which file to include.

Clue: Your compiler manual has a complete list of which functions are included in which files.

NOTE

You've already seen two built-in functions—printf() and strcpy(). (main() is not a built-in C function; main() is a function you must supply.) The #include file for printf() is STDIO.H (which stands for *standard I/O*), and the #include file for the strcpy() function is STDIO.H.

Clue: Most C compilers offer *context-sensitive help*. If yours does, you can place the cursor over a built-in function name such as strcpy() and select context-sensitive help (usually by pressing the Alt+F1 key combination). Your compiler tells you in the help message which header file you must include when you use that function.

Almost every complete program listing in this book contains the following preprocessor directive:

```
#include <stdio.h>
```

because almost every program in this book uses printf(). Chapter 6 told you to include STRING.H because the strcpy() function was discussed.

Clue: The file you include is called a *header file*. That's why most included files end in the extension .H.

If you wrote your own header files, you would use the second form of the preprocessor directive—the one that has quotation marks. If you use quotation marks, C first searches the disk directory in which your program is stored and *then* searches the built-in #include directory. Because of the search order, you can write your own header files and give them the same name as those built into C, and yours will be used instead of C's.

> **WARNING**
>
> If you write your own header files, don't put them with C's built-in #include file directory. Leave C's supplied header files intact. There is rarely a reason to override C's headers, but you might want to add some additional headers of your own.

> **NOTE**
>
> You might write your own header files when you have program statements you frequently use in many programs. Instead of typing them in every program, you can put them in a file in your program directory and #include the file where you want to use the statements.

Where Do I Put *#include* Directives?

The header files you #include are nothing more than text files that contain C code. You will learn much more about the contents of header files later, but for now understand that a header file does two things. The built-in header files help C properly execute built-in functions. The header files you write often contain code that you want to place in more than one file.

Clue: It's best to put your #include directives before main().

NOTE

The Blackjack program in Appendix B includes lots of header files because it uses lots of built-in functions. Notice the placement of the #includes: They come before main().

Defining Constants

The #define preprocessor directive defines *constants*. A C constant is really the same thing as a literal. You learned in Chapter 2 that a literal is a data value that doesn't change, like the number 4 or the string "C programming". The #define preprocessor directive lets you give names to literals. When you give a name to a literal, the named literal is known in C terminology as a *named constant* or a *defined constant*.

WARNING

In Chapter 5 you learned how to define variables by specifying their data types and giving them a name and an initial value. Constants you define with #define are *not* variables, even though they sometimes look like variables when they are used.

Here is the format of the #define directive:

```
#define CONSTANT constantDefinition
```

As with most things in C, using defined constants is easier than the format leads you to believe. Here are some sample #define directives:

```
#define AGELIMIT 21
#define MYNAME "Paula Holt"
#define PI 3.14159
```

Clue: In a nutshell, here's what #define tells C: Every place in the program that the CONSTANT appears, replace it with the constantDefinition.

The first #define just shown instructs C to find every occurrence of the word AGELIMIT and replace it with a 21. Therefore, if this statement appeared somewhere in the program after the #define:

```
if (employeeAge < AGELIMIT)
```

the compiler acts as if you typed this:

```
if (employeeAge < 21)
```

even though you didn't.

SKIP THIS, IT'S TECHNICAL

Use uppercase letters for the defined constant name. This is the one exception in C where uppercase is not only used but recommended. Because defined constants are not variables, the uppercase lets you glance through a program and tell at a glance what is a variable and what is a constant.

Clue: Assuming that you have previously defined the constant PI, the uppercase letters help keep you from doing something like this:

```
PI = 544.34;   /* Not allowed */
```

in the middle of the program. As long as you keep defined constant names in uppercase, you will know not to change them because they are *constants*.

Defined constants are good for naming values that might need to be changed between program runs. For example, if you didn't use a defined constant for AGELIMIT, but instead used an actual age limit value such as 21 throughout a program, if that age limit changed, it would be difficult to find and change every single 21. If you had used a defined constant at the top of the program and the age limit changed, you'd only need to change the #define statement to something like this:

```
#define AGELIMIT 18
```

Fun Fact

Much of the UNIX operating system (a competitor of DOS) was written in C.

WARNING

The `#define` directive is not a C command. As with `#include`, C handles your `#define` statements before your program is compiled. Therefore, if you defined PI as 3.14159 and you used PI throughout a program where you needed the value of the mathematical pi (Π), the C compiler would think *you* typed 3.14159 throughout the program when you really typed PI. PI is easier to remember (and helps eliminate typing mistakes) and is clearer to the purpose of the constant.

As long as you define a constant with `#define` before `main()` appears, the entire program will know about the constant. Therefore, if you defined PI to be the value 3.14159 before `main()`, you could use PI throughout `main()` and any other functions you write that follow `main()`, and the compiler knows to replace the PIs with 3.14159 before compiling your program.

Rewards

✖ Always `#include` the proper header file when using built-in functions.

✖ Use angled brackets (< and >) around the included filename when including compiler-supplied header files.

✖ Use quotation marks (" and ") around the included filename when including your own header files that you've stored in your source code's directory.

✖ Use uppercase characters in all defined constant names so that you can distinguish them from regular variable names.

Pitfalls

✖ Don't put `#include` statements for the built-in functions after `main()`. `#include` the header files before `main()`. You can `#include` your own header files wherever you want the code inserted.

✖ Don't treat defined constants as variables. Unlike with variables, you can't store data in a constant once it has been defined.

In Review

C's preprocessor directives make C see code that you didn't actually type. For instance, when you need the contents of another file (such as STDIO.H) that helps your program produce input and output properly, you don't have to type the contents of that file. You only have to instruct C to include the file via the #include directive.

If there is a constant value used throughout your program, such as a sales bonus limit, you should define that constant at the top of the program with #define. Instead of typing the actual number throughout the program, you have to type only the constant's name. If the limit ever changes, you have to change only the one #define line.

#include and #define are not C statements that run along with the rest of the program. They work on your source code by including text or changing defined names to actual values before C begins to compile your program.

Code Example

```
#include <stdio.h>
#include "mycode.h"
#define MINORDER 50
#define COMPNAME "Amalgamated Co."
```

Code Analysis

This section of code is composed solely of preprocessor directives. The pound sign (#) in column one is the giveaway. The first line instructs C to copy the STDIO.H file into the current program. Because angled brackets are used, the regular include directory that was created when you installed your compiler is searched. The second line uses quotation marks around the included file, which instructs C to look first in the source program's directory for the file.

Two defined constants, MINORDER and COMPNAME, are then defined. When the program must later test for or print the minimum order quantity or the company name, the defined constant names are used instead of the constants themselves.

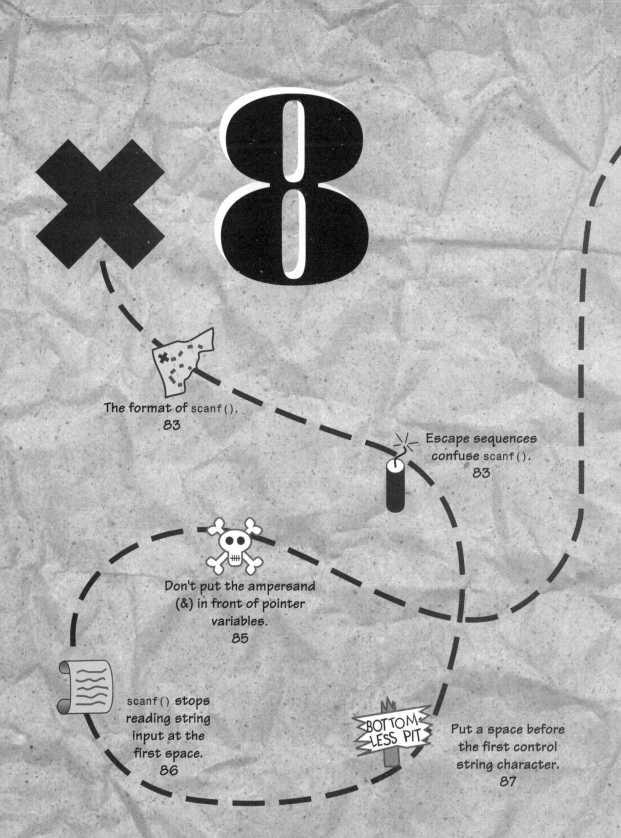

8

The format of scanf().
83

Escape sequences confuse scanf().
83

Don't put the ampersand (&) in front of pointer variables.
85

scanf() stops reading string input at the first space.
86

BOTTOM-LESS PIT

Put a space before the first control string character.
87

Can I Ask the User Questions?

With *scanf()*

printf() sends data to the screen. The scanf() function gets data from the keyboard. You must have a way to get data from your user. You can't always assign data values using assignment statements. For example, if you were writing a video rental program for use throughout the country, you couldn't assign the cost of a tape rental to a variable using the equals sign in your program because every store's rental could differ. Instead, you would have to ask the user of the program in each store location how much a tape rental costs before computing a charge.

You won't like learning scanf(), so we might as well get it over with as soon as possible. You will find that scanf() is the *craziest* function that could possibly exist! To a beginner, scanf() makes little sense, but despite its strange format, it is the easiest function to use for input at this point in the book because of its close ties to the printf() function.

Looking at *scanf()*

Figure 8.1 shows you what scanf() does. scanf() is a built-in C function that comes with all C compilers. Its header file is the same as printf()—stdio.h—so you don't have to worry about including an additional header file for scanf().

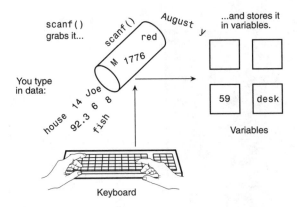

FIGURE 8.1.
scanf() fills variables with values typed by the user.

> **NOTE**
>
> scanf() is fairly easy if you know printf(). scanf() looks a lot like printf() because scanf() uses conversion codes such as %s and %d.

Clue: scanf() is the mirror-image function of printf(). Often, you will write programs that ask the user for values with a printf() and get those values with scanf(). Here is the format of scanf():

```
scanf(controlString [, data]);
```

When your program gets to scanf(), C stops and waits for the user to type values. The variables listed inside scanf() (following the controlString) will accept whatever values the user types. scanf() quits when the user presses Enter after typing values.

SKIP THIS, IT'S TECHNICAL

Even though scanf() uses the same conversion characters as printf(), never specify escape sequences such as \n, \a, or \t. Escape sequences confuse scanf(). scanf() quits getting values from the user when the user presses Enter, so you don't ever specify the \n.

Prompting for *scanf()*

Almost every scanf() you write should be preceded with printf(). If you don't issue a printf(), the program will stop and wait for input, and the user will have no idea what to do. For example, if you need to get an amount from the user, you would put a printf() function like this before scanf():

```
printf("What is the amount? ");  /* Prompt */
/* A scanf() would follow */
```

> **Clue:** A printf() before a scanf() sends a *prompt* to the user. If you don't prompt the user for the value or values you want, the user has no way of knowing what values should be typed. Generally, the printf() requests the data from the user and the scanf() gets the data that the user types.

Problems with *scanf()*

As mentioned in the first part of this chapter, scanf() is not the easiest function in the world to use. One of the first problems with scanf() is that although the user must type exactly what scanf() expects, the user rarely does this! If the scanf() needs a floating-point value, but the user types a character, there is little you can do. The floating-point variable you supply will have bad data because a character is not a floating-point value.

Fun Fact

Data-entry is the term given for grabbing user input.

For now, assume that the user *does* type what is needed. Chapter 18, "How Can I Control Input and Output?," describes some ways to overcome problems brought on by scanf() (although modern-day C programmers often resort to complete data-entry routines they write, download, or purchase elsewhere that overcomes C's difficult data-entry ability).

SKIP THIS, IT'S TECHNICAL

"I have yet to see a scanf(). When are you going to show one?" you might be asking. Get ready, because here it comes.

Here is a scanf() that gets an integer value (as you can tell from the %d integer conversion code) from the keyboard into a variable named age:

```
scanf(" %d", &age);
```

The variable age will hold whatever number the user types before pressing Enter.

The first thing to notice about scanf() is the space right before the %d. The space isn't always required here, but it never hurts, and it sometimes helps the input work better when you get numbers and characters in succession. Adding the extra space is a good habit to get into now while learning scanf().

Enough about all that. Let's get to the most obvious scanf() problem—the ampersand (&) before the variable age. Guess what? scanf() requires that you put the ampersand before all variables, even though the ampersand is *not* part of the variable name! Do it, and scanf() works; leave off the ampersand, and scanf() won't accept the user's values into the variables.

Clue: There is an exception to the ampersand rule you should know about. If you're getting input into an array using %s, as happens when you ask users for a name to be stored in a character array, you do *not* use the ampersand.

The bottom-line rule is this: If you're asking the user to type integers, floating-points, characters, doubles, or any of the other single-variable combinations (long integers and so on), put an ampersand before the variable names in the scanf(). If you are asking the user for a string into a character array, don't put the ampersand before the array name.

WARNING

You also wouldn't put the ampersand in front of *pointer* variables. Actually, an array is nothing more than a pointer variable, and that's why the ampersand isn't needed for arrays. We'll get to pointers later in this book, but if you've seen them in other languages, you know what I'm talking about. If you haven't seen a pointer variable before, and you don't know what this is all about, well, you were warned not to read this paragraph anyway! Seriously, you'll fully understand pointers and how they are like arrays after reading Chapter 25, "How Are Arrays and Pointers Different?"

> **NOTE**
>
> There's a problem with using scanf() to get character strings into
> character arrays that you should know about now. scanf() stops
> reading string input at the first space. Therefore, you can get only a
> single word at a time with scanf(). If you must ask the user for more
> than one word, such as the user's first and last name, use two
> scanf()s (with their own printf() prompts) and store the two
> names in two character arrays.

The following program asks the user for a first name, last name, age, and
weight. Notice that the character arrays have no ampersands, but that the
other two variables do. The program doesn't ask for the user's full name
because scanf() isn't capable of getting two words at once.

```c
#include <stdio.h>
main()
{
  int age;
  float weight;
  char first[15], last[15];

  printf("\nWhat is your first name? ");     /* A prompt */
  scanf(" %s", first); /* No ampersand on character arrays */
  printf("What is your last name? ");
  scanf(" %s", last);  /* No ampersand on character arrays */

  printf("How old are you? ");
  scanf(" %d", &age);  /* Ampersand required */
  printf("How much do you weigh? ");
  scanf(" %f", &weight);

  printf("\nHere is the information you entered:\n");
  printf("Name: %s %s\n", first, last);
  printf("Weight: %.0f\n", weight);  /* 0 decimal places */
                                     /* displayed         */
  printf("Age: %d", age);
  return 0; /* Always best to use this. I'll explain later */
}
```

Here is a sample execution of this program:

```
What is your first name? Joe
```

```
What is your last name? Harrison
How old are you? 41
How much do you weigh? 205

Here is the information you entered:
Name: Joe Harrison
Weight: 205
Age: 41
```

Clue: You can let the user type characters other than data values. For example, many times dates are entered with slashes or hyphens separating the day, month, and year like this: 03/05/95. You have to trust the user to type things just right. Here is a scanf() that gets a date and expects the user to type the date in *mm/dd/yy* format:

```
scanf(" %d/%d/%d", &month, &day, &year);
```

The user could type 02/28/94 or 11/22/95 but not June 5th, 1993 because the scanf() is expecting something else.

Rewards

✖ Use scanf() if you want to get data from the user by way of the keyboard.

✖ Every scanf() requires a control string that dictates how your data will look when input.

✖ Before using a scanf(), use a printf() to prompt the user for the values you want.

✖ Put an ampersand before non-array variables in a scanf().

Pitfalls

✖ Don't forget to put a space before the first control string character (for example, " %d" contains a space before the %) to ensure accurate input.

✖ Don't use an ampersand in front of array names in a scanf().

✖ Don't expect the user to type exactly what you want! If exact accuracy is needed, such as in an end-user environment where noncomputerists will be using your program, you'll want to use other means of input that are explained in Chapter 18, "How Else Can I Control Input and Output?"

In Review

This chapter's goal was to teach you how to ask for and get answers from the user. Being able to process user input is an important part of any language. scanf() performs data-entry; that is, scanf() gets the user's input and stores that input in variables.

Before using a scanf(), you will need to let the user know what kind of keyboard input you're expecting. For example, before using scanf() to get a sales amount, use a printf() to ask for the amount so the user knows what to type.

Although scanf() uses the same format codes as printf(), scanf() has extra requirements that you should understand. scanf() requires an & in front of non-array variables. Also, if you are getting strings from the user, the scanf() and %s combination can get only one word at a time.

Code Example

```
/* Asks users for their hometown, state, and year born */
printf("What town were you born in? ");
scanf(" %s", homeTown);  /* homeTown must be a
                             character array */
printf("What state were you born in? ");
scanf(" %s", state);  /* state must be a character array */
printf("What year were you born in? ");
scanf(" %d", &yearBorn);  /* yearBorn must be numeric */
```

Code Analysis

These lines of code prompt the user with a printf() before each scanf(). With the printed prompts, the user knows exactly what is required. The format code must match the variable's data type. Earlier in the program, the variables homeTown and state must have been defined as character arrays because they are to hold strings. The variable yearBorn is an int data type. (int is a large enough data type to hold year values.)

Because the first two variables are arrays, no ampersand is needed before them in the scanf()s. An & *is* needed before non-array variables such as yearBorn.

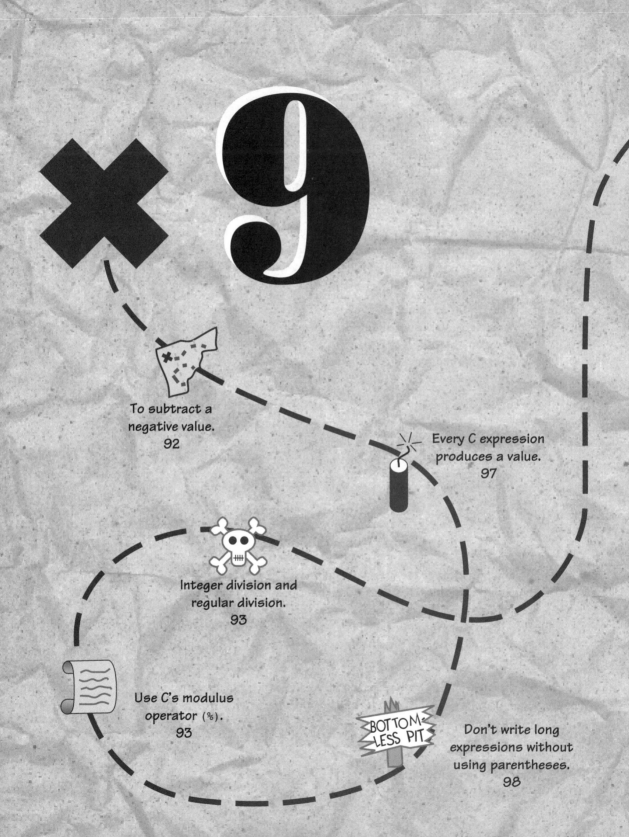

9

To subtract a
negative value.
92

Every C expression
produces a value.
97

Integer division and
regular division.
93

Use C's modulus
operator (%).
93

BOTTOM-
LESS PIT

Don't write long
expressions without
using parentheses.
98

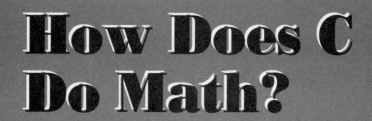

How Does C Do Math?

With Operators

There are two kinds of operators. There are the ones who help you with long distance phone calls, but we won't be discussing those. There are also C operators, which let you do math. You don't have to be a math wizard to write programs that use math operators. C does all the math for you as long as you know how to list the operators properly.

Not only should you learn to recognize math operators, but you should also learn how C orders math operators. C doesn't always calculate from left to right. This chapter explains why.

The Basics

Lots of C operators work exactly the way you expect them to. You use a plus sign (+) when you want to add, and you use a minus sign (-) when you want to subtract. An *expression* includes one or more operators. C programmers often use math expressions on the right side of the assignment operator when filling variables with values, like this:

```
totalSales = localSales + foreignSales - salesReturns;
```

C computes the answer and then stores that answer in `totalSales`.

Clue: If you want to subtract a negative value, be sure to put a space between the minus signs, like this:

```
newValue = oldValue - -factor;
```

If you omit the space, C will think you're using another operator, `--`, called the *decrement* operator, described in Chapter 13, "Are There More Operators?".

You can even put a math expression inside a `printf()`:

```
printf("In 3 years, I'll be %d years old.\n", age + 3);
```

If you want to multiply and divide, you can do so by using the * and / symbols. The following statement assigns a value to a variable using multiplication and division:

```
newFactor = fact * 1.2 / 0.5;
```

WARNING

If you put integers on *both* sides of the division symbol (/), C computes the *integer division result*. Study the following expressions to get familiar with integer division and regular division. The comments explain the results calculated from the divisions:

```
float a = 17.0;
float b = 5.0;
float answf;     /* Holds float answer */
int i = 17;
int j = 5;
int answi;       /* Holds integer answer */
answf = a / b;   /* 3.4 is stored in answf */
answi = i / j;   /* 3 is stored in answi */
```

NOTE

If you need the remainder after integer division, use C's *modulus* operator (%). Given the values just listed, the following statement puts a 2 in ansMod:

```
ansMod = i % j;  /* 2 is the remainder of 17 / 5 */
```

You now know the three ways C divides values: regular division if a noninteger is on either or both sides of the /, integer division if an integer is on both sides of the /, and modulus if the % operator is used between two integers.

Clue: You can't use % between anything but integer data types.

The following short program computes the net sale price of tires:

```
/* Computes net tire sales */
#include <stdio.h>
main()
{
  int numTires;
  float tirePrice, beforeTax, netSale;
  float taxRate = .07;        /* Sales tax */
  /* Ask user for values */
  printf("How many tires bought? ");
  scanf(" %d", &numTires);
  printf("How much is each tire? ");
  scanf(" %f", &tirePrice);
  /* Compute the sale */
  beforeTax = tirePrice * numTires;
  netSale = beforeTax + (beforeTax * taxRate);
  printf("Your total sale is %.2f\n", netSale);
  return 0;
}
```

Here is a sample run of the program:

```
How many tires bought? 4
How much is each tire? 45.99
You total sale is 196.84
```

Order of Operators

As mentioned earlier in this chapter, C doesn't always compute math operations in the order you expect. The following expression explains it in a nutshell:

```
ans = 5 + 2 * 3;  /* Puts 11 in ans */
```

If you thought that C would store 21 in ans, you're reading the expression from left to right. However, C always computes multiplication before addition! It sounds crazy, but as long as you know the rules, you'll be okay. C is following the *order of operators* table. C first multiplies 2 and 3 to get 6 and then adds 5 to get 11.

You'll find the complete order of operators table in the tearout card of this book. As you can see in the table, *, /, and % appear before + and -. Therefore, if C sees an expression with a combination of these operators, it evaluates *, /, and % before computing + and -.

Here is a difficult expression. All the variables and numbers are integers. See if you can figure out the answer by the way C would evaluate the expression:

```
ans = 5 + 2 * 4 / 2 % 3 + 10 - 3;  /* What is answer? */
```

The answer, 13, is found in Figure 9.1.

```
ans = 5 + 2 * 4 / 2 % 3 + 10 - 3
            \ /
      5 + 8 / 2 % 3 + 10 - 3
            \ /
      5 +  4  % 3 + 10 - 3
              \ /
        5 +  1  + 10 - 3
           \ /
           6  + 10 - 3
              \ /
             16 - 3
               \ /
               13
```

FIGURE 9.1.
Solving the expression the way C would.

Clue: Don't do too much at one time when evaluating such expressions for practice. As the figure shows, you should compute one operator at a time and then bring the rest of the expression down for the next round.

If an expression such as the one in Figure 9.1 contains more than one operator that sits on the same level in the order of operators table, you must use the third column, labeled Associativity, to determine how the operators are evaluated. In other words, because *, /, and % all reside on the same level, they were evaluated from left to right, as dictated by the order of operators table's Associativity column.

You might wonder why you have to learn this stuff. After all, doesn't C do your math for you? The answer is "Yes, *but...*." C does your math, but you need to know how to set up your expressions properly. The classic reason is as follows: Suppose you want to compute the average of four variables. The following will *not* work:

```
avg = i + j + k + 1 / 4;   /* Will NOT compute average! */
```

The reason is simple once you understand the order of operators. C computes the division first, so 1 / 4 is evaluated first and then i, j, and k are added to that divided result. If you want to override the order of operators, as you would do in this case, you have to learn to use ample parentheses around expressions.

Break the Rules with Parentheses

If you need to override the order of operators, you can. If you group an expression inside parentheses, C will evaluate that expression before the others. Because the order of operators table shows parentheses before any of the other math operators, parentheses have precedence, as the following statement shows:

```
ans = (5 + 2) * 3;   /* Puts 21 in ans */
```

Even though multiplication is usually performed before addition, the parentheses force C to evaluate 5 + 2 first and then multiplies the resulting 7 by 3. Therefore, if you want to average four values, you can do so by grouping the addition of the values in parentheses:

```
avg = (i + j + k + 1) / 4;   /* Computes average */
```

Clue: Use lots of parentheses. They clarify your expressions. Even if the regular operator order will suffice for your expression, parentheses will make the expression easier for you to decipher if you need to change the program later.

Assignments Everywhere

As you can see from the order of operators table, the assignment operator has precedence and associativity, as do the rest of the operators. Assignment has very low priority in the table, and it associates from right to left.

The right-to-left associativity lets you perform an interesting operation: You can assign a value to more than one variable in the same expression. To assign the value of 9 to 10 different variables, you *could* do this:

```
a = 9; b = 9; c = 9; d = 9; e = 9;
f = 9; g = 9; h = 9; i = 9; j = 9;
```

but this is easier:

```
a = b = c = d = e = f = g = h = i = j = 9;
```

Because of the right-to-left associativity, C first assigns the 9 to j and then puts the 9 in i, and so on.

Clue: C doesn't initialize variables for you. If you wanted 0 put in a bunch of variables, a multiple assignment would do it for you.

> **SKIP THIS, IT'S TECHNICAL**
>
> Every C expression produces a value. The expression j = 9; does put a 9 in j, but it also results in a completed value of 9, which is available to store somewhere else if needed. The fact that every assignment results in an expression lets you do things like this that you can't always do in other programming languages:
>
> ```
> a = 5 * (b = 2);   /* Puts a 2 in b and a 10 in a */
> ```

Rewards

✖ Use +, -, *, and / for addition, subtraction, multiplication, and division.

✖ Use % if you want the remainder of an integer division.

✖ Keep the order of operators table handy, because it determines how C evaluates expressions.

✖ Use multiple assignment operators if you have several variables to initialize.

Pitfalls

✖ Don't put two minus signs together if you want to subtract a negative number. Leave a space between them.

✖ Don't use % to compute the remainder of noninteger data division. If you divide nonintegers, the result will be an accurate floating-point answer.

✖ Don't write long expressions without using parentheses. The parentheses help show exactly what you expect, and they keep you from incorrectly relying on the order of operator table.

In Review

C provides lots of math operators that do calculations for you. Most of the operators look like their math counterparts (+, -, /, and so on), and the others are easy to learn. The primary consideration you must concern yourself with is the order of operators. C's order of operators table shows you the way C interprets the order of your calculations. You can use parentheses to override that built-in order if you like.

Code Example

```
total = cost * numberBought;
sTax = .08 * total;
grandTotal = total + sTax;
discounted = grandTotal - .10 * grandTotal;
```

Code Analysis

This series of assignment statements computes the total sale amount and the discount amount of a purchase. The cost of each item is first multiplied by the number of items bought. An 8 percent tax must be taken out of the total and then added back in. A 10 percent discount is computed from the grand total if the customer pays cash.

No parentheses are needed in any of the calculations because the natural order of operators works for the example. If you would like to make the order even clearer, you could add parentheses, such as in this rewritten last statement:

```
discounted = grandTotal - (.10 * grandTotal);
```

Part 2

The Operating Room

×10

You might have made
the variable the
wrong type.
109

You can type-
cast an entire
expression.
109

In math, nothing can
be equal to itself
plus 1.
104

Compound operators
reduce typing errors.
106

Don't mix data types.
110

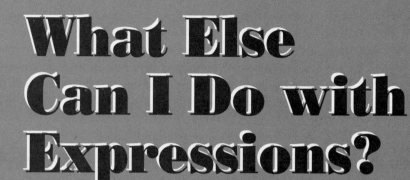

What Else Can I Do with Expressions?

Combine Operators and Give Typecasts

As you can see from the Order of Operators table on the tear-out card (at the beginning of the book), C has a rich assortment of operators. C has many operators that help C keep its command vocabulary small. There aren't many commands in C, but there are a lot more operators than in most other programming languages; whereas most computer programming languages have relatively few operators and lots of commands, C retains its succinct nature by providing many powerful operators.

This chapter explores a few more operators that you'll need as you write programs. The compound assignment operators and the typecast operator provide the vehicles for several advanced operations.

Compound Assignment

There will be many times in your programs when you have to change the value of a variable. Until now, all variables have been assigned values based on constant literal values or expressions. However, there will often be times when you must update a variable.

Suppose your program had to count the number of times a profit value goes below zero. You would need to set up a *counter variable*. A counter variable is a variable that you add one to when a certain event takes place. Every time a profit value goes negative, you might do this:

```
lossCount = lossCount + 1;   /* Adds 1 to lossCount variable */
```

> **WARNING**
>
> In math, nothing can be equal to itself plus 1! With computers, though, the previous assignment statement adds 1 to lossCount and then assigns that new value to lossCount—in effect adding 1 to lossCount's value. Remember that an equals sign means "take whatever is on the right of the equals sign and store that computed value in the variable on the left."

The following program is simple but prints the numbers from 1 to 5 using a counter assignment statement before each printf():

```
/* Counts from 1 to 5 */
#include <stdio.h>
main()
{
  int ctr = 0;      /* Start at 0 */
  ctr = ctr + 1;    /* Add 1 to counter */
  printf("ctr is at %d\n", ctr);
  ctr = ctr + 1;    /* Counter is now 2 */
  printf("ctr is at %d\n", ctr);
  ctr = ctr + 1;    /* Counter is now 3 */
  printf("ctr is at %d\n", ctr);
  ctr = ctr + 1;    /* Counter is now 4 */
  printf("ctr is at %d\n", ctr);
  ctr = ctr + 1;    /* Counter is now 5 */
  printf("ctr is at %d\n", ctr);
  return 0;
}
```

The following lines show the program's output. Notice that ctr keeps increasing (in computer lingo, it's called *incrementing*) by one with each assignment statement

```
ctr is at 1
ctr is at 2
ctr is at 3
ctr is at 4
ctr is at 5
```

By subtracting instead of adding, you can *decrement* a variable's value in a similar fashion (such as when you want to decrease totals from inventories as products are sold).

There will be other times when you'll need to *update* a variable by adding to a total or by adjusting it in some way. The following assignment statement increases the variable sales by 25 percent:

```
sales = sales * 1.25;  /* Increases sales by 25 percent */
```

C provides several *compound operators* that let you update a variable in a manner similar to the methods just described (incrementing, decrementing, and updating by more than one). However, instead of repeating the variable on *both* sides of the equals sign, you have to list the variable only once. As with much of C, some examples will help clarify what is done with the compound operators.

Clue: Chapter 15, "Are There Other Loops?," shows you how the for statement makes updating variables easier.

If you want to add 1 to a variable, you can use the *compound addition* operator, +=. These two statements produce the same result.

```
lossCount = lossCount + 1;  /* Adds 1 to lossCount variable */
```

and

```
lossCount += 1;  /* Adds 1 to lossCount variable */
```

Instead of multiplying sales by 1.25 and then assigning it to itself like this:

```
sales = sales * 1.25;  /* Increases sales by 25 percent */
```

you can use the *compound multiplication* operator, *=, to do this:

```
sales *= 1.25;  /* Increases sales by 25 percent */
```

NOTE

The compound operators are quicker to use than writing out the entire assignment because you don't have to list the same variable name on both sides of the equals sign. Also, the compound operators reduce typing errors because you don't have to type the same variable name twice in the same statement.

Table 10.1 lists all the compound assignment operators and gives examples of each. All the operators you've seen so far in this book, from addition through modulus, have corresponding compound operators.

Table 10.1. Compound assignment operators.

Compound Operator	Example	Equivalent Statement
*=	total *= 1.25;	total = total * 1.25;
/=	amt /= factor;	amt = amt / factor;

Compound Operator	Example	Equivalent Statement
%=	days %= 3;	days = days % 3;
+=	count += 1;	count = count + 1;
-=	adjust -= 0.5;	adjust = adjust - 0.5;

> **NOTE**
>
> The dispCard() function in the Blackjack game in Appendix B uses a compound addition operator to update the card count depending on the value of the last card drawn.

Watch That Order!

Look at the order of operators table and locate the compound assignment operators. You'll see that they have very low precedence. The +=, for instance, several levels lower than the +.

Initially, this might not sound like a big deal. (Actually, maybe none of this sounds like a big deal. If so, *great!* C should be easier than a lot of people would have you think.) The order of operators table can haunt the unwary C programmer. Think about how you would evaluate the second of these expressions:

```
total = 5;
total *= 2 + 3;  /* Updates the total variable */
```

At first glance, you might think that the value of total is 13 because you learned earlier that multiplication is done before addition. You're right that multiplication is done before addition, but *compound multiplication* is done *after* addition according to the order of operators. Therefore, the 2 + 3 is evaluated to get 5, and *then* that 5 is multiplied by the old value of total (which also happens to be 5) to get a total of 25, as Figure 10.1 points out.

```
total * = 2+3;
```
is the same thing as this:

```
total = total *(2 + 3);
```
because ***=** is lower than + in the table.

FIGURE 10.1.
The compound operators reside on a low level.

Typecasting: Hollywood Could Take Lessons from C

There are two kinds of typecasting: the kind that directors of movies often do (but we'll not cover that here) and also C's typecasting. A C *typecast* temporarily changes the data type of one variable to another. Here is the format of a typecast:

(*dataType*)*value*

The *dataType* can be any C data type such as int, or float. The *value* is any variable, literal, or expression. Suppose that age is an integer variable that holds 6. The following:

(float)age

converts age to a float value of 6.0. If you were using age in an expression with other floats, you should typecast age to float to maintain consistency in the expression.

> **NOTE**
>
> Because of some rounding problems that can automatically occur if you mix data types, you'll have fewer problems if you explicitly typecast all variables and literals in an expression to the same data type.

Never use a typecast with a variable on a line by itself. Typecast where a variable or an expression has to be converted to another value to properly compute a result. The preceding typecast of age might be represented like this:

```
salaryBonus = salary * (float)age / 150.0;
```

age does *not* change to a floating-point variable! age is changed only *temporarily* for this one calculation. Everywhere in the program that age is not explicitly typecast, it is still an int variable.

Clue: If you find yourself typecasting the same variable to a different data type throughout a program, you might have made the variable the wrong type to begin with.

SKIP THIS, IT'S TECHNICAL

You can typecast an entire expression. The following statement typecasts the result of an expression before assigning it to a variable:

```
value = (float)(number - 10 * yrsService);
```

The parentheses around the expression keep the typecast from casting only the variable number. C does perform some automatic typecasting. If value is defined as a float, C typecasts the preceding expression for you before storing the result in value. Nevertheless, if you want to clarify all expressions and not depend on automatic typecasting, go ahead and typecast your expressions.

Rewards

✖ Use compound assignment operators when updating variable values.

✖ Use compound assignment operators to eliminate a few typing errors and to decrease your program-writing time.

✖ Put a data type in parentheses before a variable, expression, or data value you want to typecast.

Pitfalls

✖ Don't mix data types. Instead, typecast data so that it is all the same type before evaluating it.

✖ Don't ignore the order of operators! The compound operators have low priority in the table and are done after almost every other operator finishes.

In Review

The goal of this chapter was to teach you additional operators that help you write C programs. Use the compound operators when you want to change the value of a variable. You don't have to repeat the variable name on both sides of the equals sign because a compound operator understands that you want to update the variable's value. (This saves you lots of typing and potential errors if you use long variable names such as costOfGoodsSold.)

If you want to mix variables and constants of different data types, use typecasting to produce uniform data types in expressions. Although C will typecast automatically, you won't always like the results. C might convert float to int when you wanted everything to remain float. Typecasting becomes especially critical later when you write more advanced programs that use pointers and structures.

Code Example

```c
/* Dog age calculation */
#include <stdio.h>
main()
{
  int age;
  float dogAge;
  printf("How old are you? ");
  scanf(" %d", &age);  /* Gets the user's age as an integer */
  dogAge = (float)age / 7.0;
  printf("If you were a dog, you'd only be %.1f years old!",
         dogAge);
  return 0;
}
```

Code Analysis

The code first asks the user for his or her age. Because people rarely enter fractional ages, the age value is stored in an integer variable. The age is then divided by 7.0 to get the corresponding age in dog years. (A year to a dog is like seven years to a person, which makes you wonder how Lassie has lived since the 1950s.)

Because the division produces a floating-point result, the typecast ensures that age is converted to float before the calculation is performed. Making your data types consistent is very important as you move into more advanced programming.

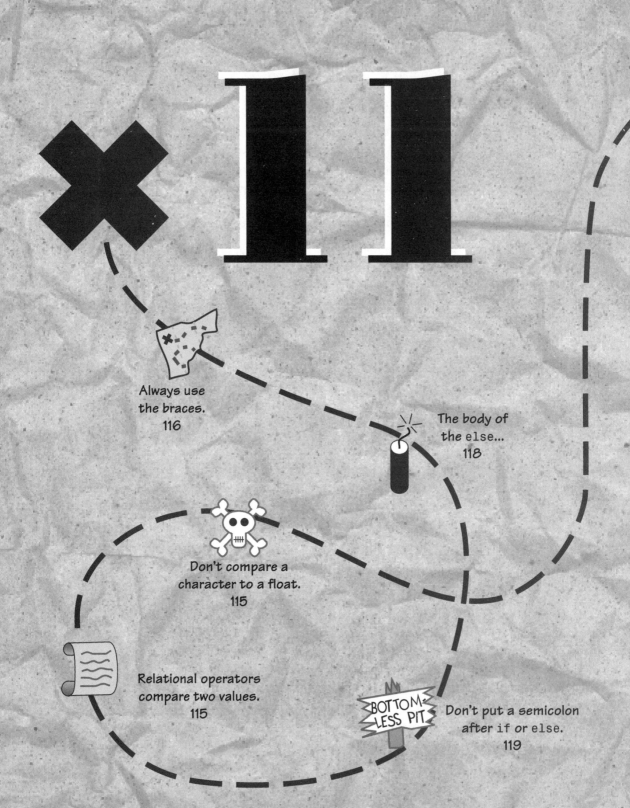

11

Can I Compare Two Values?

With Relational Operators

C provides an extremely useful statement called `if`. `if` lets your programs make decisions and execute certain statements based on the results of those decisions. By testing contents of variables, your programs can produce different output given different input.

Relational operators are also described in this chapter. Relational operators, combined with `if`, make C a powerful data-processing language. Computers would really be boring if they couldn't test data. Computers would be little more than calculators if they had no capability to decide courses of action based on data.

Testing Data

C's `if` statement works just like it does in spoken language: *If something is true, do one thing; otherwise, do something else.* Consider these statements:

> If I make enough money, we'll go to Italy.
>
> If the shoes don't fit, take them back.
>
> If it's hot outside, water the lawn.

Table 11.1 lists C's relational operators, which permit testing of data. Notice that some of the relational operators are made up of two symbols.

Table 11.1. C's relational operators.

Relational Operator	Description
`==`	Equal to
`>`	Greater than
`<`	Less than
`>=`	Greater than or equal to
`<=`	Less than or equal to
`!=`	Not equal to

> **NOTE**
>
> Relational operators compare two values. You always put a variable, literal, or expression—or a combination of any two of them—on either side of a relational operator.

Before delving into `if`, let's look at a few relational operators and see what they really mean. A regular operator produces a mathematical result. A relational operator produces a *true* or *false* result. When you compare two data values, the data values either produce a true comparison or they don't. For example, given the following values:

```
int i = 5;
int j = 10;
int k = 15;
int l = 5;
```

the following statements are *true:*

```
i == l
j < k
k > i
j != k
```

The following statements are *not* true, so they are *false:*

```
i > j
k < j
j == l
```

> **WARNING**
>
> Only like values should go on either side of the relational operator. In other words, don't compare a character to a float. If you have to compare two unlike data values, use a typecast to keep the values the same data type.

Fun Fact

To tell the difference between = and ==, remember that you need two equals signs to double-check whether something is equal.

> **WARNING**
>
> Every time C evaluates a relational operator, a value of 1 or 0 is produced. True always results in 1, and false always results in 0. The following statements would assign a 1 to the variable a and a 0 to the variable b:
>
> ```
> a = (4 < 10);  /* (4 < 10) is true, so a 1 is put in a */
>
> b = (8 == 9);  /* (8 == 9) is false, so a 0 is put in b */
> ```

You will often use relational operators in your programs because you'll often want to know if sales (stored in a variable) is more than a set goal, if payroll calculations are in line, if a product is in inventory or needs to be ordered. You have now seen only the beginning of relational operators. The next section explains how to use them.

Using *if*

The if statement uses relational operators to perform data testing. Here's the format of the if statement:

```
if (condition)
{ block of one or more C statements; }
```

The parentheses around the *condition* are required. The *condition* is a relational test like those described in the preceding section. The *block of one or more C statements* is called the *body* of the if statement. The braces around the *block of one or more C statements* are required if the body of the if contains more than a single statement.

Clue: Even though braces aren't required if an if contains just one statement, always use the braces. If you later add statements to the body of the if, the braces will be there. If the braces enclose more than one statement, the braces enclose what is known as a *compound statement.*

Here is an `if` statement:

```
if (age < 18)
  { printf("You cannot vote yet\n");
    yrs = 18 - age;  /* Calculates how many years
                          until the user can vote */
    printf("You can vote in %d years.\n", yrs); }
```

The `if` reads like this to the C programmer: "If the variable named age contains a value less than 18, print the messages and calculate the value of `yrs`. Otherwise, don't print and calculate. Whatever happens, the program continues at the statement that follows the body of the `if`" once the `if` completes its job.

> **NOTE**
>
> The `main()` function in the Blackjack program in Appendix B asks the player if he or she wants to hit or stand (in casino lingo, that means to draw another card or not). An `if` is used to determine exactly what the user wants to do.

Otherwise...: Using *else*

In the preceding section, you saw how to write a course of action that executes if the relational test is true. If the relational test were false, nothing happened. This section explains the `else` statement that you can add to `if`. Using `else`, you can specify exactly what happens when the relational test is false. Here is the format of the combined `if-else`:

```
if (condition)
  { block of one or more C statements; }
else
  { block of one or more C statements; }
```

Here is an example of `if-else`:

```
if (age < 18)
  { printf("You cannot vote yet\n");
    yrs = 18 - age;
    /* Prints an appropriate message,
       depending on user's age */
```

```
      printf("You can vote in %d years.\n", yrs); }
else
  { printf("You've made it to adulthood.\n"); }
```

If the age is less than 18, the body of the if executes. If the age is *not* less than 18, the body of the else executes.

Clue: Put semicolons only at the end of executable statements in the body of the if or the else. Never put a semicolon after the if or the else. Semicolons go only at the end of complete statements.

SKIP THIS, IT'S TECHNICAL

As with the body of the if, the body of the else doesn't require braces if it consists of a single statement; but it's a good idea to use braces anyway.

The following program computes simple income tax if the user earns more than a preset salary.

```c
/* Computes simple tax */
#include <stdio.h>
/* Defined constant holds salary level trigger */
#define MAXSAL 18000.00
main()
{
  float salary, taxAmt;
  float taxRate = .35;
  printf("How much did you earn last year? ");
  scanf(" %f", &salary);
  /* No tax for small salaries */
  if (salary >= MAXSAL)
    { taxAmt = salary * taxRate; }
  else
    { taxAmt = 0.0; }   /* None for low salary */
  printf("Your tax is %.2f\n", taxAmt);
  return 0;
}
```

Here are two runs of the program showing that the output differs depending on the amount of the user's salary:

```
How much did you earn last year? 24390.40
Your tax is 8536.64

How much did you earn last year? 16558.21
Your tax is 0.00
```

Rewards

* ✖ Use relational operators to compare data.
* ✖ Remember that a true relational result produces a 1, and a false relational result produces a 0.
* ✖ Use `if` to compare data and `else` to specify what to do if the `if` test fails.
* ✖ Put braces around the `if` body of code and around the `else` body of code. All the code in the braces either executes or does not execute depending on the relational comparison.

Pitfalls

* ✖ Don't put values of different data types on each side of a relational operator.
* ✖ Don't put a semicolon after `if` or `else`. Semicolons go only at the end of each statement, inside the body of the `if` or the `else`.

In Review

The goal of this chapter was to show you ways to test data and execute one set of code or another, depending on the result of that test. You don't always want the same code to execute every time someone runs your program because the data is not always the same. Computers must be able to look at data and process that data (which is why it's called *data processing*).

The relational operators and the `if` statement work together to produce a true or false analysis of data.

Code Example

```
printf("How much did you make last year? ");
scanf(" %f", &salary);
if (salary > 100000.0)
  { printf("Wow! You really worked hard despite ");
    printf("what some might think!"); }
else
  { sal100 = 100000.0 - salary;
    printf("Only $%.0f more to reach the century mark!",
            sal100); }
```

Code Analysis

When the user enters a salary, the program makes a decision depending on the salary's relation to $100,000. If the user earned more than $100,000 (we should all be so productive!), a congratulatory message is printed. If the user earned less than $100,000, a message prints telling the user how far away from $100,000 he or she is. (Most of us have quite a way to go!)

The `else` statement ensures that only one set of code, after `if`, executes.

12

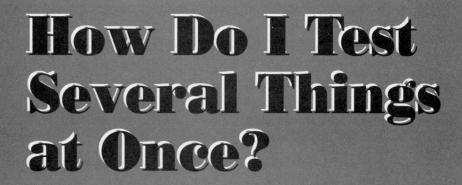

How Do I Test Several Things at Once?

With Logical Operators

Sometimes the relational operators described in Chapter 11, "How Can I Compare Two Values?," simply can't express all the testing conditions. For example, if you wanted to test whether a numeric or character variable is within a certain range, you would have to use two `if` statements, like this:

```
if (age >= 21)    /* See if 21 <= age <= 65 */
{ if (age <= 65)
    {
     printf("The age falls between 21 and 65.\n");
    }
}
```

Although there's nothing wrong with using nested `if` statements, they're not extremely straightforward and their logic is slightly more complex than you really need. By using the *logical operators* you'll read about in this chapter, you can combine more than one relational test in a single `if` statement to clarify your code.

NOTE

Don't let the terms *logical* and *relational* make you think these two groups of operators are difficult. As long as you understand how the individual operators work, you don't have to keep track of what they're called as a group.

Clue: A relational operator simply tests how two values relate (how they compare to each other). The logical operators combine relational operators.

Getting Logical

There are three logical operators (see Table 12.1). Sometimes logical operators are known as *compound relational operators* because they let you combine more than one relational operator. (See the previous Clue.)

Table 12.1. The logical operators.

Logical Operator	Meaning
&&	And
¦¦	Or
!	Not

Logical operators appear between two or more relational tests. For example, here are the first parts of three if statements that use logical operators:

```
if ((age >= 21) && (age <= 65)) {
```

and

```
if ((hrsWorked > 40) ¦¦ (sales > 25000.00)) {
```

and

```
if (!(isCharterMember)) {
```

Clue: If you combine two relational operators with a logical operator or if you use the ! (not) operator to negate a relation, the *entire* expression following the if statement requires parentheses. This is not allowed:

```
if !isCharterMember {     /* Not allowed */
```

Of course, there is more to the preceding if statements than what is shown, but to keep things simple at this point, the if bodies aren't shown.

Logical operators work just as they do in spoken language. For example, consider the spoken statements that correspond to the code lines just seen:

```
if ((age >= 21) && (age <= 65)) {
```

This could be worded in spoken language like this:

```
"If the age is at least 21 and no more than 65,..."
if ((hrsWorked > 40) ¦¦ (sales > 25000.00)) {
```

This could be worded in spoken language like this:

```
"If the hours worked are more than 40 or the sales are more than
$25000,..."
if (!(isCharterMember)) {
```

This could be worded in spoken language like this:

```
"If you aren't a charter member, you must..."
```

As you have no doubt figured out, these three spoken statements describe exactly the same tests done by the three `if` statements. You often place an *and* between two conditions, such as "If you take out the trash *and* clean your room, you can play." Figures 12.1 and 12.2 show the difference between and and or.

FIGURE 12.1.

The AND *condition requires that both sides be true.*

FIGURE 12.2.

The OR condition requires that either side be true.

> **NOTE**
>
> Reread that stern statement you might say to a child. The and condition places a strict requirement that both of the jobs must be done before the result can take place. That's what && does also. Both sides of the && must be true in order for the body of the if to execute.

Let's continue with this same line of reasoning for the ¦¦ (or) operator. You might be more lenient on the kid by saying this: "If you take out the trash *or* clean your room, you can play." The or is not as restrictive. One side or the other side of the ¦¦ must be true (and they both can be true as well). If either side is true, the result can occur. The same holds for the ¦¦ operator. One or the other side of the ¦¦ must be true (or they both can be true) in order for the body of the if to execute.

The ! (not) operator reverses a true or a false condition. True becomes false, and false becomes true. This sounds confusing, and it is! Limit the number of ! operators you use. You can always rewrite a logical expression to avoid using ! by reversing the logic. For example, the following if:

```
if ( !(sales < 3000)) {
```

is exactly the same as this if:

```
if ( sales >= 3000) {
```

As you can see, you can remove the ! and turn a negative statement into a positive test by removing the ! and using an opposite relational operator.

Clue: Suppose you wanted to write an inventory program that tests whether the number of a certain item has fallen to zero. The first part of the if might look like this:

```
if (count == 0) {
```

Because the if is true *only* if count has a value of 0, you can rewrite the statement like this:

```
if (!count) {   /* Executes if's body only if count is 0 */
```

WARNING

Again, the ! adds a little confusion to code. Even though you might save some typing effort with a fancy !, clearer code is better than trickier code and if (count == 0) { is probably better to use, despite the microsecond your program might save by using !.

Using the && operator, the following program prints one message if the user's last name begins with the letters P through S, and another message if the name begins with something else.

```c
#include <stdio.h>
main()
{
   char name[25];
   printf("What is your last name? ");
   scanf(" %s", name);

   if ((name[0] >= 'P') && (name[0] <= 'S'))
      { printf("You must go to room 2432 ");
        printf("for your tickets.\n"); }
   else
      { printf("You can get your tickets here.\n"); }
   return 0;  /* Leaves the program to DOS or C editor */
}
```

NOTE

How would the program be different if the && were changed to a ¦¦? Would the first or the second message appear? The answer is the first one. *Everybody* would be sent to room 2432. Any letter from A to Z is either more than P or less than S. The test in the preceding program has to be && because room 2432 is available only to those people whose names are between P and S.

The following section of code asks the user for a Y or N answer. The code includes an ¦¦ to ensure that the user enters a correct value.

```c
printf("Is your printer on (Y/N) ?");   /* Request Y or N */
scanf(" %c", &ans);
if ((ans == 'Y') ¦¦ (ans == 'N'))
   { /* Gets here if user typed a correct answer */
     if (ans == 'N')
        { printf("** Turn the printer on now. ***\n");
        }
   }
else
   {
     printf("You did not enter a Y or N.\n");
     exit(1);
   }
```

Clue: You can combine more than two relational operators with logical operators, but doing too much in a single statement can cause confusion. This is a little too much:

```
if ((a < 6) || (c >= 3) && (r != 9) || (p <= 1)) {
```

Try to keep your combined relational tests simple so your programs remain easy to read and maintain.

The Order of Logical Operators

Because logical operators appear in the order of operators table, they have priority at times, just as the other operators do. Studying the order of operators will show you that the `&&` operator has precedence over the `||`. Therefore, the following logic

```
if (age < 20 || sales < 1200 && hrsWorked > 15) {
```

is interpreted by C like this:

```
if ((age < 20) || ((sales < 1200) && (hrsWorked > 15))) {
```

Use ample parentheses. Parentheses help clarify the order of operators. C won't get confused if you don't use parentheses, because it knows the order of operators table very well. However, a person looking at your program has to figure out which is done first, and parentheses help group operations together.

SKIP THIS, IT'S TECHNICAL

The Blackjack game in Appendix B uses `&&` and `||` to determine the winning hands in the `findWinner()` function. Even though a lot of the program is still new to you, you should be able to read through this function's logic and get a glimpse of what's happening.

Suppose that a teacher wants to reward her students who perform well and have missed very few classes. Also, the reward requires that the students either joined three school organizations or were in two sports activities. Whew! You must admit, not only will that reward be deserved, but it's going to be difficult sorting out the possibilities.

In C code, the following `if` statement would test true if a student met the teacher's preset reward criteria:

```
if (grade > 93 && classMissed <= 3 && numActs >= 3 ¦¦ sports >=
2) {
```

That's a lot to decipher. Not only is the statement hard to read, but there is a subtle error. The ¦¦ is compared last (because ¦¦ has lower precedence than &&), but that ¦¦ should take place before the second &&. (If this is getting confusing, you're right! Long combined relational tests often are.) Here, in spoken language, is how the previous `if` operates without separating its pieces with proper parentheses:

> *"If the student's grade is more than 93 and the student missed three or fewer classes and the school activities total three or more,* OR *if the student participated in two or more sports…"*

Well, the problem is that the student only has to be in sports activities to get the reward. The last two relations (separated with the ¦¦) must be compared before the third &&. The spoken description should read like this:

> *"If the student's grade is more than 93 and the student missed three or fewer classes and* EITHER *the school activities total three or more* OR *the student participated in two or more sports…"*

The following `if`, with correct parentheses, not only makes the `if` accurate but also a little more clear:

```
if ((grade > 93) && (classMissed <= 3) && ((numActs >= 3) ¦¦
(sports >= 2)) {
```

If you like, you can break such long `if` statements into two or more lines like this:

```
if ((grade > 93) && (classMissed <= 3) &&
   ((numActs >= 3) ¦¦ (sports >= 2)) {
```

Some C programmers even find that two `if` statements are clearer than four relational tests, such as these statements:

```
if ((grade > 93) && (classMissed <= 3)
   { if ((numActs >= 3) || (sports >= 2))
       { /* Reward the student */ }
```

The style you end up with depends mostly on what you like best, what you are the most comfortable with, and what appears to be the most maintainable.

Rewards

✖ Use logical operators to connect relational operators.

✖ Use && when both sides of the operator have to be true in order for the entire condition to be true.

✖ Use || when either one side or the other side (or both) have to be true in order for the entire condition to be true.

Pitfalls

✖ Don't overdo the use of !. Most negative logic can be reversed (so < becomes >= and > becomes <=) to get rid of the not operator.

✖ Don't combine too many relational operators in a single expression.

In Review

This chapter's goal was to teach you the logical operators. Although relational operators test data, the logical operators, && and ¦¦, let you combine more than one relational test into a single statement and execute code accordingly.

As you saw in this chapter, we often use logical-like operators in real life. Often, we make decisions based on several conditions.

Code Example

```
printf("What is your grade average for last semester? ");
scanf(" %f", &avg);
printf("How many hours did you take? ");
scanf(" %d", &hours);
if ((avg > 90.0) && (hours > 15))
    { printf("You are a top-notch student!\n");
      printf("Keep up the good work!"); }
```

Code Analysis

The code's intention is a simple example of another teacher's program to give good students some encouragement. These two relations are tested: the student's grade-point average and the number of hours the student took. The grade-point average alone is not enough to encourage the student because the student might have taken only a single course. Just because the student took a lot of courses doesn't mean the student excelled, either.

Therefore, *both* the grade-point average and the number of hours taken are combined into one compound relational test using the && operator. If the student's average is good *and* the student takes a lot of courses, the student is encouraged to continue.

This example is easier than the code in the last section of the book because you should keep if tests simple instead of combining three or more relational operations.

13

Group parts of the
conditional operator.
136

Only variables can be
incremented or
decremented.
139

Take the assignment out.
137

The conditional
requires less typing.
137

BOTTOM-
LESS PIT

The placement of
prefix and postfix.
142

Are There More Operators?

Additional C Operators

Have patience! You've learned about almost all of the C operators. With the exception of a few more advanced operators that you'll read about in Chapter 24, "What's the Point?," this chapter rounds out the order of operators table and explains *conditional operators, increment operators,* and *decrement operators.*

C's operators sometimes substitute for more wordy commands that you would use in other programming languages. Not only can an assortment of operators speed your program development time, they also compile more efficiently and run faster than commands. The C operators do a lot to make C the efficient language that it is.

Goodbye *if-else*; Hello Conditional

The conditional operator is the only C operator that requires *three* arguments. Whereas division, multiplication, and most of the others require two values to work, the conditional operator requires three. Although the format of the conditional operator looks complex, you will see that it streamlines some logic and is actually straightforward to use.

The conditional operator looks like this: ?:. Here is its format:

```
relation ? trueStatement : falseStatement;
```

The `relation` is any relational test such as age >= 21 or sales <= 25000.0. You also can combine the relational operators with the logical operators you learned about in Chapter 12, "How Do I Test Several Things at Once?" The `trueStatement` is any valid C statement, and the `falseStatement` is also any valid C statement. Here is an example of a conditional operator:

```
(total <= 3850.0) ? (total *= 1.10): (total *= 1.05);
```

Clue: The parentheses are not required, but they do help group the three parts of the conditional operator so that you can see them easier.

If the test in the first set of parentheses is true, the *trueStatement* executes. If the test in the first set of parentheses is false, the *falseStatement* executes. The conditional operator you just saw does *exactly* the same thing as this if-else statement:

```
if (total <= 3850.0)
  { total *= 1.10; }
else
  { total *= 1.05; }
```

This statement tells C to multiply total by 1.10 or by 1.05, depending on the result of the relational test.

NOTE

Just about any if-else statement can be rewritten as a conditional statement. The conditional requires less typing, you won't accidentally leave off a brace somewhere, and the conditional runs more efficiently than an if-else because it compiles into more compact code.

Clue: The format of the conditional operator is obvious when you think of it like this: The question mark asks a question. Keeping this in mind, you could state the earlier example as follows: *Is the total <= 3850.0? If so, do the first thing; otherwise, do the second.*

WARNING

C programmers don't like the redundancy you saw in the earlier use of the conditional operator. As you can see, the total variable appears twice. Both times it is being assigned a value. When you face such a situation, take the assignment out of the conditional operator's statements:

```
total *= (total <= 3850.0) ? (1.10): (1.05);
```

137

Don't replace every single `if-else` with a conditional operator. Many times `if-else` is more readable, and some conditional statements are just too complex to squeeze easily into a conditional operator. However, when a simple `if-else` is all that's needed, the conditional operator provides a nice alternative.

The conditional operator offers one additional advantage over `if`: The conditional often can appear in places where `if` can't go. The following `printf` prints a trailing s if the number of pears is more than one:

```
printf("I ate %d pear%s", numPear, (numPear>1) ? ("s.") : ("."));
```

If the value in `numPear` is greater than 1, you'll see something like this printed:

```
I ate 4 pears.
```

but if there is only one pear, you'll see this:

```
I ate 1 pear.
```

> **NOTE**
>
> Maybe you're wondering why the conditional operator is `?:`, but the question mark and colon *never* appear next to each other. Well, that's just the way it is. It would be too cumbersome to go around saying that the conditional operator looks like a question mark and a colon with some stuff in between.

The Small-Change Operators: ++ and - -

Although the conditional operator works on three arguments, the *increment* and *decrement* operators work on only one. The increment operator adds 1 to a variable, and the decrement operator subtracts 1 from a variable. That's it, 'nuff said. Almost....

Incrementing and decrementing variables are things you would need to do if you were counting items (such as the number of customers who shopped in your store yesterday) or counting down (such as removing items from an inventory as people buy them). In Chapter 10, "What Else Can I Do with Expressions?," you read how to increment and decrement variables using compound operators. Here, you will learn two operators that can more easily do the same. The increment operator is ++ and the decrement operator is --. If you want to add one to the variable count, here's how you do it:

```
count++;
```

You also can do this:

```
++count;
```

The decrement operator does the same thing, only the 1 is subtracted from the variable. You can do this:

```
count--;
```

You also can do this:

```
--count;
```

As you can see, the operators can go on either side of the variable. If the operator is on the left, it's called a *prefix increment* or *prefix decrement* operator. If the operator is on the right, it's known as a *postfix increment* or *postfix decrement* operator.

SKIP THIS, IT'S TECHNICAL

Never apply an increment or decrement operator to a literal constant or an expression. Only variables can be incremented or decremented. You would never see this:

```
--14;   /* Don't do this! */
```

Prefix and postfix operators produce identical results when used by themselves. It is only when you combine them with other expressions that a small "gotcha" appears. Consider the following code:

```
int i = 2, j = 5, n;
n = ++i * j;
```

The question is, what is n when the statements finish executing? It's easy to see what's in j because j doesn't change and still holds 5. The ++ ensures that i is always incremented, so you know that i becomes 3. The trick is determining exactly when i increments. If i increments before the multiplication, n becomes 15, but if i increments after the multiplication, n becomes 10.

The answer lies in the *prefix* and *postfix* placements. If the ++ or -- is *prefix,* C computes it before anything else on the line. If the ++ or -- is *postfix,* C computes it after everything else on the line finishes. Because the ++ in the preceding code is prefix, i increments to 3 before being multiplied by j. The following statement increments i *after* multiplying i by j and storing the answer in n:

```
n = i++ * j;   /* Puts 10 in n and 3 in i */
```

Being able to increment a variable in the same expression as you use the variable means less work on the programmer's part. The preceding statement replaces the following two statements that you would have to write in other programming languages:

```
n = i * j   /*No comment*/
i = i + 1
```

> **WARNING**
>
> The ++ and -- operators are extremely efficient. If you care about such things (most of us don't), ++ and -- compile into only one machine language statement, whereas adding or subtracting 1 using +1 or -1 doesn't always compile so efficiently.

Fun Fact

sizeof() *doesn't look like an operator at all. It looks (and acts) like a function call.*

Sizing Up the Situation

You use sizeof() to find the number of memory locations it takes to store values of any data type. Although most C compilers use 2 bytes to store integers, not all do. To find out for sure exactly how much memory is being used by integers and floating points, you can use sizeof(). The following statements do just that:

```
i = sizeof(int);    /* Puts size of integers into i */
f = sizeof(float);  /* Puts size of floats into f */
```

`sizeof()` works on variables as well as data types. If you need to know how much memory that variables and arrays take, you can apply the `sizeof()` operator to them. The following section of code shows you how:

```
char name[] = "George Paul";
int i = 7;
printf("The size of i is %d\n", sizeof(i));
printf("The size of name is %d", sizeof(name));
```

length 8

Here is one possible output from this code:

```
The size of i is 2
The size of name is 12
```

size of

Depending on your computer and C compiler, your output might differ because of the differences in integer sizes. Notice that the character array size is 12, which includes the null zero.

Clue: The length of a string and the size of a string are two different values. The length is the number of bytes up to but not including the null zero, and it is found via `strlen()`. The size of a string is the number of characters it takes to hold the string, including the null zero.

SKIP THIS, IT'S TECHNICAL

Although `sizeof()` might seem worthless right now, you'll see how it comes in handy as you progress in C.

Rewards

✖ Use the conditional operator in place of simple `if-else` statements to improve efficiency.

✖ The conditional operator requires three arguments. Extra parentheses help clarify these three arguments by separating them from each other.

✖ Use ++ and -- to increment and decrement variables instead of adding and subtracting 1 using assignment or the += and -= operators. ++ and -- are extremely efficient.

Pitfalls

✖ Don't duplicate assignment statements on each side of the conditional operator's :. Pull the variable and the assignment operator completely out of the conditional operator and place them on the left of the conditional to improve efficiency.

✖ Don't think that prefix and postfix always produce the same values. Prefix and postfix are identical only when a single variable is involved. If you combine ++ or -- with other variables and expressions, the placement of prefix and postfix is critical to get the result you want.

In Review

The goal of this chapter was to round out your knowledge of C's operators and show you most of the ones remaining to be learned. The longest C operator, ?:, and the shortest C operators, -- and ++, were taught. Understanding these operators doesn't take a lot of work, yet the operators are powerful and substitute for complete statements in other languages. One of C's operators doesn't look like an operator at all. The sizeof() operator returns the number of memory locations consumed by whatever is in its parentheses.

Code Example

```
/* Works with an age and integer */
#include <stdio.h>
main()
{
  int age, intSize;
  float gift;
  printf("\nHow old are you? ");
  scanf(" %d", &age);
  if (age < 18)
    { gift = 5.00; }
  else
    { gift = 10.00; }
  gift = (age < 18) ? 5.00 : 10.00;   /* Does the same
                                         as the if */
  printf("Your gift is $%.2f\n", gift);
  age++;   /* Adds 1 to age */
  printf("In a year, you'll be %d years old.\n", age);
  intSize = sizeof(int);
  printf("Integers take %d memory locations.", intSize);
  return 0;
}
```

Code Analysis

The if statement is redundant. If you were to remove the if statement, the program would perform exactly the way it does with the if. The conditional operator does the same thing in one statement that the if does in four. The conditional operator assigns a gift of either $5 or $10, depending on the age of the user.

One is then added to the user's age so that users can see their age a year from now (as if they couldn't do this themselves!). Lastly, the code prints a message telling the user how much memory is taken up by integers on the machine running the program.

Part 3

Keeping Control

The body of the
while.
150

The do and while
act like wrappers.
154

while and if are two
separate statements.
151

If the condition
is false.
152

An infinite loop
will occur.
155

How Can I Do the Same Stuff Over and Over?

With *while* and *do-while* Loops

Now that you've learned the operators, you're ready to play "loop-the-loop" with your programs. A *loop* is simply a section of code that repeats a few times. You don't want a loop to repeat forever. That's called an *infinite loop*. The loops you write (if you write them properly, and of course you will) should come to a conclusion when they finish doing the job you set them up to do.

Why would you want a program to loop? The answer becomes clear when you think about the advantage of using a computer for tasks that people wouldn't want to do. Computers never get bored, so you should give them mundane and repetitive tasks and leave the tasks that require thought to people. You wouldn't want to pay someone to add a list of hundreds of payroll figures, and few people would want to do it anyway. Computer programs can do that kind of repetitive work. People can then analyze the results when the computer loop finishes calculating all the figures.

If you want to add a list of figures, print company sales totals for the past 12 months, or add up the number of students who enroll in a computer class, you need to use a loop. This chapter explains two common C loops that use the while command.

while We Repeat

The while statement always appears at the beginning or the end of a loop. The easiest type of loop that uses while is called the while loop. (The other is called the do-while loop. You'll see it a little later.) Here is the format of while:

```
while (condition)
{ block of one or more C statements; }
```

The condition is a relational test that is exactly like the relational test condition you learned for if. The block of one or more C statements is called the *body* of the while.

Clue: The body of the while repeats as long as the condition is true. Remember how the if works: The body of the if executes if the condition is true. The body of the if executes only once, however; whereas the body of the while can execute lots of times.

Figure 14.1 helps explain the similarities and differences between if and while. The formats of the two commands are similar in that braces are required if the body of the while has more than one statement. Even if the body of the while contains only a single statement, you should enclose the body in braces so the braces will still be there if you add statements to the while later. Never put a semicolon after the while's parenthesis. The semicolon follows only the statements inside the body of the while.

```
Using if:
  if(amount < 25)
    {
    printf("Amount is too small.\n");
    wrongVal++; MOVE ALONG
    }
```
⟶ Executes only one time but only then if amount is less than 25.

```
Using while:
  while (amount < 25)
    {
    printf("Amount is too small.\n");

    wrongVal++;

    printf("Try again...What is new amount?\n");

    scanf("%d",&amount); GO BACK
    }
```
Keeps repeating as long as amount is less than 25.

FIGURE 14.1.
The if body executes once, and the while *body can repeat more than once.*

WARNING

The two statements in Figure 14.1 are similar, but they don't do the same thing. while and if are two separate statements that do two separate things.

You *must* somehow change a variable inside the while loop's *condition*. If you don't, the while will loop forever because it will test the same *condition* each time through the loop. Therefore, you avoid infinite loops by making sure the body of the while loop changes something in the *condition* so that eventually the *condition* will become false and the program will continue with the statements that follow the while loop.

> **NOTE**
>
> As with `if`, the `while` might *never* execute! If the *condition* is false going into `while` the first time, the body of the `while` doesn't execute.

Using *while*

If you want to repeat a section of code until a certain condition becomes false, `while` is the way to go. The Blackjack program in Appendix B contains a slick use of `while` in the `dispTitle()` function to clear the screen. The function is repeated here for your review:

```
/* Clears everything off the screen */
void dispTitle(void)
{
  int i = 0;
  while (i < 25)    /* Clears screen by printing 25 blank */
  { printf("\n");   /* lines to "push off" stuff that      */
    i++; }          /* might be left over on the screen    */
                    /* before this program                 */
  printf("\n\n*Step right up to the Blackjack tables*\n\n");
  return;
}
```

> **WARNING**
>
> Almost every C compiler has a built-in function that clears the screen. The problem is that none of these screen-clearing functions are compatible with the ANSI C standard. Therefore, I used another method to erase the screen before each Blackjack game. A `while` loop prints 25 newlines. When the cursor gets to the bottom of a screen, the screen scrolls upward, and what was on the screen gets pushed off the top. This simple and generic screen-clearing function, written using `while`, works with all ANSI C compilers, such as the one you probably have.

> **NOTE**
>
> The looping method for screen clearing is not really elegant, but it's about the most generic way possible to clear the screen. If you want to dig through your compiler's manual and replace this `while` loop with your compiler's screen-clearing function, go ahead.

Back to the actual `while` code needed to clear the screen: The variable `i` is initially set to 0. The first time `while` executes, `i` is less than 25, so the `while` *condition* is true and the body of the `while` executes. In the body, a newline is sent to the screen and `i` is incremented. The second time the *condition* is tested, `i` has a value of 1, but 1 is still less than 25, so the body executes again. The body continues to execute until `i` is incremented to 25. Because 25 is not less than 25 (they are equal), the *condition* becomes false and the loop stops repeating. The rest of the program is then free to execute.

Clue: If `i` were not incremented in this screen-clearing `while`, the `printf()` would execute forever or until you pressed Ctrl+Break to stop it.

Using *do-while*

`while` also can be used in conjunction with the `do` statement. When used as a pair, the statements normally are called do-while statements or the `do-while` loop. The `do-while` behaves almost exactly like the `while` loop. Here is the format of `do-while`:

```
do
   { block of one or more C statements; }
while (condition)
```

> ### SKIP THIS, IT'S TECHNICAL
> The do and while act like wrappers around the body of the loop.
> Again, braces are required if the body has more than a single
> statement.

Use a do-while in place of a while only when the body of the loop *must ex-ecute at least one time*. The condition is located at the *bottom* of the do-while
loop, so C can't test the condition until the loop finishes the first time.

The Blackjack program asks the user to type an H or an S—in other words
to *hit* (that's casino lingo for drawing another card) or stand. However, us-ers don't always type what they're supposed to. Therefore, when you request
user input that has a fixed number of possibilities, such as an H or an S, you
should check what the user enters to make sure it's one of the answers you're
expecting. Here is a sample do-while, similar to that used in the Blackjack
program, that keeps asking the user for an answer until the user gets it right:

```
do {
  ans = getAns("Hit or stand (H/S)? ");
} while ((ans != 'S') && (ans != 'H'));  /* Loop if bad
                                            answer */
```

The strange-looking getAns() function call simply executes a function that
displays the Hit or stand (H/S)? message and gets a character from the
user into ans. For now, study the formation of the do-while because that is
the center of your concern here.

Clue: Chapter 19, "Can You Tell Me More About Strings?," ex-plains how to test for an uppercase Y or N or a lowercase y or n with
a built-in function named toupper().

Rewards

- ✖ Use while or do-while when you need to repeat a section of code.
- ✖ Make sure that the body of the while or do-while loop changes something in the *condition*, or the loop will repeat forever.
- ✖ Remember that loops differ from if because the body of an if executes only once instead of lots of times if the *condition* is true.

Pitfalls

- ✖ Don't put a semicolon after the while *condition*'s closing parenthesis. If you do, an infinite loop will occur.
- ✖ Don't assume that the user will answer questions the way you expect. Keep asking for an answer until the user types what you need.

155

In Review

The goal of this chapter was to show you how to repeat sections of code. The while and do-while loops both repeat statements within their statement bodies. All code between the while and do-while braces repeats instead of executing only once. Both the while and do-while statements cause their code sections to repeat while a given relational condition is true.

The difference between the two statements lies in the placement of the relational test that controls the loops. The while statement tests the relation at the top of the loop, and the do-while statement tests the relation at the bottom of the loop, forcing all its statements to execute at least once.

Code Example

```
/* Prints 1 to 20 twice */
#include <stdio.h>
main()
{
  int ctrl = 1;
  while (ctr <= 20)
    { printf("%d \n", ctr);
      ctr++; }
  ctr = 1;
  do
    { printf("%d \n", ctr);
      ctr++; }
  while (ctr <= 20);
  return 0;
}
```

Code Analysis

The code shows both kinds of loops presented in this chapter. The program prints the numbers from 1 to 20 twice. The first half of the program uses while to control the loop, and the second half uses do-while to control the loop. As you can see, both kinds of loops can do the very same thing. The choice of while and do-while is often trivial. You would choose one over the other only when the first cycle was important and you wanted the loop to execute at least once (with do-while), or maybe not at all.

By the way, if the printf() functions included ctr's increment like this:

```
{ printf("%d \n", ctr++); }
```

you would not need the increment statements that appear on lines by themselves. The separate increments, however, make the program a little easier to read, and readability is more important that extreme efficiency in most cases.

Are There Other Loops?

The *for* Loop

There is another type of C loop called the for loop. A for loop offers more control than while and do-while. With a for loop, you can specify exactly how many times you want to loop; whereas with while loops, you must continue looping as long as a condition is true.

There is room for all three kinds of loops in C programs. There are times when one loop fits one program's requirements better than another. For example, if you wrote a program to handle customer orders as customers purchase items from the inventory, you would need to use a while loop. The program would process orders *while* customers came through the door. If 100 customers happened to buy things, the while loop would run 100 times. At the end of the day, you might want to add the 100 customer purchases to get a total for the day. You could then use a for loop because you would then know exactly how many times to loop.

> **NOTE**
>
> By incrementing counter variables, you can simulate a for loop with a while loop. You also can simulate a while with a for! Therefore, the kind of loop you use ultimately depends on which kind you feel comfortable with at the time.

for Repeat's Sake!

As you can see from the lame title of this section, the for loop is important for controlling repeating sections of code. The format of for is a little strange:

```
for (startExpression; testExpression; countExpression)
{ block of one or more C statements; }
```

Perhaps a short example with actual code would be easier to understand:

```
for (ctr = 1; ctr <= 10; ctr++)
  { printf("Still counting... ");
    printf("%d\n", ctr);
}
```

or   0 <10

Gabe Mankin

6160

handwritten: E AIC

handwritten: regelin

Here's the way this `for` statement works: When the `for` begins, the *startExpression,* which is `ctr = 1;`, executes. The *startExpression* is executed *only once* in any `for` loop. The *testExpression* is then tested. In this example, the *testExpression* is `ctr <= 10;`. If it is true—and it will be true the first time in this code—the body of the `for` loop executes. When the body of the loop finishes, the *countExpression* is executed (`ctr` is incremented).

Clue: As you can see, indenting the body of a `for` loop helps separate the body of the loop from the rest of the program making the loop more readable. (The same is true for the other kinds of loops, such as `do-while` loops.)

> **WARNING**
>
> That's a lot to absorb in one full swoop—even in one paragraph. Let's make it easy. Follow the line in Figure 15.1, which shows in what order `for` executes. While following the line, reread the preceding paragraph. It should then make more sense to you.

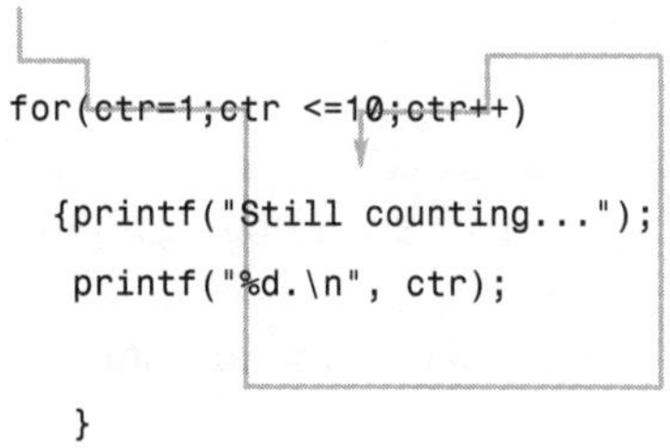

```
for(ctr=1;ctr <=10;ctr++)

    {printf("Still counting...");
    printf("%d.\n", ctr);


    }
```

FIGURE 15.1.
Following the order of `for`.

handwritten: printf(Enter dolla~
handwritten: Scanf (%d ", & mony

Here is the very same loop written as a while statement:

```
ctr = 1;
while (ctr <= 10)
  { printf("Still counting... ");
    printf("%d\n", ctr);
    ctr++;
}
```

Here is the output of this code:

```
Still counting...1
Still counting...2
Still counting...3
Still counting...4
Still counting...5
Still counting...6
Still counting...7
Still counting...8
Still counting...9
Still counting...10
```

Clue: If you follow Figure 15.1's guiding line and read the preceding while loop, you'll see how the for and while do the same thing. The `ctr = 1;` that precedes the while is the first statement executed in the for.

SKIP THIS, IT'S TECHNICAL

A do-while loop can't really represent the for loop because the relational test is performed *before* the body of the for loop and after in the do-while. The do-while's test, as you might recall from the end of Chapter 14, "How Can I Do the Same Stuff Over and Over?" always resides at the bottom of the loop.

Working with *for*

The for loop reads a lot like the way you speak in everyday life. Consider this statement:

> For each of our 45 employees, calculate the pay and print a check.

This statement leaves no room for ambiguity. There will be 45 employees, 45 pay calculations, and 45 checks printed. for loops don't always count *up* as the preceding one did with ctr. Here is a for loop that counts *down* before printing a message:

```
for (cDown = 10; cDown > 0; cDown--)
   { printf("%d\n", cDown); }
printf("Blast off!\n");
```

Here is the output of this code:

```
10
9
8
7
6
5
4
3
2
1
Blast off!
```

Fun Fact

If you were programming in BASIC or QBasic, you'd need a **next** for each **for** statement. In C, you don't!

163

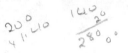

Clue: If the last expression in the for parentheses decrements in some way, the initial value must be greater than the test value in order for the loop to execute. In the previous for statement, the initial value of 10 is greater than the *testExpression*'s 0 comparison.

The following for loop counts up by 3s, beginning with 1:

```c
for (i = 1; i < 18; i += 3)
{ printf("%d ", i); }  /* Prints 1, 4, 7, 10, 13, 16 */
```

The following code produces an interesting effect:

```c
for (outer = 1; outer <= 3; outer++)
  { for (inner = 1; inner <= 5; inner++)
    { printf("%d ", inner);
  }
  printf("\n"); /* a newline every 5 times */
}
```

Here is the code's output:

```
1 2 3 4 5
1 2 3 4 5
1 2 3 4 5
```

If you put a for loop in the body of another loop, you are *nesting* the loops. In effect, the inner loop executes as many times as the outer loop dictates. You might need a nested for loop if you wanted to print three lists of your top five customers. The outer loop would move from one to three, while the inner loop would print the top five customers.

The Blackjack game in Appendix B uses a for loop to initialize 52 cards. Here is the code that does that:

```c
for (sub = 0; sub <= 51; sub++)  {  /* Counts from 0 to 51 */
  val = (val == 14) ? 1 : val; /* If val is 14, reset to 1 */
  cards[sub] = val;
  val++;  }
```

You have yet to learn about noncharacter arrays (a special kind of variable list, which is what cards[] is), but you can see that the for loop counts up, starting at 0, until sub is equal to 51 (for 52 cards total). The line with the long ?: conditional operator ensures that val never goes higher than 14. Four sets of numbers from 1 to 13 (making a total of 52) are assigned to the initial card deck. The numbers 1 through 13 indicate cards from the Ace to the King.

Rewards

✖ Use a `for` loop when you want to increment or decrement a variable through a loop.

✖ Remember that the `for` loop's relational test is performed at the top of the loop.

✖ Use a nested loop if you want to loop a certain number of times.

Pitfalls

✖ Don't forget the semicolons inside the `for` loop. `for` requires them.

✖ Don't use an initial value that is less than the test value if you want to count down with `for`.

In Review

The goal of this chapter was to show you an additional way to form a loop of statements in C. The for statement gives you a little more control over the loop than either while or do-while. The for statement controls a loop with a variable that is initialized and changed according to the expressions in the for statement.

Code Example

```
for (chap = 1; chap <= 15; chap++)
  { printf ("You're done with Chapter %d \n", chap); }
```

Code Analysis

Here's what the code produces:

```
You're done with Chapter 1
You're done with Chapter 2
You're done with Chapter 3
:
```

and so on until the message You're done with Chapter 15 prints. The for statement causes the loop control variable chap to increment from its initial value of 1 to its final value of 15. Once chap becomes larger than 15, the for statement terminates the loop and the program continues from there.

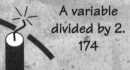

What if I Want to Stop in the Middle of a Loop?

Use *break* and *continue*

This chapter doesn't teach you how to use another kind of loop. Instead, this chapter extends the information you learned in the last two chapters. There are ways to control the while loop in addition to a relational test, and you can change the way a for loop operates via means other than the counter variable.

The break and continue statements let you control loops for those special occasions when you want to quit a loop early or repeat a loop sooner than it would normally repeat.

Take a *break*

The break statement rarely, if ever, appears on a line by itself. Typically, break appears in the body of an if statement. The reason will be made clear shortly. Here is the format of break:

```
break;
```

> **WARNING**
>
> break is easy, isn't it? Yep, not much to it. However, keep in mind that break usually resides in the body of an if. In a way, if is the first part of almost every break.

break always appears inside a loop. The purpose of break is to terminate the current loop. When a loop ends, the code following the body of the loop takes over. When break appears inside a loop's body, break terminates that loop immediately and the rest of the program continues.

Here is a for loop that normally would print 10 numbers. Instead of 10, however, the break causes the loop to stop after printing five numbers.

```
for (i = 0; i < 10; i++)
  { printf("%d ", i);
    if (i == 4)
      { break; }  /* Quits loop after i becomes 4 */
}
/* Rest of program goes here */
```

As a real-world example, suppose a teacher wrote a program to average her 25 students' test scores. The following program keeps a running total of the 25 students. If, however, a student or two missed the test, the teacher wouldn't want to average the entire 25 student scores. If the teacher enters a -1.0 for a test score, the -1.0 triggers the break statement and the loop terminates early.

```c
/* Test Scoring */
#include <stdio.h>
main()
{
  int numTest;
  float stTest, avg, total = 0.0;
  /* Asks for up to 25 tests */
  for (numTest = 0; numTest < 25; numTest++)
  { printf("What is the next student's test score? ");
    scanf(" %f", &stTest);
    if (stTest < 0.0)
      { break; }  /* Quits early if no more students */
    total += stTest;
  }
  avg = total / numTest;
  printf("\nThe average is %.1f%%.\n", avg);
  return 0;  /* Exits the program */
}
```

Before I discuss the program, take a look at a sample run of it:

```
What is the next student's test score? 89.9
What is the next student's test score? 92.5
What is the next student's test score? 51.0
What is the next student's test score? 86.4
What is the next student's test score? 78.6
What is the next student's test score? -1

The average is 79.7%.
```

The teacher had a lot of sick students that day! If all 25 students had shown up, the for loop would have ensured that exactly 25 test scores were asked for. However, because only five took the test, the teacher had to let the program know, via a negative number in this case, that she was done entering the scores and that she now wanted an average.

Fun Fact

Now that you know about the **break** statement, you can use it to get out of infinite loops.

Clue: To get the percent sign at the end of the final average, two %s have to be used in the `printf()` control string. C interprets a percent sign as a control code unless you put two of them together, as done in this program. Then it still interprets the first percent sign as a control code for the second. In other words, the percent sign is a control code for itself.

WARNING

break simply offers an early termination of a while, do-while, or for loop. break can't exit from if, which isn't a loop statement. Figure 16.1 helps show the action of break.

```
                      printf("How many numbers do you want to see?");
                      scanf("%d",&num);
                      for (i=1; i<10;i++)
Normal              ┌──► {
flow of             │      printf("Counting up...%d\n" ,i);
the loop            │      if (i== num)
                    │         {break;} ──────────────────┐  If break
                    └──── }                               │  executes
                      /* Rest of program follows*/ ◄──────┘
```

FIGURE 16.1.
break terminates a loop earlier than usual.

Let's *continue* Working

Whereas break causes a loop to *break* early, continue forces a loop to *continue* early. (So *that's* why they're named that way!) Depending on the complexity of your for, while, or do-while loop, you might not want to execute the *entire body of the loop every iteration.* continue says, in effect, "C, please ignore the rest of this loop's body this iteration of the loop. Go back up to the top of the loop and start the next loop cycle."

Clue: The word *iteration* is a fancy computer name for the cycle of a loop. Programmers sometimes think they will keep their jobs if they use words that nobody else understands.

The following program shows off continue nicely. The program contains a for loop that counts from 1 to 10. If the loop variable contains an odd number, the message I'm rather odd... prints and the continue instructs C to ignore the rest of the loop body because it prints Even up! for the even numbers that are left.

```c
/* Odd and even */
#include <stdio.h>
main()
{
  int i;
  for (i = 1; i <= 10; i++)
    { if ((i%2) == 1)  /* i is odd if true */
        { printf("I'm rather odd...\n");
          continue;
        }
      printf("Even up!\n");
    }
  return 0;  /* Exits the program */
}
```

Here is the program's output:

```
I'm rather odd...
Even up!
I'm rather odd...
Even up!
I'm rather odd...
Even up!
I'm rather odd...
Even up!
I'm rather odd...
Even up!
```

NOTE

As with `break`, `continue` is rarely used without a preceding `if` statement of some kind. If you *always* wanted to `continue`, you wouldn't have entered the last part of the loop's body. You want to use `continue` only in some cycles of the loop.

SKIP THIS, IT'S TECHNICAL

Look again at how the preceding program knew that the loop variable was odd. The remainder of a variable divided by 2 is always 1 for odd numbers and 0 for even ones.

Rewards

✖ Use `break` to terminate `for`, `while`, or `do-while` loops early.

✖ Use `continue` to force a new cycle of a loop.

Pitfalls

✖ Don't use `break` or `continue` without some sort of relational test before them.

In Review

The goal of this chapter was to teach you how to control loops better with the break and continue statements. The while, do-while, and for loops all can be terminated early with break or continued early with continue. Although you will want many of the loops you write to execute until their natural conclusions, you need to change the way they loop or stop looping.

Code Example

```
/* Divisibility check */
#include <stdio.h>
main()
{
  int i;
  for (i = 1; i < 100; i++)
  {
    printf ("Testing %d\n", i);
    /* Checks if the number is divisible by 3 AND 4 */
    if ((i % 3 == 0) && (i % 4) == 0)
      { printf ("Found it!\n");
        break; }
    /* Checks whether the number is divisible by 3 */
    if (i % 3 == 0)
      { printf ("I am divisible by 3.\n");
        printf ("But that's only half the test!\n");
        continue; }
    /* Checks whether the number is divisible by 4 */
    if (i % 4 == 0)
      { printf ("I am divisible by 4.\n");
        printf ("One out of two isn't bad!\n");
        continue; }
    printf ("I'm not divisible by 3 or 4!\n");
  }
  return 0;
}
```

Code Analysis

The code presented here cycles through the numbers from 1 to 100 and reports the first number that is divisible by both 3 and 4. If the number is divisible by 3 only or by 4 only, a message is printed saying so, and the loop (via continue) cycles again. The break statement toward the top of the loop forces the early conclusion of the for statement, if the number is found to be divisible by both 3 and 4.

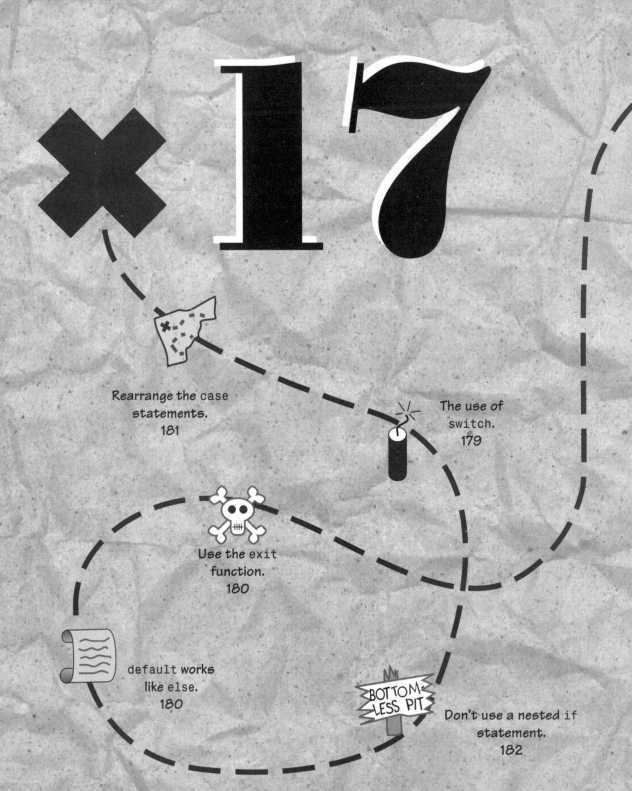

×17

How Can I Test Lots of Values?

With the *switch* Statement

The if statement is great for simple testing of data, especially if your data tests have only two or three possibilities. You can use if to test for more than two values, but if you do, you have to nest several if statements inside one another, and that can get confusing and hard to maintain.

Consider for a moment how you execute code based on a user's response to a menu. A menu is a list of options from which to select, such as this one:

```
What do you want to do?
  1. Add information
  2. Change information
  3. Print information
  4. Delete information
  5. Quit the program
What is your choice?
```

It would take four if-else statements, nested inside one another, to handle all these conditions as you can see here:

```
if (userAns == 1)
  { /* Perform the add routine */ }
else
  if (userAns == 2)
    { /* Perform the change routine */ }
  else
    if (userAns == 3)
      { /* Perform the print routine */ }
    else
      if (userAns == 4)
        { /* Perform the delete routine */ }
      else
        { /* Perform the quit routine */ }
```

There is nothing wrong with nested ifs, but the C switch statement is clearer for multiple conditions.

Making the *switch*

The switch statement has one of the longest formats of any statement in C (or just about any other language). Here is the format of switch:

```
switch (expression)
  { case (expression1): { one or more C statements; }
    case (expression2): { one or more C statements; }
```

```
case (expression3): { one or more C statements; }
   /* If there are more case statements,
      they would go here  */
default: { one or more C statements; }
}
```

SKIP THIS, IT'S TECHNICAL

As with most statements, the actual use of switch is a lot less intimidating than its format leads you to believe.

The menu shown earlier is perfect for a series of function calls. The problem is that this book has yet to discuss function calls, except for a handful of built-in functions such as printf() and scanf(). The following simple switch statement prints an appropriate message, depending on the choice the user makes. Ordinarily, a function call would replace the printf() statements you see after each case. After you read Chapter 31, "How Do Functions Share Data?", you'll understand how to use function calls to perform case actions.

```
/* Menu printing statements go here */
do
{  printf("What is your choice? ");
   scanf(" %d", &choice);
   switch (choice)
   { case (1) : printf("You are adding.\n");
               break;
     case (2) : printf("You are changing.\n");
               break;
     case (3) : printf("You are printing.\n");
               break;
     case (4) : printf("You are deleting.\n");
               break;
     case (5) : exit(1);   /* Quits program.
                             Requires stdlib.h */
               break;
     default  : printf("I don't know the ");
               printf("option %d.\n", choice);
               printf("Try again.\n");
               break;
   }
} while ((choice < 1) ¦¦ (choice > 5));
/* Rest of program would follow */
```

The case statements determine courses of action based on the value of choice. For example, if choice equals 2, the message You are changing. prints. If choice equals 5, the program quits using the built-in exit() function.

> **WARNING**
>
> Anytime you need to terminate a program before its natural conclusion, use the exit() function. The value you place in exit()'s parentheses will be returned to your operating system. Most beginning programmers ignore the return value and put either a 0 or 1 in the parentheses. You must #include <stdlib.h> in every program that uses exit().

The do-while loop keeps the user honest. If the user enters something other than a number from 1 to 5, the I don't know message prints, thanks to the default keyword. C ensures that if none of the other cases matches the variable listed after switch, the default's statements execute.

> **NOTE**
>
> default works like else in a way. else takes care of an action if an if test is false, and default takes care of an action if none of the other case conditions successfully match the switch variable. Although default is optional (as is else), it's a good programming practice to use a default to handle unexpected switch values.

Clue: The switch variable can be either an integer or a character variable. Do not use a float or a double for the switch test.

break and *switch*

The switch statement shown earlier has several break statements scattered throughout the code. The breaks ensure that only one case executes. Without the break statements, the switch would "fall through" to the other case statements. Here is what would happen if the break statements were removed from the switch and the user answered with a choice of 2:

```
You are changing.
You are printing.
You are deleting.
```

The break keeps switch case statements from running together.

> **NOTE**
>
> The only reason the default condition's message did not print is that the exit() function executed inside case (5).

Efficiency Considerations

case statements don't have to be arranged in any order. Even default doesn't have to be the last case statement. As a matter of fact, the break after the default statement isn't needed as long as default appears at the end of switch. However, putting break after default helps ensure that you move both statements if you ever rearrange the case statements. If you were to put default higher in the order of case statements, default would require a break so that the rest of the case statements wouldn't execute.

Clue: You might rearrange the case statements for efficiency. Put the most-common case possibilities toward the top of the switch statement so C won't have to search down into the case statements to find a matching case.

The dispCard() function in the Blackjack program in Appendix B uses a switch to print face cards and update the points in each hand.

Rewards

✖ Use `switch` to code menu selections and other types of applications that need to select from a variety of values.

✖ Use an integer or character value in `switch` because `float` and `double` values can't be matched properly.

✖ Put `break` at the end of each `case` if you don't want the subsequent `case` statements to execute.

Pitfalls

✖ Don't use nested `if` statements when a `switch` statement will work instead. `switch` is a clearer statement.

In Review

The goal of this chapter was to explain C's switch statement. switch analyzes the value of an integer or character variable and executes one of several sections of code called *cases*. You can write equivalent code using embedded if statements, but switch is clearer—especially when your program needs to analyze a user's response to a menu and execute sections of code accordingly.

Code Example

```
/* Tax code display */
#include <stdio.h>
main()
{
  char choice;
  printf("Are you filing a single, joint, or ");
  printf("married return (s, j, m)? ");
  do
    { scanf(" %c", &choice);
      switch (choice)
      { case ('s') : printf("You get a $1,000 deduction.\n");
                     break;
        case ('j') : printf("You get a $3,000 deduction.\n");
                     break;
        case ('m') : printf("You get a $5,000 deduction.\n");
                     break;
        default    : printf("I don't know the ");
                     printf("option %c.\n", choice);
                     printf("Try again.\n");
                     break;
      }
  } while ((choice != 's') && (choice != 'j') &&
                             (choice != 'm'));
  return 0;
}
```

Code Analysis

The code first asks the user a question that has three possible answers. Depending on the result of the answer, s, j, or m, the program prints an appropriate tax-related message.

A switch statement should always be written to handle the unexpected. The default case takes over if the user enters anything other than s, j, or m, and the do-while ensures that the question keeps being asked until the user answers with one of the three answers.

If you test this program yourself, please be sure to enter a lowercase answer for the filing choice so the switch can properly match your answer with the appropriate case.

18

The second `for` loop continues.
190

`getch()` *does not echo the input characters to the screen.*
193

Use `int` and you'll be safe.
190

Aren't you glad you learned about `break`?
191

Don't use a character I/O function with character variables.
194

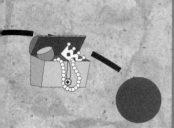

How Else Can I Control Input and Output?

With Built-In I/O Functions

There are more ways to produce input and output than with the scanf() and printf() functions. This chapter shows you some of C's built-in I/O functions that you can use to control I/O. You can use these simple functions to build powerful data-entry routines of your own.

These functions offer the *primitive* ability to input and output one character at a time. Of course, you also can use the %c format specifier with scanf() and printf() for single characters; however, the character I/O functions explained here are a little easier to use, and they provide some capabilities that scanf() and printf() don't offer.

putchar() and *getchar()*

getchar() gets a single character from the keyboard, and putchar() sends a single character to the screen. Figure 18.1 shows you what happens when you use these functions. They work basically the way you think they would. You can use them just about anytime you want to print or input a single character into a variable.

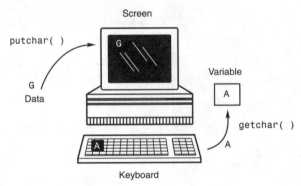

FIGURE 18.1.
getchar() *and* putchar() *input and output single characters.*

Clue: Always include the STDIO.H header file when using this chapter's I/O functions, just as you do for printf() and scanf().

NOTE

The name getchar() sounds like "get character," and putchar() sounds like "put character." Looks as though the designers of C knew what they were doing!

The following program prints C is fun, a character at a time, using putchar() to print each element of the character array in sequence. Notice that strlen() is used to ensure that the for doesn't output past the end of the string.

```
#include <stdio.h>
#include <string.h>
main()
{
  int i;
  char msg[] = "C is fun";
  for (i = 0; i < strlen(msg); i++)
    { putchar(msg[i]); }  /* Outputs a single character */
        putchar('\n');   /* Must do because putchar() doesn't */
                return 0;  /* All done */
}
```

The getchar() function returns the character input from the keyboard. Therefore, you usually assign the character to a variable or you do something else with it. You can put getchar() on a line by itself like this:

```
getchar();  /* Does nothing with the character you get */
```

but most C compilers warn you that this statement is rather useless. The getchar() function would get a character from the keyboard, but then nothing would be done with the character.

WARNING

The Blackjack program in Appendix B contains a getchar() on a line by itself in getAns(). Believe it or not, this is not necessarily inconsistent with the preceding paragraph. You'll see why in a few moments.

Here is a program that gets a character one at a time from the keyboard and stores the collected characters in a character array. A series of putchar() functions then prints the array backwards.

```
#include <stdio.h>
#include <string.h>
main()
{
  int i;
  int msg[25];
  printf("Type up to 25 characters then press Enter...\n");
  for (i = 0; i < 25; i++)
    { msg[i] = getchar();  /* Gets a character at a time */
      if (msg[i] == '\n')
        {
          i--;
          break; }  /* Quits if user presses Enter */
    }
  putchar('\n');  /* Prints a blank line */
  for (; i >= 0; i--)
    { putchar(msg[i]); }  /* Prints a character at a time */
  putchar('\n');
  return 0;  /* All done */
}
```

Clue: Notice that the second for loop variable i has no initial value! Actually, it does. i contains the last array subscript entered in the previous getchar()'s for loop. Therefore, the second for loop continues with the value of i left by the first for loop.

WARNING

The getchar() input character typically is defined as an int, as done here. Integers and characters are about the only C data types you can use interchangeably without worry of typecasts. In some advanced applications, getchar() can return a value that won't work in a char data type, so use int and you'll be safe.

NOTE

Aren't you glad you learned about break? The program keeps getting a character at a time until the user presses Enter (which produces a newline \n escape sequence). break stops the loop.

The Newline Consideration

Although getchar() gets a single character, control isn't returned to your program until the user presses Enter. The getchar() function actually instructs C to accept input into a *buffer,* which is a memory area reserved for input. The buffer isn't released until the user presses Enter, and then the buffer's contents are released a character at a time. This means two things. One, the user can press the Backspace key to correct bad character input as long as he or she hasn't pressed Enter. Two, the Enter keypress is left on the input buffer if you don't get rid of it.

Getting rid of the Enter keypress is a problem that all beginning C programmers must face. There are several solutions, but none are extremely elegant. Consider the following segment of a program:

```
printf("What are your two initials?\n");
firstInit = getchar();
lastInit  = getchar();
```

You would think that if the user typed GT, the G would go in the variable firstInit and the T would go in lastInit, but that's not what happens. The first getchar() doesn't finish until the user presses Enter because the G was going to the buffer. Only when the user presses Enter does the G leave the buffer and go to the program; but *then* the Enter is *still* on the buffer! Therefore, the second getchar() sends that Enter (actually, the \n that represents Enter) to lastInit! The T is still left for a subsequent getchar() (if there is one).

Clue: One way to fix this problem is to insert an extra `getchar()` that captures the Enter but doesn't do anything with it. That's why the Blackjack program in Appendix B has a `getchar()` on a line by itself—to capture the Enter and clear the buffer to make room for the next character input.

Here is a workaround for the initial-getting problem:

```
printf("What are your two initials?\n");
firstInit = getchar();
nl = getchar();   /* Grabs the newline */
lastInit  = getchar();
nl = getchar();   /* Grabs the newline */
```

This code requires that the user press Enter between each initial. You don't have to do anything with the `nl` variable because `nl` exists only to hold the in-between newline. As done in the Blackjack game, you don't even have to save the newline keypress in a variable. The following code works just like the last:

```
printf("What are your two initials?\n");
firstInit = getchar();
getchar();   /* Discards the newline */
lastInit  = getchar();
getchar();   /* Discards the newline */
```

Some C compilers issue warning messages when you compile programs with a stand-alone `getchar()` on lines by themselves. As long as you use these `getchar()`s for discarding Enter keypresses, you can ignore the compiler warnings.

You also can request the two initials by requiring the Enter keypress *after* the user enters the two initials like this:

```
printf("What are your two initials?\n");
firstInit = getchar();
lastInit  = getchar();
getchar();   /* Discards the newline */
```

If the user types GP and then presses Enter, the G will reside in the `firstInit` variable and the P in the `lastInit` variable.

A Little Faster: *getch()*

A character input function named getch() helps eliminate the leftover Enter keypress that getchar() leaves. getch() is *unbuffered*—that is, getch() gets whatever keypress the user types immediately and doesn't wait for an Enter keypress. The drawback to getch() is that the user can't press the Backspace key to correct bad input. For example, with getchar(), a user could press Backspace if he or she typed a B instead of a D. The B would be taken off the buffer by the Backspace, and the D would be left for getchar() to get once Enter was pressed. Because getch() does *not* buffer input, there is no chance of pressing Backspace. The following code gets two characters without an Enter keypress following each one:

```
printf("What are your two initials?\n");
firstInit = getch();
lastInit  = getch();
```

getch() is a little faster than getchar() because it doesn't wait for an Enter keypress before grabbing the user's keystrokes and continuing. You therefore don't need a stand-alone getch() to get rid of the \n as you do with getchar().

> **SKIP THIS, IT'S TECHNICAL**
>
> getch() does *not* echo the input characters to the screen as getchar() does. Therefore, you must follow getch() with a mirror-image putch() if you want the user to see on-screen the character he or she typed. To echo the initials, you could do this:
>
> ```
> printf("What are your two initials?\n");
> firstInit = getch();
> putch(firstInit);
> lastInit  = getch();
> putch(lastInit);
> ```

The next chapter explains more built-in functions, including two that quickly input and output strings as easily as this chapter's I/O functions work with characters.

Rewards

✖ Use getchar() and putchar() to input and output single characters.

✖ Use a stand-alone getchar() to get rid of the Enter keypress if you don't want to capture it. You also can create a loop to call getchar() *until* the return value is \n, as shown in the sample code.

✖ Use getch() to get *unbuffered* single characters as soon as the user types them.

Pitfalls

✖ Don't use a character I/O function with character variables. Use an int variable instead.

✖ Don't forget to print character input using putch() if you want that input echoed on the screen as the user types.

In Review

This chapter's goal was to explain a few additional input and output functions. The functions presented here are character I/O functions. Unlike scanf() and printf(), the getchar(), getch(), putchar(), and putch() functions input and output single characters at a time.

You'll often find the getch() and getchar() functions used inside large input routines that build input. This means that these functions get a character at a time from the keyboard and add those characters to an array that is checked against a string value of some kind.

Code Example

```
printf("I'm going to print a report now.\n");
printf("Is your printer turned on (y/n)? ");
ans = getch();  /* Gets the user's answer */
if (ans == 'n')
  { printf("I'll wait. Press Enter when you have it on...\n");
    ans = getch();  /* Waits for Enter keypress */
}
/* The report printing code would follow */
```

Code Analysis

This code asks the user a yes-or-no question and waits for the user to respond with a y or an n. The if ensures that the message prints if the user enters n. If the user does not yet have the printer on, the program waits to give the user a chance to turn the printer on. (A report couldn't be printed otherwise.) The user lets the program know when the printer is turned on by pressing Enter.

×19

islower **tests for lowercase values.**
199

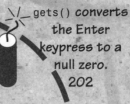

gets() **converts the Enter keypress to a null zero.**
202

You are responsible for making sure the first array is large enough.
201

Use a string literal.
201

BOTTOM-LESS PIT

Don't put a newline inside the puts() **string.**
203

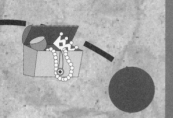

Can You Tell Me More About Strings?

C's Built-In Character and String Functions

This chapter shows you ways to take work off your shoulders and put it on C's. C includes lots of helpful built-in functions in addition to ones like `strlen()`, `getchar()`, and `printf()` that you've read about so far.

There are many more built-in functions than there is room for in a single chapter. This chapter explains the most common and helpful character and string functions. In the next chapter, you'll learn about some numeric functions.

Character-Testing Functions

There are several built-in *character-testing functions*. Now that you know how to use `getchar()` and `getch()` to get single characters, the character-testing functions can help you determine exactly what kind of input characters your program receives. You can set up `if` logic to execute certain courses of action based on the results of the character tests.

Clue: You should include the CTYPE.H header file at the top of any program that uses the character functions described here.

The `isalpha()` function returns true (which is 1 to C) if the value in its parentheses is an alphabetic character a through z (or the uppercase A through Z) and returns false (which is 0 to C) if the value in parentheses is any other character. Consider this `if`:

```
if (isalpha(inChar))
  { printf("Your input was a letter.\n"); }
```

The message prints only if `inChar` contains an alphabetic letter.

C has a corresponding function named `isdigit()` that returns true if the character in the parentheses is a number from 0 through 9. The following `if` prints A number if `inChar` contains a digit:

```
if (isdigit(inChar))
  { printf("A number\n"); }
```

> **NOTE**
>
> Do you see why these are called *character-testing* functions? Both `isalpha()` and `isdigit()` test character content and return the relational result of the test.

Is the Case Correct?

The `isupper()` and `islower()` functions let you know if a variable contains an upper- or lowercase value. Using `isupper()` keeps you from having to write long `if` statements like this:

```
if ((inLetter >= 'A') && (inLetter <= 'Z'))
  { printf("Letter is uppercase\n"); }
```

Instead, use `isupper()` in place of the logical comparison:

```
if (isupper(inLetter))
  { printf("Letter is uppercase\n"); }
```

Clue: `islower()` tests for lowercase values in the same way as `isupper()` tests for uppercase values.

You might want to use `isupper()` to ensure that your user enters an initial uppercase letter when entering names.

Case-Changing Functions

There are two important character-changing functions (also called *character-mapping functions*) that return their arguments changed a bit. Unlike `isupper()` and `islower()`, which only *test* character values and return a true or false result of the test, `toupper()` and `tolower()` return their arguments converted to different case. `toupper()` returns its parentheses argument as uppercase. `tolower()` returns its parentheses argument as lowercase.

The following program segment prints yes or no depending on the user's input. Without the toupper() function, the code is extra long.

```
if ((userInput == 'Y') || (userInput == 'y'))
  { printf("yes\n"); }
else
  { printf("no\n"); }
```

The next set of statements uses the toupper() function to streamline the if's logical test for lowercase letters:

```
if (toupper(userInput) == 'Y') /* No need to */
  { printf("yes\n"); }          /* test lower */
else
  { printf("no\n"); }
```

Clue: The Blackjack program uses toupper() in the getAns() function to return the uppercase version of whatever value the user types:

```
return toupper(ans);
```

String Functions

The STRING.H header file contains descriptions for more functions than just strcpy() and strlen(). This section explains the strcat() function that lets you merge two character arrays as long as the arrays hold strings. strcat() stands for *string concatenation.*

strcat() takes one string and appends it to, or adds it onto the end of, another string. Here is a code fragment that shows what happens with strcat():

```
char first[25] = "Peter";
char last[25] = " Parker";
strcat(first, last);  /* Adds last to the end of first */
printf("I am %s\n", first);
```

Here is the output of this code:

```
Peter Parker
```

strcat() requires two string arguments. strcat() takes the second string and tacks it onto the end of the first one. The reason the space appears before the last name is only because the last array is initialized with a space before the last name in the second line.

> **WARNING**
>
> You are responsible for making sure that the first array is large enough to hold *both* strings. If you attempt to concatenate a second string to the end of another string, and the second string is not defined with enough characters to hold the two strings, strange and unpredictable results can happen.

> **NOTE**
>
> Because the second argument for strcat() is not changed, you can use a string literal in place of a character array for the second argument if you like.

An easy way to print and get strings is provided by the puts() and gets() functions. Their descriptions are in STDIO.H, so you don't have to add an additional header file for puts() and gets(). puts() sends a string to the screen, and gets() gets a string from the keyboard. The following program demonstrates gets() and puts(). As you look through it, notice that neither printf() nor scanf() is required to input and print strings.

```c
/* Get and put strings */
#include <stdio.h>
#include <string.h>
main()
{
  char city[15];
  char st[3];  /* Leave 1 for null zero */
  char fullLocation[18] = "";  /* Put empty string here */
  puts("What town do you live in? ");
  gets(city);
  puts("What state do you live in? (2-letter abbreviation)");
  gets(st);
  /* Concatenates the strings */
```

```
        strcat(fullLocation, city);  /* Adds a comma and a space */
        strcat(fullLocation, ", ");  /* to end of city */
        strcat(fullLocation, st);  /* Adds the state
                                       to end of city */
        puts("\nYou live in ");
        puts(fullLocation);
        return 0;
}
```

Clue: strcat() has to be used three times: once to add the city, once for the comma, and once to tack the state onto the end of the city.

Here is the output from a sample run of this program:

```
What town do you live in?
Jacksonville
What state do you live in? (2-letter abbreviation)
FL

You live in
Jacksonville, FL
```

Clue: puts() automatically puts a newline at the end of every string it prints. You don't have to add a \n at the end of an output string unless you want an extra blank line printed.

SKIP THIS, IT'S TECHNICAL

gets() converts the Enter keypress to a null zero to ensure that the data obtained from the keyboard winds up being a null-terminated string instead of an array of single characters.

One of the most important reasons to use gets() over scanf() is that you can ask the user for strings that contain embedded spaces, such as a full name (first and last name). scanf() cannot accept strings with spaces; scanf() stops getting user input at the first space.

Rewards

✖ Use C's built-in character-testing and character-mapping functions so your programs won't have to work as hard to determine the case of character data.

✖ Use `gets()` to get strings and `puts()` to print strings.

✖ Use `gets()` when you must get strings that might contain spaces. Remember that `scanf()` cannot grab strings with spaces.

✖ Use `strcat()` to merge two strings.

Pitfalls

✖ Don't concatenate two strings with `strcat()` unless you're positive that the first character array can hold the strings after they're merged.

✖ Don't put a newline inside the `puts()` string unless you want an extra line printed. `puts()` automatically adds a newline to the end of strings.

In Review

The goal of this chapter was to show you some built-in character and string functions that help you test and change strings. A string is a literal list of characters, explicitly stated inside quotation marks or stored in a character array. The string functions presented in this chapter work on both string literals and arrays.

There are functions that test characters for digits and letters, convert uppercase and lowercase characters to their opposites, concatenate (merge) strings, and allow for quick input and output of strings.

Code Example

```
/* Convert to upper and lowercase */
#include <stdio.h>
#include <conio.h>
#include <ctype.h>
#include <string.h>
main()
{
  char name[25], nameNew[25];
  char ans;
  int i;
  printf("What is your name? ");
  gets(name);
  printf("Are you sure that %s is your name (y/n)? ", name);
  ans = getch();
  if (toupper(ans) == 'Y')
    { for (i = 0; i <= strlen(name); i++)
        { nameNew[i] = toupper(name[i]); }
      printf("Your name in uppercase letters is %s.\n", nameNew);
    }
  return 0;
}
```

Code Analysis

This code first asks the user for his or her name. The name is entered using a gets() function. The user can enter both a first and last name because gets() is used instead of scanf(). If the user verifies that the name is entered correctly, the for statement converts each character in the name to an uppercase letter. The for loop steps through the array, sending each character through the toupper() function and storing the uppercase letters in an array named nameNew.

20

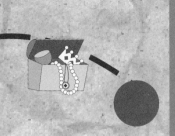

Can C Do My Math Homework?

The Built-In Numeric Functions Show You

This chapter extends your knowledge of built-in functions to the numeric functions. C helps you do math that the C operators can't do alone. More than anything else, the C built-in numeric functions supply routines that you don't have to write yourself.

A lot of C's built-in math functions are highly technical. Not that their uses are difficult, but their purposes might be. Unless you need trigonometric and advanced math functions, you might not find a use for many of the functions described in this chapter.

Clue: Some people program in C for years and never need many of these functions. You should read this chapter's material to get an idea of what C can accomplish so you'll know what's available if you ever do need these powerful functions.

Practicing Your Math

All the functions this chapter describes require the use of the MATH.H header file. Be sure to include MATH.H along with STDIO.H if you use a math function. The first few math functions are not so much math functions as they are numeric functions. These functions convert numbers to and from other numbers.

The `floor()` and `ceil()` functions are called the *floor* and *ceiling* functions, respectively. They "push down" and "push up" non-integers to their next lower or next higher integer values. For example, if you wanted to compute how many dollar bills are in a certain amount of change (that includes dollars and cents), you could use `floor()` on the amount. The following code does just that:

```
change = amtPaid - cost;   /* Floating-point values */
dollars = floor(change);
printf("The change includes %f dollar bills.\n", dollars);
```

> **WARNING**
>
> Although `ceil()` and `floor()` convert their arguments to integers, each function returns a `float` value! That's why the `dollars` variable was printed using the `%f` conversion code.

The `ceil()` function (which is the opposite of `floor()`) finds the next highest integer. Both `ceil()` and `floor()` work with negative values too, as the following few lines show:

```
lowVal1 = floor(18.5);    /* Stores  18.0 */
lowVal2 = floor(-18.5);   /* Stores -19.0 */
hiVal1 = ceil(18.5);      /* Stores  19.0 */
hiVal2 = ceil(-18.5);     /* Stores -18.0 */
```

> **NOTE**
>
> The negative values make sense when you think about the direction of negative numbers. The next integer *down* from -18.5 is -19. The next integer *up* from -18.5 is -18.
>
> See, these functions aren't so bad, and they come in handy when you need them.

Doing More Conversions

Two other numeric functions convert numbers to other values. The `fabs()` function returns the floating-point *absolute value*. When you first hear about absolute value, it sounds like something you'll never need. The absolute value of a number, whether it is negative or positive, is the positive version of the number. Both of these `printf()` functions print 25:

```
printf("Absolute value of 25.0 is %.0f.\n", fabs(25.0));
printf("Absolute value of -25.0 is %.0f.\n", fabs(-25.0));
```

NOTE

The floating-point answers print without decimal places because of the `.0` inside the `%f` conversion codes.

Clue: Absolute values are useful for computing differences in ages, weights, and distances. For example, the difference between two people's ages is always a positive number, no matter how you subtract one from the other.

Two additional mathematical functions might come in handy, even if you don't do heavy scientific and math programming. The `pow()` function raises a value to a power, and the `sqrt()` function returns the square root of a value.

Clue: You can't compute the square root of a negative number. The `fabs()` function can help ensure that you don't try to take the square root of a negative number by converting the number to a positive value before you compute the square root.

SKIP THIS, IT'S TECHNICAL

Perhaps a picture will bring back fond high school algebra memories. Figure 20.1 shows the familiar math symbols used for `pow()` and `sqrt()`.

The following code prints the value of 10 raised to the third power and the square root of 64:

```
printf("10 raised to the 3rd power is %.0f.\n",
       pow(10.0, 3.0));
printf("The square root of 64 is %.0f.\n", sqrt(64.0));
```

Here is the output of these `printf()` functions:

```
10 raised to the 3rd power is 1000.
The square root of 64 is 8.
```

If a C programmer does this: A mathematician does this:

$$x = \texttt{pow(4, 6);} \qquad x = 4^6$$

$$x = \texttt{sqrt(value);} \qquad x = \sqrt{\text{value}}$$

FIGURE 20.1.
Looking at the math symbols for `pow()` *and* `sqrt()`.

Getting Into Trig and Other Really Hard Stuff

Only a handful of readers will need the trigonometric and logarithmic functions. If you know you won't, or if you hope you won't, go ahead and skip to the next section. Those of you who need them now won't require much explanation, so not much is given.

The primary trigonometric functions are explained in Table 20.1. They each require an argument expressed in radians.

Table 20.1. C's trigonometric functions.

Function	Description
`cos(x)`	Returns the cosine of the angle x.
`sin(x)`	Returns the sine of the angle x.
`tan(x)`	Returns the tangent of the angle x.

SKIP THIS, IT'S TECHNICAL

If you want to supply an argument in degrees instead of in radians, you can convert from degrees to radians with this formula:

radians = degrees * (3.14159 / 180.0);

The primary log functions are shown in Table 20.2.

Table 20.2. C's logarithmic functions.

Function	Description
exp(x)	Returns e, the base of the natural logarithm, raised to a power specified by x (e^x).
log(x)	Returns the natural logarithm of the argument x, mathematically written as ln(x). x must be positive.
log10(x)	Returns the base-10 logarithm of the argument x, mathematically written as $\log_{10}(x)$. x must be positive.

The following program prints the results of the six trig and log functions:

```
/* Trig and log functions */
#include <stdio.h>
#include <math.h>
main()
{
  printf("The trig functions:\n");
  printf("  The cosine of 1 is %.3f\n", cos(1));
  printf("  The sine of 1 is %.3f\n", sin(1));
  printf("  The tangent of 1 is %.3f\n", tan(1));
  printf("The log functions:\n");
  printf("  e raised to 1 is %.3f\n", exp(1));
  printf("  The natural log of 2 is %.3f\n", log(2));
  printf("  The base-10 log of 2 is %.3f\n", log10(2));
  return 0;
}
```

Here is the output. Does C compute these values faster than you can with pencil and paper?

```
The trig functions:
  The cosine of 1 is 0.540
  The sine of 1 is 0.841
  The tangent of 1 is 1.557
The log functions:
  e raised to 1 is 2.718
  The natural log of 2 is 0.693
  The base-10 log of 2 is 0.301
```

Getting Random

For games and simulation programs, you often need to generate random values. C's built-in `rand()` function does just that. It returns a random number from 0 to 32767. The `rand()` function requires the STDLIB.H (*standard library*) header file. If you want to narrow the random numbers, you can use % (the modulus operator) to do so. The following expression puts a random number from 1 to 6 in the variable `dice`:

```
dice = (rand() % 5) + 1;   /* From 1 to 6 */
```

> **WARNING**
>
> Because a die can have a value from 1 to 6, the modulus operator returns the integer division remainder (0 through 5), and then a 1 is added to produce a die value.

There's one crazy thing you must do if you want a *truly* random value. It is described next.

> **NOTE**
>
> You might always want a different set of random numbers produced each time a program runs. Games need such randomness. However, many simulations and scientific studies need to repeat the same set of random numbers. rand() will always do that if you don't seed the random-number generator.

213

To *seed* the random-number generator means to give it an initial base value from which the rand() function can offset with a random number. Use srand() to seed the random-number generator. The number inside srand()'s parentheses must be different every time you run the program unless you want to produce the same set of random values.

The trick to giving srand() a different number each run is to put the exact time of day inside srand()'s parentheses. Your computer keeps track of the time of day down to hundredths of a second.

Because there's no time to go into much detail, let's cut to the chase and see how most C programmers produce truly random values. The following code is similar to a section from the Blackjack game in Appendix B. The comments explain things that need clarifying at this point.

```
time_t t;  /* Goes with your variable definitions
             such as int i;                        */
srand(time(&t));                /* Seeds with the time of day */
subDraw = (rand() % (numCards));  /* Ensures that a random
                                     card is drawn from a
                                     52-card deck         */
```

Clue: You must include TIME.H before seeding the random-number generator with the time of day, as done here.

NOTE

The bottom line is this: If you add the two weird-looking time statements shown here, rand() will always be random and will produce different results every time you run a program.

Rewards

✖ Use the built-in numeric functions when you can so that you won't have to write code to perform the same calculations.

✖ Lots of the numeric functions such as floor(), ceil(), and fabs() convert one number to another.

✖ Be sure to seed the random-number generator with the time of day if you want random numbers with rand() to be different every time you run a program.

Pitfalls

✖ Don't feel that you must master the trig and log functions if you don't need them now. Many C programmers never use them.

✖ Don't use an integer variable to hold the return value from this chapter's math functions (unless you typecast the function return values) because they return floats or doubles even though some, like ceil(), produce whole-number results.

In Review

The goal of this chapter was to explain lots of built-in math functions that can make numeric data processing easier. C contains a rich assortment of integer functions, numeric conversion functions, time and date functions, and random-number generating functions.

You don't have to understand every function in this chapter at this time. You might write hundreds of C programs and never use many of these functions. Nevertheless, they are in C if you need them.

Code Example

```
#include <math.h>
po2 = pow(2.0, 2.0);
printf("2 raised to the 2nd power is %.0f\n", po2);
s2 = sqrt(49);
printf("The square root of 49 is %.0f\n", s2);
si628 = sin(6.28);
printf("The sine of 6.28 is %f\n", si628);
r01 = rand();
printf("A random number from 1 to 32767 is %f\n", r01);
```

Code Analysis

These code lines give quick examples of how you would use some of the math functions described in this chapter. The program contains four pairs of statements. Each pair contains a function call and the output of that function call's resulting value.

Notice that rand() is the only function in the code that doesn't accept an argument. If the rand() function based its answer on a value you passed, rand() wouldn't be very random.

Part 4

C Programs and Lots of Data

21

val holds the values
as they are assigned.
227

Always specify
the number of
subscripts
when you define
an array.
225

Make your arrays big
enough to hold
values.
223

The first
subscript of all
C arrays begins
at 0.
224

BOTTOM-
LESS PIT

Don't use an
array until you
have
initialized it.
228

How Does C Work with Lists?

Using Arrays

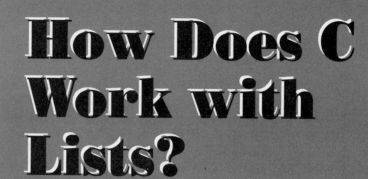

The really nice thing about this chapter is that it covers absolutely nothing new. You've worked with arrays when you've stored strings in character arrays throughout this book. This chapter simply hones that concept of arrays and demonstrates that you can create an array of any data type, not just the `char` data type.

As you know, an array of characters is just a list of characters that has a name. Similarly, an array of integers is just a list of integers that has a name, and an array of floating-point values is just a list of floating-point values that has a name. Instead of referring to each of the array elements by a different name, you only have to refer to them by the array name and distinguish them with a subscript enclosed in brackets.

Reviewing Arrays

All arrays contain values called *elements*. An array can contain *only* elements that are of the same type. In other words, you can't have an array that has a floating-point value, a character value, and an integer value.

Define arrays almost the same way you define regular non-array variables. To define a regular variable, you only have to specify its data type next to the variable name:

```
int i;    /* Defines a non-array variable */
```

To define an array, you must add brackets (`[]`) after the name and specify the maximum number of elements that you will ever store in the array:

```
int i[25];   /* Defines the array */
```

If you want to initialize a character array with an initial string, you know that you can do this:

```
char name[6] = "Italy";  /* Leave room for the null! */
```

WARNING

Once you define an array to a certain size, don't try to store more elements than were allowed in the original size. After defining `name` as just done, the `strcpy()` function will *let* you store a string longer than *Italy* in name, but the result would be disastrous because other data in memory could be overwritten unintentionally. If another variable happened to be defined immediately after name, that other variable's data will be overwritten if you try to store a too-long string into name.

Clue: If the initial array needs to be larger than the initial value you assign, specify a larger array size when you define the array, like this:

```
char name[80] = "Italy";   /* Leaves lots of
                              extra room */
```

Doing this makes room for a string much longer than *Italy* if you want to store a longer string in name. For example, you might want to use gets() to get a string from the user, that could easily be longer than *Italy*.

WARNING

Make your arrays big enough to hold enough values, but don't overdo it. Don't make your arrays larger than you think you'll really need. Arrays can consume a large amount of memory, and the more elements you reserve, the less memory you have for your program and other variables.

You can initialize an array one element at a time when you define an array by enclosing the array's data elements in braces and following the array name with an equals sign. For example, the following statement both defines an integer array *and* initializes it with five values:

```
int vals[5] = {10, 40, 70, 90, 120};
```

SKIP THIS, IT'S TECHNICAL

As a review, Figure 21.1 shows what vals looks like in memory after the definition. The numbers in brackets indicate subscripts. No null zero is at the end of the array because null zeros terminate only strings stored in character arrays.

The vals array

10	vals[0]
40	vals[1]
70	vals[2]
90	vals[3]
120	vals[4]

FIGURE 21.1.
After defining and initializing the vals *array.*

NOTE

The first subscript of all C arrays begins at 0.

The following statement defines and initializes two arrays—a floating-point array and a double floating-point array. Because C is free-form, you can continue the initialization list over more than one line, as is done for annualSal.

```
float money[10] = {6.23, 2.45, 8.01, 2.97, 6.41};
double annualSal[6] = {43565.78, 75674.23, 90001.34,
                       10923.45, 39845.82};
```

You also can define and initialize a character array with individual characters:

```
char grades[5] = {'A', 'B', 'C', 'D', 'F'};
```

Because a null zero is not in the last character element, grades consists of individual characters, but not a string. If the last elements were initialized with '\0', which represents the null zero, you could have treated grades as a string and printed it with puts(), or printf() and the %s conversion code. The following name definition puts a string in name:

```
char italCity[7] = {'V', 'e', 'r', 'o', 'n', 'a', '\0'};
```

You have to admit that initializing such a character array with a string is easier to do like this:

```
char italCity[7] = "Verona";   /* Automatic null zero */
```

We should be getting back to numeric arrays, which are the primary focus of this chapter. Is there a null zero at the end of the following array named nums?

```
int nums[4] = {5, 1, 3, 0};
```

There is *not* a null zero at the end of nums! Be careful, nums is not a character array, and a string is not being stored there. The zero at the end of the array is a regular numeric zero. The bit-pattern (that's fancy computer lingo for the internal representation of data) is exactly like that of a null zero. But you would never treat nums as if there were a string in nums, because nums is defined as an integer numeric array.

SKIP THIS, IT'S TECHNICAL

Always specify the number of subscripts when you define an array! There is one exception to this rule, however: If you assign an initial value or set of values to the array *at the time you define the array*, you can leave the brackets empty:

```
int ages[5] = {5, 27, 40, 65, 92};  /* Correct */

int ages[];  /* Incorrect */

int ages[] = {5, 27, 40, 65, 92};  /* Correct */
```

NOTE

`sizeof()` returns the number of bytes you *reserved* for the array, *not* the number of elements in which you have stored a value. For example, if floating-point values consume 4 bytes on your computer, an 8-element floating-point array will take a total of 32 bytes of memory, and 32 is the value returned if you apply `sizeof()` to the array after you define the array.

Clue: If you want to zero out every element of an array, you can do so with a shortcut that C provides:

```
float amount[100] = {0.0};  /* Zeroes-out all of
                                the array */
```

If you don't initialize an array, C won't either. Until you put values into an array, you have no idea exactly what's in the array. The only exception to this rule is that most C compilers zero out all elements of an array if you initialize at least one of the array's values when you define the array. The previous clue works because one value was stored in amount's first element's position and C filled in the rest with zeros. (Even if the first elements were initialized with `123.45`, C would have filled the remaining elements with zeros.)

Putting Values in Arrays

You don't always know the contents of an array at the time you define it. Often, array values come from a disk file, calculations, or a user's input. Character arrays are easy to fill with strings because C supplies the `strcpy()` function. You can fill other types of arrays a single element at a time. There is no shortcut function, such as `strcpy()`, that puts lots of integers or floating-point values in an array.

The following code defines an array of integers and asks the user for values that are stored in that array. Array elements, unlike regular variables that all have different names, are easy to work with because you can use a loop to count the subscripts, as done here:

```
int ages[3];
for (i = 0; i < 3; i++)
  { printf("What is the age of child #%d? ", i+1);
    scanf(" %d", &ages[i]);  /* Gets next age from user */
  }
```

Clue: The `initCardsScreen()` function in the Blackjack program (see Appendix B) uses a conditional operator to produce various numeric values that represent cards in the deck:

```
val = (val == 14) ? 1 : val; /* If val is 14,
                                 reset to 1 */
```

The program keeps incrementing `val`. However, if `val` becomes 14, this conditional statement resets `val` back to 1. The values 1 through 13 represent the 13 cards in each suit (the Ace through the King). Four groups of values from 1 to 13 fill the card array, and `val` holds the values as they are assigned.

We're Not Done Yet

This chapter explained the purpose of arrays. The next chapter explains exactly how to sort arrays in the order you want them and how to search arrays for a specific value.

Rewards

- ✖ Use arrays to hold lists of values of the same data type.
- ✖ Refer to the individual elements of an array with a subscript.
- ✖ Write `for` loops if you want to "step through" every array element, whether it be to initialize, print, or change the array elements.

Pitfalls

✖ In an array, don't use more elements than defined subscripts.

✖ Don't use an array until you have initialized it with values.

In Review

The goal of this chapter was to teach you how to store data in lists called *arrays*. An array is nothing more than a bunch of variables. Each variable has the same name (the array name). You distinguish between the variables in the array (the array *elements*) with a numeric *subscript*. The first array element has a subscript of 0, and the rest count up from there.

Arrays are characterized by brackets that follow the array names. The array subscripts go inside the brackets when you need to refer to an individual array element.

Code Example

```
int i;
float grades[10];  /* Creates the array */
float avg = 0;
for (i = 0; i < 10; i++)
  { printf("What is student number %d's grade? ", i+1);
    scanf(" %f", &grades[i]);  /* Gets each grade
                                  from teacher */
    avg += grades[i];  /* Adds to total scores */
  }
  avg /= 10;  /* Computes average */
  printf("\nThe average of all grades is %.2f.\n", avg);
```

Code Analysis

This code first creates work variables that hold an integer counter for the for loop—the grades array that will hold 10 grades—and the floating-point variable avg that will hold the average of those grades.

The program then asks the teacher for each of the 10 students' grades in the for loop. The last statement in the loop adds each grade to a running total of the grades. The total variable, named avg, is finally divided by 10 at the end of the program to hold the average of the grades.

22

The found variable is
often called a flag
variable.
236

Jot down
variable values.
235

The program's for
loop might end.
236

Find values
that you put in
the arrays.
233

BOTTOM-
LESS PIT

A match may
not be found.
237

How Can I Search for Data?

Step Through Arrays

You bought this book to learn C as painlessly as possible—and that's what has been happening. (You knew that *something* was happening, right?) Nevertheless, you won't become an ace programmer if you aren't exposed a bit to searching and sorting values. Complete books have been written on searching and sorting techniques, and the next two chapters present only the simplest techniques. Be forewarned, however, that before you're done, this and the next chapter may raise more questions than they answer. If you enjoy searching and sorting, look at Appendix A, which lists several more books that help strengthen your searching and sorting abilities with C.

You'll find that this and the next chapter are a little different from a lot of the others. Instead of teaching you new C features, these chapters demonstrate the use of C language elements you've been learning throughout this book. The chapters focus on arrays. You will see applications of the array concepts you learned in Chapter 21. Once these chapters strengthen your array understanding, Chapter 25 explains a C alternative to arrays that sometimes comes in handy.

Filling Arrays

As mentioned in Chapter 21, your programs will use several means to fill arrays. Some arrays, such as the day counts in each of the 12 months, historical temperature readings, and last year's sales records, are known in advance. You might initialize arrays with such values when you define the arrays, or when you use assignment statements.

You will also be filling arrays with values entered by your program's users. A customer-order fulfillment program would get its data only as customers place orders. A scientific lab would only know test values after the scientists gather their results.

Other data values might come from disk files. Customer records, inventory values, and school transcript information is just too voluminous for users to enter each time a program is run.

In reality, your programs can and will fill arrays using a combination of all three of these methods:

✖ Assignment

✖ User data-entry

✖ Disk files

In this book, the programs have to be kept simple. Until you learn about disk files, you'll see arrays filled with assignment statements, and possibly simple user data-entry (and *you'll* be the user!).

> **NOTE**
>
> At this point, it's important for you to concentrate on what you do with arrays after the arrays get filled with values. One of the most important things to do is *find* values that you put in the arrays.

Finders Keepers

Think about the following scenario: Your program contains an array that holds customer ID numbers and an array that holds the same number of customer balances. Such arrays are often called *parallel arrays* because the arrays are in synch; that is, element number 14 in the customer ID array contains the customer number that owes a balance found in element 14 of the balance array.

The customer balance program might fill the two arrays from disk data when the program first starts. As a customer places a new order, it's your program's job to find that customer balance and stop the order if the customer owes more than $100 already (the deadbeat!).

Fun Fact

The search value is called the key.

In a nutshell, here is the program's job:

1. Ask for a customer ID number (the key).

2. Search the array for a customer balance that matches the key value.

3. Inform you if the customer already owes more than $100.

The following program does just that. Actually, the program only maintains a list of 10 customers because you're not yet ready to tackle disk input (but you're almost there!). The program initializes the arrays when the arrays are first defined; so maintaining only 10 array element pairs (the customer ID and the corresponding balance arrays) keeps the array definitions simple.

> **NOTE**
>
> As with the sorting program you'll see in the next chapter, this program is a little longer than the others so far in the book; but you're ready to look through a longer program because you've had *such* a good teacher so far!

Study this program before typing it in and running it. See if you can get the gist of the program from the code and comments. Following this code listing is an explanation.

Fun Fact

This program uses a sequential search technique.

```
/* Searches for balances */
#include <stdio.h>
main()
{
    int ctr;  /* Loop counter */
    int idSearch;  /* Customer to look for (the key) */
    int found = 0; /* 1 (true) if customer is found */

    /* Defines the ten elements in each of the parallel arrays */
    int custID[10] = {313, 453, 502, 101, 892,
                          475, 792, 912, 343, 633 };
    float custBal[10] = {  0.00,  45.43,  71.23, 301.56,  9.08,
                          192.41, 389.00, 229.67,  18.31, 59.54};

    /* Interact with the user looking for a balance */
    printf("\n\n*** Customer Balance Lookup ***\n");
    printf("What is the customer number? ");
    scanf(" %d", &idSearch);

    /* Now, look for the balance in the arrays */
    for (ctr=0; ctr<10; ctr++)
    {  if (idSearch == custID[ctr])     /* Found? */
       {  found = 1;        /* Yes, found is true */
          break;            /* No more search needed */
       }
    } /* Not found yet, loop again to try another match */

    /* If the for-loop finishes, the customer ID was
        found or all customers were searched unsuccessfully  */
```

```
   if (found)            /* Cleaner than if (found == 1) */
     { if (custBal[ctr] > 100.00)
         { printf("\n** That customer's balance is $%.2f.\n",
                  custBal[ctr]);
           printf("   No credit!\n");
         }
       else    /* Balance is less than 100.00 */
         { printf("\n**The customer's credit is good!\n");
         }
     }
   else   /* Not found */
     { printf("** You must have typed an incorrect customer
              ID.");
       printf("\n   ID %3d was not found in list.\n", idSearch);
     }
   return 0;
}
```

SKIP THIS, IT'S TECHNICAL

Yes, this program is long. However, most of this book has shown you small examples of code. It would be a good exercise for you to step through this program and figure out what it's doing. Use a pencil and paper to jot down variable values.

There are three possibilities to this program's attempted customer search:

❌ The customer's balance is less than $100.

❌ The customer's balance is too high (more than $100).

❌ The customer's ID is not even in the list.

Here are three runs of the program showing each of the three possibilities.

```
*** Customer Balance Lookup ***
What is the customer number? 343

**The customer's credit is good!


*** Customer Balance Lookup ***
What is the customer number? 583
** You must have typed an incorrect customer ID.
   ID 583 was not found in list.
```

```
*** Customer Balance Lookup ***
What is the customer number? 101

** That customer's balance is $301.56.
   No credit!
```

The first part of the program defines and initializes two arrays with the customer ID numbers and matching balances. As you know, when you first define arrays, you can then use the assignment operator, =, to assign the array's data.

After printing a title and asking for a customer ID number, the program uses a `for` loop to step through the parallel arrays looking for the user's entered customer ID. If discovered, a `found` variable is set to true (1) for later use. Otherwise, `found` remains false (0).

Clue: The `found` variable is often called a *flag* variable because it flags (signals) to the rest of the program whether the customer ID was or was not found.

WARNING

The program's `for` loop might end without the customer being found. The code following the `for` loop would have no way of knowing if the `for`'s `break` triggered an early `for` loop exit (meaning the customer was found) or if the `for` ended normally. Therefore, the `found` variable lets the code following the `for` loop know if the `for` found the customer or not.

Once the `for` loop ends, the customer is found (or not found). If found, the following two conditions are possible:

- ✖ The balance is already too high.
- ✖ The balance is okay for more credit.

No matter which condition is the true condition, the user is informed of the result. If the customer was not found, the user is told that, and the program ends.

How was that for a *real-world* program? Too difficult you say? Look it over once or twice more. You'll see that the program performs the same steps (albeit in seemingly more detail) that you would follow if you were scanning through a list of customers by hand.

Clue: What's *really* important is that if there were a thousand, or even ten thousand customers, and the arrays were initialized from a disk file, the same search code would work! The amount of data doesn't affect the logic of this program (only the way the arrays are initialized with data).

Clue: The previous program's search is a *sequential search* because the customer ID array is searched from beginning to end until a match is found. There are more advanced searches that you'll learn about as your programming skills improve. In the next chapter, you'll see how sorting an array helps speed some array searches. There are also advanced search techniques called *binary searches* and *Fibonacci searches*.

Rewards

✖ Filling arrays is only the first step; once filled, your program must get to the data.

✖ Until you learn more about searches, use a sequential search because it is the easiest search technique to master first.

Pitfalls

✖ Don't forget that a match may not be found. Always assume that your search value may not be in the list of values and always include the code needed to handle an unfound value.

In Review

The goal of this chapter was to show you how to find values in arrays. You saw how to find array values based on a *key*. The key is a value entered by the user. You'll often search through parallel arrays, as done here. One array (the key array) holds the values for which you'll search. If the search is successful, other arrays supply needed data and you can report the results back to the user. If the search is unsuccessful, you need to let the user know that also.

Code Example

```c
/* Searches for letters */
#include <stdio.h>
#include <stdlib.h>
main()
{
  char letters[50];
  char userInit;
  int ctr, nl, numInits=0;
  /* Store random letters from A to Z */
  for (ctr=0; ctr<50; ctr++)
    { letters[ctr] = 65 + (rand() % 26); }
  /* Get the user's search initial */
  printf("What is your first initial? ");
  userInit = getchar();
  nl = getchar();   /* To discard the newline */
  /* Find the number of occurrences */
  for (ctr=0; ctr<50; ctr++)
    { if (letters[ctr] == userInit)
        { numInits++; }
    }
  printf("\nIn the array, there were %d of your initials.\n",
        numInits);
  return 0;
}
```

Code Analysis

This program first uses the `rand()` function to store letters of the alphabet in 50 character array elements. The formula `rand() % 26` produces numbers from 0 to 25. These numbers are added to 65 to produce ASCII table values from 65 to 90, which match the uppercase letters from A to Z.

Once 50 random letters are stored in the letters array, the program asks the user for her or his first initial. A for loop then searches through the array looking for matches. One is added to the numInits variable each time a match is found. Once the program searches through all the array elements, a printf() prints the total matches found.

23

`rand()` produces
different results
between compilers.
245

Sort the list in
descending
order.
246

Keeping arrays
sorted is not always
easy.
250

To alphabetize
a list of char-
acters.
246

BOTTOM-
LESS PIT

Keep your arrays
sorted.
251

How Can I Arrange and Alphabetize?

The Bubble Sort Does the Trick

Sorting is the computer term given to ordering lists of values. Not only must you be able to find data in arrays, you often need to arrange array data in a certain order. Computers are perfect for sorting and alphabetizing data, and arrays provide the vehicles for holding sorted data.

Your programs don't always hold array data in the order you want to see that data. For example, students don't enroll in alphabetical last-name order, even though most colleges print lists of students that way. Therefore, once student data is collected, the school's computer programs must somehow arrange that data in last-name order for reports.

This chapter explains the easiest of computer sorting techniques called the *bubble sort.*

Putting Your House in Order: Sorting

If you want to alphabetize a list of letters or names, or put a list of sales values into *ascending* order (ascending means from low to high, and *descending* means from high to low), you should use a sorting routine. Of course, the list of values that you sort will be stored in an array because array values are so easily rearranged by their subscripts.

Think about how you'd put a deck of cards in order if you threw them up in the air and let them fall. You would pick them up, one by one, looking at how the current card fit in with the others in your hand. Often you would rearrange some cards that you already held. The same type of process is used for sorting an array; often you have to rearrange values that are in the array.

There are several computer methods for sorting values. This chapter teaches you about the *bubble sort.* The bubble sort isn't extremely efficient compared to other sorts, but it's the easiest to understand. The name *bubble sort* comes from the nature of the sort. During a sort, the lower values "float" up the list each time a pass is made through the data. Figure 23.1 shows the process of sorting five numbers using a bubble sort.

Before sorting:
```
50
32
93
 2
74
```

During first pass, C compares the first value
to the second. Because 32 is less than 50, they
switch places:
```
32
50
93
 2
74
```

It then compares 32 and 93 and leaves them
where they are. Next, C compares 32 and 2. Because
2 is the lesser value, 32 and 2 switch places:
```
 2
50
93
32
74
```

Finally, it compares 2, the new first value in
the list, to 74 and leaves them.

After first pass:
```
 2
50
93
32
74
```

During second pass, C compares the second value, 50,
to 93 and leaves them. It then compares 50 to 32 and
switches them:
```
 2
32
93
50
74
```

C then compares the second value, 32, to 74 and
leaves them.

After second pass:
```
 2
32
93
50
74
```

This process continues until all the numbers
have been sorted.

After third pass:
```
 2
32
50
93
74
```

After fourth pass:
```
 2
32
50
74
93    (sorted)
```

FIGURE 23.1.

During each pass, the lower values "float" to the top of the array.

The next program sorts a list of 10 numbers. The numbers are randomly generated using rand(). The bubble sort routine is little more than a nested for loop. The inner loop walks through the list, swapping any pair of values that is out of order down the list. The outer loop causes the inner loop to run several times (one time for each item in the list).

Fun Fact

Other sorting methods include the QuickSort, the Heapsort, and the Shell-Metzner sort.

An added bonus that is common to many improved bubble sort routines is the testing to see if a swap took place during any iteration of the inner loop. If no swap took place, the outer loop finishes early (via a break statement). Therefore, if the loop is sorted to begin with, or if only a few passes are needed to sort the list, the outer loop doesn't have to finish all its planned repetitions.

```c
#include <stdio.h>
#include <stdlib.h>
/* Program that sorts a list of 10 numbers */
main()
{
    int ctr, inner, outer, didSwap, temp;
    int nums[10];   /* Will hold the 10 numbers */

    /* Fills array with random numbers from 1 to 100 */
    for (ctr = 0; ctr < 10; ctr++)
      { nums[ctr] = (rand() % 99) + 1; }

    /* Prints the list before it is sorted */
    puts("\nHere is the list before the sort:");
    for (ctr = 0; ctr < 10; ctr++)
      { printf("%d\n", nums[ctr]); }

    /* Sorts the array */
    for (outer = 0; outer < 9; outer++)
      { didSwap = 0;   /* Becomes 1 (true) if list
                              is not yet ordered */
        for (inner = outer; inner < 10; inner++)
          {  if (nums[inner] < nums[outer])
                 {  temp = nums[inner];
                    nums[inner] = nums[outer];
                    nums[outer] = temp;
                    didSwap = 1;   /* True because a swap
                                        took place */
                 }
          }
        if (didSwap == 0)  /* Quits if list is now sorted */
          { break; }
      }
```

```
/* Prints the list after it is sorted */
  printf("\nHere is the list after the sort:\n");
  for (ctr = 0; ctr < 10; ctr++)
    { printf("%d\n", nums[ctr]); }
  return 0;
}
```

The output from this sorting program is as follows:

```
Here is the list before the sort:
71
54
58
29
31
78
2
77
82
71

Here is the list after the sort:
2
29
31
54
58
71
71
77
78
82
```

Clue: Your output might be different than that shown in the preceding example because rand() produces different results between compilers. The important thing to look for is the set of 10 random values your program generates, which should be sorted upon completion of the program.

Here is the swapping of the variables inside the inner loop:

```
temp = nums[inner];
nums[inner] = nums[outer];
nums[outer] = temp;
```

In other words, if a swap needs to take place (the first of the two values being compared is higher than the second of the two values), the program must swap `nums[inner]` with `nums[outer]`.

You might wonder why an extra variable, `temp`, was needed to swap two variables' values. A natural (and incorrect) tendency when swapping two variables might be this:

```
nums[inner] = nums[outer];  /* Does NOT swap the */
nums[outer] = nums[inner];  /* two values        */
```

The first assignment wipes out the value of `nums[inner]` so that the second assignment has nothing to assign. Therefore, a third variable is required to swap any two variables.

SKIP THIS, IT'S TECHNICAL

If you wanted to sort the list in descending order, you would only have to change the less-than sign (<) to a greater-than sign (>) right before the swapping code:

```
/* Top of program would go here */
{  if (nums[inner] > nums[outer])
     /* Rest of program follows */
```

NOTE

If you wanted to alphabetize a list of characters, you could do so by testing and swapping character array values, just as you've done here. In Chapter 25, "How Are Arrays and Pointers Different?" you will learn how to store lists of string data that you can sort.

Faster Searches

Sometimes, sorting data speeds your data searching. In the last chapter, you saw a program that searched a customer ID array for a matching user's value.

If a match was found, a corresponding customer balance (in another array) was used for a credit check. The customer ID values were not stored in any order.

There was the possibility that the user's entered customer ID might not have been found. Perhaps the user entered the customer ID incorrectly, or the customer ID had not been stored in the array. Every element in the entire customer ID array had to be searched before the programmer could realize that the customer ID was not going to be found.

If, however, the arrays were sorted in customer ID order before the search began, the program would not always have to look at each array element before deciding that a match can't be made. If the customer ID array were sorted, and the user's customer ID were passed when looking through a search, the program would know right then that a match would not be found. Consider the following list of unsorted customer IDs:

313
532
178
902
422
562

Suppose the program had to look for the customer ID 413. With an unsorted array, a program would have to match the ID 413 to each element in the array.

If the arrays contained hundreds or thousands of values instead of only six, the computer would take longer to realize unmatched searches because each search would require that each element be looked at. However, if the values were always sorted, a program would not always have to scan through the entire list before realizing a match would not be found. Here is the same list of values sorted numerically, from low to high customer IDs:

178
313
422
532
562
902

A sorted list makes the search faster. Now if you search for customer ID 413, your program can stop searching after looking at only three array values. 422 is the third element, and because 422 is greater than 413, your program can stop searching. It can stop searching because 422 comes after 413.

> **NOTE**
>
> In extreme cases, searching a sorted array is not necessarily faster than sorting using an unsorted array. For instance if you were searching within the previous list for customer ID 998, your program would have to search all six values before realizing that 998 is not in the list.

The following program is a combination of the customer ID searching program shown in the previous chapter and the sorting routine shown in this chapter. The customer ID values are sorted and then the user is asked for a customer ID to find. The program then determines if the customer's balance is less than $100. If, however, the ID is not in the list, the program terminates the search early. Keep in mind that having only 10 array values makes this program seem like overkill; but if there were tens of thousands of customers, the code would not be different.

```c
/* Searches a sorted list for balances */
#include <stdio.h>
main()
{
  int ctr;  /* Loop counter */
  int idSearch;  /* Customer to look for (the key) */
  int found = 0; /* 1 (true) if customer is found */

  /* Defines the ten elements in each of the parallel arrays */
  int custID[10] = {313, 453, 502, 101, 892,
                    475, 792, 912, 343, 633 };
  float custBal[10] = {  0.00,  45.43,  71.23, 301.56,  9.08,
                       192.41, 389.00, 229.67,  18.31, 59.54};
  int tempID, inner, outer, didSwap;   /* For sorting */
  float tempBal;                       /* and swapping */

  /* First, sort the arrays by customer ID */
    for (outer = 0; outer < 9; outer++)
      { didSwap = 0;  /* Becomes 1 (true) if list
                         is not yet ordered */
```

```
        for (inner = outer; inner < 10; inner++)
          {  if (custID[inner] < custID[outer])
             {  tempID = custID[inner];     /* Must swap    */
                tempBal = custBal[inner]; /* BOTH arrays! */
                custID[inner] = custID[outer];
                custBal[inner] = custBal[outer];
                custID[outer] = tempID;
                custBal[outer] = tempBal;
                didSwap = 1;  /* True because a swap
                                     took place */
             }
          }
        if (didSwap == 0)  /* Quits if list is now sorted */
          { break; }
     }
/* Interact with the user looking for a balance */
printf("\n\n*** Customer Balance Lookup ***\n");
printf("What is the customer number? ");
scanf(" %d", &idSearch);

/* Now, look for the balance in the arrays */
for (ctr=0; ctr<10; ctr++)    /* Search maximum of 10 values */
{  if (idSearch == custID[ctr])    /* Found? */
     {  found = 1;       /* Yes, found is true */
        break;           /* No more search needed */
     }
   if (custID[ctr] > idSearch)  /* Don't go too far */
     { break; }  /* Know early the ID isn't in the list */
} /* Not found yet, loop again to try another match */

/* If the for-loop finishes, the customer ID was
    found or all customers were searched unsuccessfully  */

if (found)           /* Cleaner than if (found == 1) */
  { if (custBal[ctr] > 100.00)
     { printf("\n** That customer's balance is $%.2f.\n",
           custBal[ctr]);
       printf("   No credit!\n");
     }
    else    /* Balance is less than 100.00 */
     { printf("\n**The customer's credit is good!\n");
     }
  }
  else   /* Not found */
    { printf("** You must have typed an incorrect customer
ID.");
      printf("\n   ID %3d was not found in list.\n", idSearch);
    }
  return 0;
}
```

NOTE

Other than the Blackjack game in Appendix B, the preceding program is this book's hardest to understand. Mastering this program puts you at a level above that of *absolute beginner*. Congratulations, and hats off to you once you master the logic presented here. See, programming in C isn't difficult after all!

Before seeing this program, you mastered both array searching and array sorting. This program simply puts the two procedures together. About the only additional job this program does is keep the two parallel arrays in synch during the search. As you can see from the body of the search code, when customer ID elements are swapped (within the custID array), the corresponding (via the subscript) element in the customer balance array is searched.

An early search termination could take place because of the following:

```
if (custID[ctr] > idSearch)    /* Don't go too far */
  { break; }   /* Know early the ID isn't in the list */
```

When there are several thousand array elements, such an if saves a lot of processing time.

WARNING

Keeping arrays sorted is not always easy or efficient. For instance, you don't want your program sorting a large array every time you add, change, or delete a value from the array. After storing several thousand values in an array, sorting the array after adding each value takes too much time, even for fast computers. There are advanced ways of manipulating arrays so that you always insert items in sorted order. (However, such techniques are way beyond the scope of this book.) You're doing well without complicating things too much here.

Rewards

✖ Use an ascending sort when you want to arrange array values from low to high.

✖ Use a descending sort when you want to arrange array values from high to low.

✖ The nested for loop, such as the one you saw in this chapter, is a perfect statement to produce a bubble sort.

Pitfalls

✖ Don't swap the values of two variables unless you introduce a third work variable to hold the in-between value.

✖ Sorting routines doesn't have to be hard. Start with the one listed in this chapter and adapt it to your own needs.

✖ Don't forget to keep your arrays sorted. You'll speed up searching for values.

In Review

The goal of this chapter was to familiarize you with the bubble sort method of ordering and alphabetizing values in arrays. You don't need any new C commands to sort values. Sorting is one of the primary array advantages. It shows that arrays are a better storage method than separately named variables. The array subscripts let you step through the array and swap values, when needed, to sort the array.

Code Example

```
/* Sorts the array backwards (in descending order) */
for (outer = 0; outer < 9; outer++)
  { didSwap = 0;   /* Becomes 1 (true) if list
                        is not yet ordered */
for (inner = outer; inner < 10; inner++)
  {  if (nums[inner] > nums[outer])   /* Descending
                                            test */
     { temp = nums[inner];   /* Swaps if needed */
       nums[inner] = nums[outer];
       nums[outer] = temp;
       didSwap = 1;   /* True because a swap
                           took place */
   }
 }
 if (didSwap == 0)   /* Quits if list is now sorted */
   { break; }
}
```

Code Analysis

This section of code forms the complete descending sort code needed to sort this chapter's list of 10 random numbers backwards. The only difference between a descending sort and an ascending sort is the if comparison at the top of the swapping code.

This if statement is marked by the comment /* Descending test */. The nested loops test pairs of numbers in the list. If the lowest value in the pair of numbers is greater than the second value in the pair, the swap code executes to reverse the two values. (The swapping code consists of the four lines marked by the /* Swaps if needed */ comment.)

24

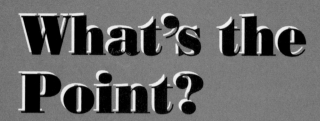

What's the Point?

Using Pointers, You'll Find Out

Pointer variables, often called *pointers,* let you do much more with C than you can with programming languages that don't support pointers. When you first learn about pointers, you'll probably ask, "What's the point?" (Even after you master them, you still might ask the same thing!) Actually, pointers provide the means for the true power of C programming. This book exposes the tip of the pointer iceberg. The concepts you learn here will form the foundation of your C programming future.

Fun Fact

Languages such as BASIC, FORTRAN, and COBOL don't support pointers.

Memory Addresses

Inside your computer is a bunch of memory. The memory holds your program as it executes, and it also holds your program's variables. Just as every house has a different address, every memory location has a different address. Not coincidentally, the memory locations have their own *addresses* as well. As with house addresses, the memory addresses are all unique; no two are the same.

Figure 24.1 shows you the look of a computer's memory. The address has nothing to do with the data stored in that address. All computer addresses begin at zero and increment from there.

```
                              Addresses
                                  .
                Memory            .
              ┌─────────┐         0
              │         │
              │         │         1
              │         │
              │  DOS    │         2
              │         │
              │   C     │         3
              │         │
              │ Program │         4
              │         │
              │  Data   │         5
              │         │
              │         │         6
              │         │
              └─────────┘         7

                            Top of memory
```

FIGURE 24.1.
The computer contains lots of memory, and each memory location has a unique address.

256

As you can see from Figure 24.1, your memory acts a little like one big hardware array, with each address being a different subscript and each memory location being a different array element.

When you define variables, C finds an unused place in memory and attaches a name to that memory location. That's a good thing. Instead of having to remember that an order number is stored at memory address 34532, you only have to remember the name orderNum (assuming you named the variable orderNum when you defined the variable). The name orderNum is *much* easier to remember than a number.

Clue: The support of variable names is just one of many programming shortcuts that compilers provide.

WARNING

Figure 24.1 is somewhat misleading. PC addresses are often *segmented* into *segments* and *offsets*. The PC's memory is divided into segments that represent sections of memory in the same way that chapters in a book represent sections of the book. The offset is a second number added to the segment's address to get to a particular memory location. Someday we'll program computers that use a strict *flat memory model*, which is a fancy way of saying we'll be able to throw that segment stuff out the door and get back to the basics of giving every memory location a sequential address starting at 0 and continuing until the memory runs out.

Defining Pointer Variables

As with any other type of variable, you must define a pointer variable before you can use it. Before going further, you need to learn two new operators. Table 24.1 shows them along with their descriptions.

Table 24.1. The pointer operators.

Operator	Description
&	Address-of operator
*	Dereferencing operator

SKIP THIS, IT'S TECHNICAL

You've seen the * before. How does C know the difference between multiplication and dereferencing? The context of how you use them determines how C interprets them. You've also seen the & before scanf() variables. The & in scanf() is the address-of operator. scanf() requires that you send it the address of non-array variables.

The following shows how you would define an integer and a floating-point variable:

```
int num;
float value;
```

To define an integer pointer variable and a floating-point pointer variable, you simply insert an *:

```
int * pNum;    /* Defines two pointer variables */
float * pValue;
```

NOTE

There's nothing special about the names of pointer variables. Lots of C programmers like to preface pointer variable names with a p, as done here, but you can name them anything you like. The p simply reminds you they are pointer variables and not regular variables.

Clue: All data types have corresponding pointer data types. There are character pointers, long integer pointers, and so on.

Pointer variables hold addresses of other variables. That's their primary purpose. Use the address-of operator, &, to assign the address of one variable to a pointer. Until you assign an address of a variable to a pointer, the pointer is uninitialized and you can't use it for anything.

The following code defines an integer variable named age and stores a 19 in age. Then a pointer named pAge is defined and initialized to point to age. The address-of operator reads just like it sounds. The second line that follows tells C to put the address of age into pAge.

```
int age = 19;        /* Stores a 19 in age */
int * pAge = &age;   /* Links up the pointer */
```

You have no idea exactly what address C will store age at. However, whatever address C uses, pAge will hold that address. When a pointer variable holds the address of another variable, it in effect *points* to that variable. Assuming that age is stored at the address 18826 (only C knows exactly where it is stored), Figure 24.2 shows what the resulting memory would look like.

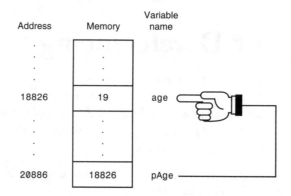

FIGURE 24.2.
The variable pAge points to age if pAge holds the address of age.

NOTE

Just because you define two variables back-to-back doesn't mean that C stores them back-to-back in memory. C *might* store them together, but it also might not.

> **WARNING**
> *Never* try to set the address of one type of variable to a pointer variable of a different type. C will only let you assign the address of one type of variable to a pointer defined with the same data type.

The * isn't part of a pointer variable's name. You will use the * *dereferencing operator* for several things, but in the pointer definition, the * exists only to tell C that the variable is a pointer and not a regular variable. The following four statements do *exactly the same thing* as the previous two statements. Notice that you don't use * to store the address of a variable into a pointer variable unless you are also defining the pointer at the same time.

```
int age;      /* Defines a regular integer */
int * pAge;   /* Defines a pointer to an integer */
age = 19;     /* Stores 19 in age */
pAge = &age;  /* Links up the pointer */
```

Using the Dereferencing *

As soon as you link up a pointer to another variable, you can work with the other value by *dereferencing* the pointer. Programmers never use an easy word when a hard one will do just as well (and confuse more people). Dereferencing just means that you use the pointer to get to the other variable. When you dereference, use the * dereferencing operator.

In a nutshell, here are two ways to change the value of age (assuming the variables are defined as described earlier):

```
age = 25;
```

and

```
*pAge = 25;  /* Stores 25 where pAge points */
```

Notice that you can use a variable name to store a value or dereference a pointer that points to the variable. You also can use a variable's value in the same way. Here are two ways to print the contents of age:

```
printf("The age is %d.\n", age);
```

and

```
printf("The age is %d.\n", *pAge);
```

The dereferencing operator is used when a function works with a pointer variable that it is sent. In Chapter 32, you'll learn how to pass pointers to functions. When a function uses a pointer variable that is sent from another function, you must use the dereferencing operator before the variable name everywhere it appears. The Blackjack program in Appendix B does this in the dealCard() function. The following lines from this function show the dereferencing operator being used:

```
subDraw = (rand() % (*numCards));   /* From 0 to numcards */
cardDrawn = cards[subDraw];
cards[subDraw] = cards[*numCards - 1];   /* Puts top
                                            card in */
```

Rewards

* ✖ Get comfortable with memory addresses because they form the basis of pointer usage.

* ✖ Use the & to produce the address of a variable.

* ✖ Use the * to define a pointer variable and to dereference a pointer variable. *pAge and age reference the same memory location as long as you've made pAge point to age.

Pitfalls

* ✖ Don't try to make a pointer variable of one data type point to a variable of a different data type.

* ✖ Don't worry about the *exact* address that C uses for variable storage. If you use &, C will take care of the rest.

* ✖ Don't forget to use * when dereferencing your pointer, or you'll get the wrong value.

* ✖ Don't get too far ahead. You will fully appreciate pointers only after programming in C for a while. At this point (pun not intended!), pointers will not seem to help at all. The only thing you might feel a little better about is knowing what the & inside scanf() really means.

In Review

The goal of this chapter was to introduce you to pointer variables. A pointer variable is nothing more than a variable that holds the location of another variable. You can refer to the pointed-to variable by its name, or by dereferencing the pointer.

Pointers have many uses in C, especially in advanced C programming. As you'll learn in the next chapter, arrays are nothing more than pointers in disguise. Because pointers offer more flexibility than arrays, many C programmers stop using arrays once they master pointers.

Code Example

```c
char initial = 'G';  /* Defines a character variable */
char * pInitial;  /* Defines a character pointer variable */
float score = 97.4;  /* Defines a floating-point variable */
float * pScore;  /* Defines a floating-point pointer variable */
pInitial = & initial;  /* Links the pointer to the data */
pScore = &score;
printf("The initial is %c.\n", *pInitial);
*pScore = 85.0;  /* Changes score, not pScore! */
```

Code Analysis

The code initializes two nonpointer variables—a character variable named initial and a floating-point variable named score. The code also defines two pointer variables and makes those pointer variables point to the regular variables.

As you can see in the last two statements, you can use a pointer variable to get to the contents of other variables. The printf() does not print the value of pInitial; rather, printf() prints the value of initial. The score variable, not pScore, is changed to 85.0 as well because of the dereferencing of the pointer.

25

Use `fgets()` to read strings from data files.
271

Integers usually take more than 1 byte of memory storage.
268

You can't change a constant.
267

Assign strings new values without using `strcpy()`
269

BOTTOM-LESS PIT

Don't use a built-in function to fill a character's location.
273

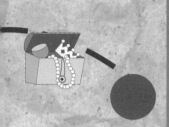

How Are Arrays and Pointers Different?

They're the Same Thing in C

Fun Fact

A calendar is a real-life example of an array with 12 elements that store data.

This chapter teaches how C's array and pointer variables share a lot of principles. As a matter of fact, an array is a special kind of pointer. Because of their similarities, you can use pointer notation to get to array values, and you can use array notation to get to pointed-at values.

Perhaps the most important reason to learn how arrays and pointers overlap is for character-string handling. By combining pointer notation (using the dereferencing operation) and array notation (using subscripts), you can store lists of character strings and reference them as easily as you reference array values of other data types.

Also, once you master the *heap*—a special place in memory that you'll get an introduction to in the next chapter—you'll see that pointers are the only way to get to heap memory, where you put data values.

Array Names Are Pointers

An array name is nothing more than a pointer to the first element in that array. The array name is not exactly a pointer *variable*, though. Array names are known as *pointer constants*. The following statement defines an integer array and initializes it:

```
int vals[5] = {10, 20, 30, 40, 50};
```

You can reference the array by subscript notation. That much you know already. However, C does more than just attach subscripts to the values in memory. C sets up a pointer to the array and names that point to `vals`. You can never change the contents of `vals`; it is like a fixed pointer variable whose address is locked in by C. Figure 25.1 shows you what C really does when you define and initialize `vals`.

Because the array name is a pointer (that can't be changed), you can print the first value in the array like this:

```
printf("The first value is %d.\n", vals[0]);
```

But more importantly for this chapter, you can print the first array value like this too:

```
printf("The first value is %d.\n", *vals);
```

As you'll see in a moment, this is also equivalent and accesses `vals[0]`:

```
printf("The first value is %d.\n", *(vals+0));
```

		Addresses
		.
		.
vals	46204	32054
	.	.
	.	.
vals[0]	10	46204
vals[1]	20	46206
vals[2]	30	46208
vals[3]	40	46210
vals[4]	50	46212
	.	
	.	

FIGURE 25.1.
The array name is a pointer to the first value in the array.

> **WARNING**
> The fact that an array is a fixed constant pointer is why you can't put an array name on the left side of an equals sign. You can't change a constant. (Remember, though, that C relaxes this rule only when you first define the array, because C has yet to fix the array at a specific address.)

Getting Down in the List

Because an array name is nothing more than a pointer to the *first* value in the array, if you want the second value, you only have to add 1 to the array name and dereference *that* location. This set of `printf()` lines

```
printf("The first array value is %d.\n", vals[0]);
printf("The second array value is %d.\n", vals[1]);
printf("The third array value is %d.\n", vals[2]);
printf("The fourth array value is %d.\n", vals[3]);
printf("The fifth array value is %d.\n", vals[4]);
```

does *exactly* the same as these:

```
printf("The first array value is %d.\n", *(vals + 0));
printf("The second array value is %d.\n", *(vals + 1));
printf("The third array value is %d.\n", *(vals + 2));
printf("The fourth array value is %d.\n", *(vals + 3));
printf("The fifth array value is %d.\n", *(vals + 4));
```

If vals is a pointer constant (and it is), and the pointer constant holds a number that is the address to the array's first element, adding 1 or 2 (or whatever) to vals before dereferencing vals adds 1 or 2 to the address pointed to by vals.

Clue: If you're wondering about the importance of all this mess, hang tight. In a moment you'll see how C's pointer notation lets you make C act *almost* as if it has string variables.

SKIP THIS, IT'S TECHNICAL

As you might remember, integers usually take more than 1 byte of memory storage. The preceding printf()s appear to add 1 to the address inside vals to get to the next dereferenced memory location; but C helps you out here. C adds one int size when you add 1 to an int pointer (and one double size when you add 1 to a double pointer, and so on). The expression *(vals + 2) tells C that you want the *third integer* in the list that vals points to.

Characters and Pointers

The following two statements set up almost the same thing in memory. The only difference is that in the second statement, pName is a pointer *variable*, not a pointer constant:

```
char name[] = "Andrew B. Mayfair";    /* name points to A */
char * pName = "Andrew B. Mayfair";   /* pName points to A */
```

Because pName is a pointer variable, you *can* put it on the left side of an equals sign! Therefore, you don't always have to use strcpy() if you want to assign a character pointer a new string value. The character pointer will only point to the first character in the string. However, %s and all the string functions work with character pointers just as easily as with character arrays (since the two are the same thing) because these functions know to stop at the null zero.

To put a different name in the name array, you have to use strcpy() or assign the string one character at a time, but to make pName point to a different name, you get to do this:

```
pName = "Theodore M. Brooks";
```

Clue: The only reason string assignment works is that C puts all your program's string literals into memory somewhere and then *replaces* them in your program with their addresses. C is not really putting Theodore M. Brooks into pName because pName can hold only addresses. C is putting the *address* of Theodore M. Brooks into pName.

NOTE

Yea! You now have a way to assign strings new values without using strcpy(). It took a little work to get here, but aren't you glad you made it? If so, settle down, because there is just one catch (isn't there always?).

Be Careful with Lengths

It's okay to store string literals in character arrays as just described. The new strings that you assign with = can be shorter or longer than the previous strings. That's nice, because you might recall that you can't store a string into a character array that is longer than the array you reserved initially.

You must be extremely careful, however, *not* to let the *program* store strings longer than the first string you point to with the character pointer. This is a little complex, but keep following along because this chapter stays as simple and short as possible. Never set up a character pointer variable like this:

```
main()
{
char * name = "Tom Roberts";
/* Rest of program follows */
```

and then later let the user enter a new string with gets() like this:

```
gets(name);  /* Not very safe */
```

The problem with this statement is that the user might enter a string longer than Tom Roberts, the first string assigned to the character pointer. Although a character pointer can point to strings of any length, the gets() function, along with scanf(), strcpy(), and strcat(), doesn't know that it's being sent a character pointer. Because they might be sent a character array that can't change location, these functions map the newly created string directly over the location of the string in name. If a string longer than name is entered, other data areas could be overwritten.

> **WARNING**
>
> Yes, this is a little tedious. You might have to read this section again later after you get more comfortable with pointers and arrays.

If you want to have the advantage of a character pointer—that is, if you want to be able to assign string literals to the pointer and still have the safety of arrays so you can use the character pointer to get user input—you can do so with a little trick.

If you want to store user input in a string pointed to by a pointer, first reserve enough storage for that input string. The easiest way to do this is to reserve a character array and then assign a character pointer to the beginning element of that array:

```
char input[81];  /* Holds a string as long
                    as 80 characters */
char *iptr = input;  /* Also could have done this:
                        char *iptr = &input[0]; */
```

Now you can input a string by using the pointer:

```
gets(iptr);  /* Makes sure that iptr points to
                the string typed by the user */
```

as long as the string entered by the user is not longer than 81 bytes long. There is a nice string-input function you can use to ensure that entered strings don't get longer than 81 characters, including the null zero. Use `fgets()` if you want to limit the number of characters accepted from the user. `fgets()` works like `gets()`, except that you specify a length argument. The following statement shows `fgets()` in action:

```
fgets(iptr, 81, stdin);  /*Gets up to 80 chars and adds null
                            zero */
```

The second value is the maximum number of characters you want to save from the user's input. Always leave one for the string's null zero. The pointer `iptr` can point to a string as long as 81 characters. If the user enters a string less than 81 characters, `iptr` points to that string with no problem. If, however, the user goes wild and enters a string 200 characters long, `iptr` points only to the first 80, followed by a null zero at the 81st position that `fgets()` added, and the rest of the user's input is ignored.

Clue: You can use `fgets()` to read strings from data files. The third value of `fgets()` can be a disk file pointer, but you'll learn about disk pointers later in the book. For now, use `stdin` as the third value you send to `fgets()` so that `fgets()` goes to the keyboard for input and not somewhere else.

You also can assign the pointer string literals using the assignment like this:

```
iptr = "William Harper Littlejohn";
```

Arrays of Pointers

If you want to use a bunch of pointers, create an array of them. An array of pointers is just as easy to define as an array of any other kind of data, except that you must include the * operator after the data type name. The following statements reserve an array of 25 integer pointers and an array of 25 character pointers:

```
int * ipara[25];   /* 25 pointers to integers */
char * cpara[25];  /* 25 pointers to characters */
```

The array of characters is most interesting because you can store a list of strings in the array. More accurately, you can *point* to various strings. The following program illustrates two things: how to initialize an array of strings at definition time and how to print them using a for loop:

```
#include <stdio.h>
main()
{
  int i;
  char * names[5] = {"Joe Swadley", "Richard Wikert",
                     "Keith Miller", "Dean Davenport",
                     "Stacy Wiquet"};
  for (i = 0; i < 5; i++)
    { printf("Name %d: %s\n", i, names[i]); }
  return 0;
}
```

Here is the output from this program:

```
Name 0: Joe Swadley
Name 1: Richard Wikert
Name 2: Keith Miller
Name 3: Dean Davenport
Name 4: Stacy Wiquet
```

Figure 25.2 shows how the program sets up the names array in memory. Each element is nothing more than a character pointer that contains the address of a different person's name. It's important that you understand names does not hold strings, just pointers to strings.

See, even though there is no such thing as a string array in C (because there are no string variables), storing character pointers in names makes the program act as though names is a string array.

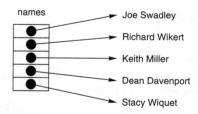

FIGURE 25.2.
The names array contains pointers to strings.

Rewards

* ✖ Use character pointers if you want to assign string literals directly.
* ✖ Use either array subscript notation or pointer dereferencing to access array and pointer values.
* ✖ Take a break. This was a lot of material!

Pitfalls

* ✖ Don't use a built-in function to fill a character pointer's location unless that character pointer was originally set up to point to a long string.

In Review

The goal of this chapter was to get you thinking about the similarities between arrays and pointers. An array name is really just a pointer that points to the first element in the array. Unlike pointer variables, an array name can't change. This is the primary reason an array name can't appear on the left side of an equals sign.

Using pointers allows more flexibility than arrays. You can directly assign a string literal to a character pointer variable, whereas you must use the `strcpy()` function to assign strings to arrays. You'll see many uses for pointer variables throughout your C programming career.

Code Example

```c
char * days[7];
days[0] = "Sunday";
days[1] = "Monday";
days[2] = "Tuesday";
days[3] = "Wednesday";
days[4] = "Thursday";
days[5] = "Friday";
days[6] = "Saturday";
printf("Enter a number from 1 to 7: ");
scanf(" %d", &dayNum);
if (dayNum >= 1 && dayNum <= 7)
  { printf("That day is %s\n", days[dayNum - 1]); }
else
  { printf("You didn't enter a good number.\n"); }
```

Code Analysis

The array of seven pointer variables is created and then assigned to the seven days of the week string literals. The strings could have been assigned when days was defined, but this code assigns each string one at a time, just to show you how it can be done.

The program then asks for a number. If the user enters a number from 1 to 7, the matching day element is printed. Because array elements begin at 0, 1 has to be subtracted from the user's number to match a day of the week name.

26

Don't assign variable
names to heap
memory.
278

Each set of
allocated
memory will be
contiguous.
284

Mastering the heap
takes practice.
281

You can use
the `malloc()`
function.
284

BOTTOM
LESS PIT

Don't always rely on
regular arrays.
288

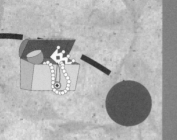

Where's More Memory?

Try the Heap

Absolute beginners to C aren't the only ones who might, at first, find this chapter's concepts confusing. Even advanced C programmers get mixed up when dealing with the *heap*. The heap is the collection of unused memory in your computer. The memory left over—after your program, your program's variables, and your operating system's workspace—comprises your computer's available heap space, as Figure 26.1 shows.

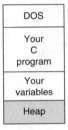

| DOS |
| Your C program |
| Your variables |
| Heap |

FIGURE 26.1.
The heap is unused memory.

There will be many times when you'll want access to the heap because there will be times when your program will need more memory than you initially defined in variables and arrays. This chapter gives you some insight into why and how you would want to use heap memory instead of variables.

Clue: You don't assign variable names to heap memory. The only way to access data stored in heap memory is through pointer variables. Aren't you glad you learned about pointers already? Without pointers, you couldn't learn about the heap.

NOTE

The free heap memory is called *free heap* or *unallocated heap* memory. The part of the heap in use by your program at any one time is called the *allocated heap*. Your program might use varying amounts of heap space as the program executes. So far, no program in this book used the heap.

Thinking of the Heap

Now that you've learned what the heap is—the unused section of contiguous memory—throw out what you've learned! You'll more quickly grasp how to use the heap if you think of the heap as just one big *heap of free memory* stacked up in a pile. The next paragraph explains why.

You'll be allocating (using) and deallocating (freeing back up) heap memory as your program runs. When you request heap memory, you don't know exactly *from where* on the heap the new memory will come. Therefore, if one statement in your program grabs heap memory, and then the *very next statement* also grabs another section of heap memory, that second section of the heap may not physically reside right after the first section you allocated.

Clue: Just like scooping dirt from a big heap, one shovel does not pick up dirt granules that were *right* below of the last shovel of dirt. Also, when you throw the shovel of dirt back on the heap, that dirt doesn't go right back to where it was. Although this analogy might seem to stretch the concept of computer memory, you'll find that you'll understand the heap much better if you think of the heap of memory like you think of the heap of dirt: You have no idea exactly where the memory you allocate and deallocate will come from or go back to. You know only that the memory comes and goes from the heap.

If you allocate 10 bytes of heap memory at once, those 10 bytes will be contiguous. The important thing to know is that the *next* section of heap memory you allocate will not necessarily follow the first, so you shouldn't count on anything like that.

Your operating system uses heap memory along with your program. If you work on a networked computer, or use a multitasking operating environment such as Windows, other tasks may be grabbing heap memory along with your program. Therefore, another routine may have come in between two of your heap-allocation statements and allocated or deallocated memory.

You will have to keep track of the memory you allocate. You do this with pointer variables. For instance, if you want to allocate 20 integers on the heap, you'll use an integer pointer. If you want to allocate 400 floating-point values on the heap, you'll use a floating-point pointer. The pointer will always point to the first heap value of the section you just allocated. Therefore, a single pointer points to the start of the section of heap you allocate. If you want to access the memory after the first value on the heap, you can use pointer notation or array notation to get to the rest of the heap section you allocated. (See, the last chapter's pointer/array discussion really *does* come in handy!)

But WHY Do I Need the Heap?

Okay, before learning exactly *how* you allocate and deallocate heap memory, you probably want more rationalization about why you even need to worry about the heap. After all, the variables, pointers, and arrays you've learned about so far have sufficed nicely for program data.

The heap memory will not always replace the variables and arrays you've been learning about. The problem with the variables you've learned about so far is that you must know *in advance* exactly what kind and how many variables you will want. Remember, you must define all variables before you use them. If you define an array to hold 100 customer IDs, but the user has 101 customers to enter, your program can't just expand the array at runtime. Some programmer (like *you*) has to change the array definition and recompile the program before the array can hold more values.

With the heap memory, however, you don't have to know in advance how much memory is needed. Like an accordion, the heap memory your program uses can grow or shrink as needed. If you need another 100 elements to hold a new batch of customers, your program can allocate that new batch at runtime without needing another compilation.

> **WARNING**
>
> This book won't try to fool you into thinking all your questions will be answered in this chapter. Mastering the heap takes practice and, in reality, programs that really need the heap are beyond the scope of this book. Nevertheless, when you finish this chapter, you'll have a more solid understanding of how to access the heap than you would get from most books because of the approach that's used. (Perilous Perry might take you on a rough journey, but he'll always get you back safely!)

Commercial programs such as spreadsheets and word processors must rely heavily on the heap. After all, the programmer who designs the program cannot know exactly how large or small a spreadsheet or word processing document will be. Therefore, as you type data into a spreadsheet or word processor, the underlying program allocates more data. Probably, the program does not allocate the data 1 byte at a time as you type, because memory allocation is not always extremely efficient when done 1 byte at a time. More than likely, the program will allocate memory in chunks of code, such as 100-byte or 500-byte sections.

So why can't the programmers simply allocate huge arrays that can hold a huge spreadsheet or document instead of messing with the heap? For one thing, memory is one of the most precious resources in your computer. As we move into networked and windowed environments, memory becomes even more precious. Your programs can't allocate huge arrays for those rare occasions when a user *might* need that much memory. All that memory would be used solely by your program, and other tasks could not access that allocated memory.

> **NOTE**
>
> The heap enables your program to use only as much memory as it needs. When your user needs more memory, (for instance, to enter more data), your program can allocate the memory. When your user is finished using that much memory (such as clearing a document to start a new one in a word processor), you can deallocate the memory, making it available for other tasks that might have a need for the memory.

Fun Fact

Word processors almost exclusively use heap memory.

How Do I Allocate the Heap?

You must learn only two new functions to use the heap. The malloc() (for *memory allocate*) function allocates heap memory, and the free() function deallocates heap memory.

Clue: Be sure to include the STDLIB.H header file in all the programs you write that use malloc() and free().

We might as well get to the rough part. malloc() is not the most *user-friendly* function for newcomers to understand. Perhaps looking at an example of malloc() would be the best place to start. Suppose you were writing a temperature-averaging program for a local weather forecaster. The more temperature readings the user enters, the more accurate the correct prediction will be. You decide that you will allocate 10 integers to hold the first 10 temperature readings. If the user wants to enter more, your program can allocate another batch of 10, and so on.

You first need a pointer to the 10 heap values. The values are integers, so you need an integer pointer. You'll need to define the integer pointer like this:

```
int * temps;  /* Will point to the first heap value */
```

Here is how you can allocate 10 integers on the heap using malloc():

```
temps = (int *) malloc(10 * sizeof(int));  /* Yikes! */
```

That's a lot of code just to get 10 integers. The line is actually fairly easy to understand when you see it broken into pieces. The malloc() function requires only a single value—the number of bytes you want allocated. Therefore, if you wanted 10 bytes, you could do this:

```
malloc(10).
```

The problem is that the previous description did not require 10 bytes, but 10 *integers*. How many bytes of memory do 10 integers require? 10? 20? The answer, of course, is that *it depends*. Only sizeof() knows for sure.

Therefore, if you want 10 integers allocated, you must tell `malloc()` that you want 10 sets of bytes allocated, with each set of bytes being enough for an integer. Therefore, the previous line included the following `malloc()` function call:

```
malloc(10 * sizeof(int))
```

This part of the statement told `malloc()` to allocate, or set aside, 10 contiguous integer locations on the heap. In a way, the computer puts a fence around those 10 integer locations so that subsequent `malloc()` calls do not intrude on this allocated memory. Now that you've mastered that last half of the `malloc()` statement, there's not much left to understand. The first part of `malloc()` is fairly easy.

`malloc()` will always do the following two steps (assuming there is enough heap memory to satisfy your allocation request):

1. Allocate the number of bytes you request and make sure that no other program can overwrite that memory until your program frees it.

2. Assign your pointer to the first allocated value.

Figure 26.2 shows the result of the previous temperature `malloc()` function call. As you can see from the figure, the heap of memory (shown here as just that, a *heap*) now contains a fenced-off area of 10 integers, and the integer pointer variable named `temps` points to the first integer. Subsequent `malloc()` function calls will go to other parts of the heap and will not tread on the allocated 10 integers.

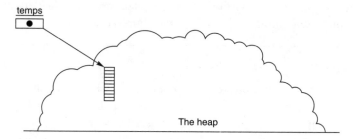

FIGURE 26.2.
After allocating the 10 integers.

SKIP THIS, IT'S TECHNICAL

What do you *do* with the 10 integers you just allocated? Treat them like an array! You can store data by referring to temps[0], temps[1], and so on. You know from the last chapter that you access contiguous memory using array notation, even if that memory begins with a pointer. Also, remember that each *set* of allocated memory will be contiguous, so the 10 integers will follow each other just as if you allocated temps as a 10-integer array.

There is still one slight problem with the malloc() allocation. The left-hand portion of the temperature malloc() has yet to be explained. What is the (int *) for?

The (int *) is a typecast. You've seen other kinds of typecasts in this book. To convert a float value to an int, you place (int) before the floating-point value like this:

```
aVal = (int)salary;
```

The * inside a typecast means that the typecast is a pointer typecast. malloc() always returns a *character* pointer. If you want to use malloc() to allocate integers, floating points, or any kind of data other than char, you have to typecast the malloc() so the pointer variable that receives the allocation (such as temps) receives the correct pointer data type. temps is an integer pointer; you should not assign temps to malloc()'s allocated memory unless you typecast malloc() into an integer pointer. Therefore, the left side of the previous malloc() simply tells malloc() that an integer pointer, not the default character pointer, will point to the first of the allocated values.

NOTE

Besides defining an array at the top of main(), what have you gained by using malloc()? For one thing, you can use the malloc() function anywhere in your program, not just where you define variables and arrays. Therefore, when your program is ready for 100 double values, you can allocate those 100 double values. If you used a regular array, you would need a statement like this:

```
double myVals[100];   /* A regular array of 100 doubles */
```

towards the top of main(). Those 100 double values would sit around for the life of the program taking up valuable memory resources from the rest of the system, even if the program only needed the 100 double values for a short time. With malloc(), you need to define only the pointer that points to the top of the allocated memory for the program's life, not the entire array.

If There's Not Enough Heap Memory

In extreme cases, there may not be enough heap memory to satisfy malloc()'s request. The user's computer may not have a lot of memory, another task might be using a lot of memory, or your program may have previously allocated everything already. If malloc() fails, its pointer variable will point to a null value, 0. Therefore, many programmers follow a malloc() with an if like this:

```
temps = (int *) malloc(10 * sizeof(int));  /* Yikes! */
if (temps == 0)
  { printf("Oops! Not enough memory.\n");
    exit(1);    /* Exit the program early */
  }
/* Rest of program continues */
```

If malloc() works, temps contains a valid address that points to the start of the allocated heap. If malloc() fails, the invalid address of 0 is pointed to (heap memory never begins at address zero) and the error prints on-screen.

Clue: Often, programmers use the *not* operator, !, instead of testing a value against 0, as done here. Therefore, the previous if test would more likely be coded like this:

```
if (!temps)     /* Means, if not true */
```

Freeing Heap Memory

When you're done with the heap memory, give it back to the system. Use `free()` to do that. `free()` is a lot easier than `malloc()`. To free the 10 integers allocated with the previous `malloc()`, use `free()` in the following manner:

```
free(temps);    /* Gives the memory back to the heap */
```

If you originally allocated 10 values, 10 are freed. If the `malloc()` that allocated memory for `temps` had allocated 1,000 values, all 1,000 would be freed. Once freed, you can't get the memory back; remember, `free()` tosses the allocated memory back onto the heap of memory, and once tossed, the memory might be grabbed by another task (always remember the dirt heap analogy). If you use `temps` after the previous `free()`, you run the risk of overwriting memory and, possibly, locking up your computer, requiring rebooting.

If you fail to free allocated memory, your operating system will reclaim that memory once your program ends. However, forgetting to call `free()` defeats the purpose of using heap memory in the first place. The goal of the heap is to give your program the opportunity to allocate memory at the point the memory is needed and deallocate that memory when you're through with it.

Multiple Allocations

Often, an array of pointers helps you allocate many different sets of heap memory. Going back to the weather forecaster's problem, suppose the forecaster wanted to enter historical temperature readings for several different cities. The forecaster, though, has a different number of readings for each of the different cities.

An array of pointers is useful for such a problem. Here is how you could allocate an array of 50 pointers:

```
int * temps[50];    /* 50 integer pointers */
```

The array will *not* hold 50 integers (because of the dereferencing operator in the definition); instead, the array holds 50 pointers. The first pointer is called temps[0], the second pointer is temps[1], and so on. Each of the array elements (each pointer) can point to a different set of allocated heap memory. Therefore, even though the 50 pointer array elements must be defined for all of main(), you can allocate and free the data pointed to as you need extra memory.

Consider the following section of code that might be used by the forecaster:

```
for (ctr=0; ctr<50; ctr++)
  { puts("How many readings for the city?");
    scanf(" %d", &num);

    /* Allocate that many heap values */
    temps[ctr] = (int *)malloc(num * sizeof(int));

    /* It is here that the code would ask for each
       temperature reading for this city */
  }
/* Calculations would go here */

/* Once done with the heap memory, deallocate it */
for (ctr=0; ctr<50; ctr++)
  { free(temps[ctr]); }
```

Of course, such code requires massive data-entry. The values would most likely come from a historical disk file instead of from the user. Nevertheless, the code gives you insight into the advanced data structures available by using the heap. Also, real-world programs aren't usually of the 20-line variety you often see in this book. Real-world programs, although not necessarily harder than those here, are usually many pages long. Throughout the program, some sections may need extra memory, whereas other sections do not need the memory. The heap lets you use memory efficiently.

Figure 26.3 shows you what the heap memory might look like during the allocating of the temps array memory (after the first four of the fifty malloc() calls). As you can see, temps belongs to the program's data area, but the memory pointed to by each temps element belongs to the heap. You can free up the data pointed to by temps when you no longer need the extra workspace.

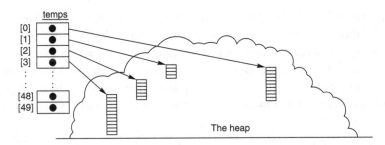

FIGURE 26.3.
Each temps *element points to a different part of the heap.*

Rewards

✖ Use malloc() and free() to allocate and release heap memory.

✖ Tell malloc() exactly how large each allocation must be by using the sizeof() operator inside malloc()'s parentheses.

✖ Allocate only the pointer variables at the top of your function along with the other variables. Put the data itself on the heap when you need data values other than simple loop counters and totals.

✖ If you must track several *chunks* of heap memory, use an array of pointers. Each array element can point to a different amount of heap space.

✖ Check to make sure malloc() worked properly. malloc() returns a 0 if the allocation fails.

Pitfalls

✖ Don't always rely on regular arrays to hold a program's data. Sometimes, a program needs data for just a short time, and using the heap will make better use of your memory resources.

✖ Don't get discouraged if the heap is beyond your grasp at this point. Using the heap is considered one of the most difficult parts of C programming, and yet, as you saw in this chapter, using the heap isn't *that* hard.

In Review

Are you thoroughly confused yet, or do you want more information on `malloc()` and `free()`? Well, memory allocation isn't as easy as a `puts()` function call, but you've seen about all there is to `malloc()` and `free()`. You have a long future ahead of you as a C programmer, and `malloc()` will probably confuse you a few more times before `malloc()` becomes second nature.

Nevertheless, hopefully memory allocation and deallocation makes more sense to you now than before you started this chapter. (I know, you had never *heard* of memory allocation before this chapter!) As you progress in your C programming career, keep your eyes open for other programmer's examples of `malloc()` and `free()`.

In review, `malloc()` allocates heap memory for your programs. You access that heap via a pointer variable, and you can then get to the rest of the allocated memory using array notation based on the pointer assigned by the `malloc()`.

When you are done with heap memory, deallocate that memory with the `free()` function. `free()` tosses the memory back to the heap so other tasks can use it.

Code Example

```
#include <stdlib.h>
iPtr = (int *)malloc(100 * sizeof(int));
if (!iPtr)
  { puts("The integer allocation failed.");
    exit(1);
  }
fPtr = (float *)malloc(50 * sizeof(float));
if (!fPtr)
  { puts("The float allocation failed.");
    exit(1);
  }
dPtr = (double *)malloc(450 * sizeof(double));
if (!dPtr)
  { puts("The double allocation failed.");
    exit(1);
  }
```

```
/* You now have allocated a total of 600 heap values */
for (ctr=0; ctr<100; ctr++)
  { iPtr[ctr] = ctr; }   /* Store 0 through 99 */
for (ctr=0; ctr<50; ctr++)
  { *(fPtr+ctr) = (float)ctr; }   /* Store 0 through 49 */
for (ctr=0; ctr<450; ctr++)
  { iPtr[ctr] = (double)ctr; }   /* Store 0 through 449 */
free(iPtr);
free(fPtr);
free(dPtr);
```

Code Analysis

This code allocates three groups of heap memory. The iPtr integer pointer variable points to the first of the 100 allocated integer heap values, fPtr points to the first of the 50 allocated floating-point values, and dPtr points to the first of the 450 allocated double floating-point values.

After each malloc(), the pointer value is checked to make sure that the allocation worked successfully.

Three for loops then store sequential numbers, starting at 0, in the allocated memory. The integer loop counter ctr is used to initialize the three sections of the heap, so a float and double typecast is used to convert ctr to the correct data type before storing the value on the heap. Just for grins, the floating-point heap was initialized using pointer notation instead of array notation.

Remember to deallocate heap memory when you're done with it. The three free() function calls deallocate all 600 values allocated by the previous three malloc() calls.

27

How Do I Store Lots of Data?

With Structures

Arrays and pointers are nice for lists of values, but those values must all be of the same data type. There will be times when you have different data types that must go together and be treated as a whole.

A perfect example is a customer record. For each customer, you would have to track a name (character array), balance (double floating-point), address (character array), city (character array), state (character array), and zip code (character array or long integer). Although you would want to be able to initialize and print individual items within the customer record, you would also want to access the customer record as a whole, such as when you would write it to a customer disk file (which is explained in the next chapter).

The C *structure* is the vehicle by which you group data such as would appear in a customer record, *and* get to all the individual parts, called *members*. If you have many occurrences of that data and many customers, you would need an array of structures.

> **NOTE**
>
> Other programming languages have equivalent data groupings called *records*. The designers of C wanted to call these data groupings *structures*, however, so that's what they are in C.

Fun Fact

QBasic stores structures in dimensioned types.

Many times, a C structure holds data that you might store on 3x5 cards in a cardfile. Without a computer, a company might very well maintain a cardfile box with cards that contain a customer's name, balance, address, city, state, and zip code, like the customer structure just described. Later in this chapter, you'll see how C structures are stored in memory, and you'll see even more similarities to the cardfile cards.

Defining a Structure

The first thing you must do is tell C exactly what your structure will look like. When you define variables of built-in data types such as ints, you don't have to tell C what an int is because C already knows. When you want to define a structure, however, you must first tell C exactly what your structure looks like. Then and only then can you define variables for that structure.

SKIP THIS, IT'S TECHNICAL

Try to view a structure as just a group of individual data types. The entire structure has a name and can be considered a single value (such as a customer) taken as a whole. The individual members of the structure are built-in data types, such as `int` and `char` arrays, that could represent an age and a name. You can access the individual members if you want to.

Clue: Not only is a structure like a cardfile, but you also can see that a structure is a lot like a paper form with blanks to fill in. A blank form, such as one you might fill out when applying for a credit card, is useless by itself. If the credit card company prints 10,000 forms, that doesn't mean they have 10,000 customers. Only when someone fills out the form is there a customer, and only when you define a variable for the structure you describe will C give memory space to a structure variable.

To define an `int` variable, you only have to do this:

```
int i;
```

You don't first have to tell C what an `int` is. To define a structure variable, you must first define what the structure looks like and assign a data type name, such as `customer`, to C. After defining the structure's format, you can define a variable.

The `struct` statement defines the look (or layout) of a structure. Here is the format of `struct`:

```
struct [structure tag] {
  member definition;
  member definition;
   :
  member definition;
};
```

Title of worksheet — Subject

what's in the worksheet — Information

Fun Fact

Members are called fields in other programming languages.

structure tag = subject / topic
members = information

Again, the struct defines only the layout, or the *look*, of a structure. The *structure tag* is a name you give to that particular structure's look, but the *structure tag* has nothing to do with a structure variable name you might create later. After you define the format of a structure, you can define variables.

The member definitions are nothing more than regular built-in data type definitions such as int age;. Instead of defining variables, though, you are defining *members,* in effect giving a name to that particular part of the structure.

WARNING

You *can* define a variable at the same time as the struct declaration statement, but most C programmers don't do so. If you want to define a variable for the structure at the same time you declare the structure format itself, insert one or more variable names before the struct statement's closing semicolon.

NOTE

Structures are a lot to absorb. The example that follows will aid your understanding.

Let's say you're writing a program to track a simple retail computer inventory. You need to track a computer manufacturer, model, amount of disk space (in megabytes), amount of memory space (in megabytes), quantity, cost, and retail price.

First you must use struct to define a structure. Here is a good candidate:

defining a structure

```
struct invStruct {
    char manuf[25];   /* Manufacturer name */
    char model[15];   /* Model code */
    int  diskSpace;   /* Disk space in megabytes */
    int  memSpace;    /* Memory space in megabytes */
    int  quantity;    /* Number in the inventory */
    float cost;       /* Cost of computer */
    float price;      /* Retail price of computer */
};
```

Figure 27.1 shows you what this structure format looks like.

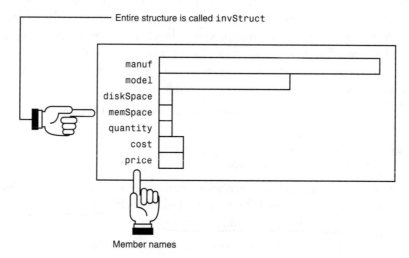

FIGURE 27.1.

The format of the invStruct structure.

The previous structure definition does *not* define seven variables! The previous structure definition defines a single structure data type. Remember, you don't have to tell C what an integer looks like before defining an integer variable; you *must*, however, tell C what an invStruct looks like before defining variables for that structure data type. The previous struct statement tells C what the user's invStruct is supposed to look like. Once C learns the structure's format, C can then define variables that take on the format of that structure when the user is ready to define variables.

If you create a structure that you might use again sometime, consider putting it in its own header file, or in a header file along with other common structures. Use #include to pull that header file into any source code that needs it. If you ever need to change the structure definition, you have to look in only one place to change it—in its header file.

Clue: That advice alone is worth the price of this book!

297

Often, a programmer puts structure declarations, such as the previous one for invStruct, before main() and then defines variables for that structure in main() and in any other functions below main(). To create variables for the structure, you must do the same thing you do when you create variables for any data type: Put the structure name before a variable list. Because there is no data type named invStruct, you must tell C that invStruct is a struct name. You can define three structure variables like this:

```
#include "c:\inv.h"  /* Includes the structure definition */
main()
{
  struct invStruct item1, item2, item3;
  /* Rest of program would follow */
```

Now there are three variables into which you can put data. These variables are structure variables named item1, item2, and item3. If you wanted to define 500 structure variables, you would use an array:

```
#include "c:\inv.h"  /* Includes the structure definition */
main()
{
  struct invStruct items[500];
  /* Rest of program would follow */
```

Remember, the structure definition must go in the INV.H header file if you take this approach. Otherwise, you must place the structure definition directly inside the program before the structure variables like this:

```
struct invStruct {          — title & worksheet
  char manuf[25];   /* Manufacturer name */
  char model[15];   /* Model code */
  int  diskSpace;   /* Disk space in megabytes */
  int  memSpace;    /* Memory space in megabytes */
  int  quantity;    /* Number in the inventory */
  float cost;       /* Cost of computer */
  float price;      /* Retail price of computer */
};
main()
{
  struct invStruct items[500];  ← Title & work sheet & what's in
  /* Rest of program would follow */         worksheet
```

As long as the struct definition appears before main(), you can define invStruct structure variables throughout the rest of the program in any function you write. (The last part of this book explains how to write programs that contain more functions than main().)

Perhaps you will need pointers to three structures instead of structure variables? Define them like this:

```
main()
{
  struct invStruct *item1, *item2, *item3;
  /* Rest of program would follow */
```

(handwritten annotation: ← pointers to 3 structures)

(handwritten annotation in margin: What is heap structure)

`item1`, `item2`, and `item3` now can point to three structure variables. You can then reserve heap memory for the structures instead of using actual variables. (`sizeof()` works for structure variables to allow for heap structure data.) The following three statements reserve three heap structure areas and makes `item1`, `item2`, and `item3` point to those three heap values:

```
item1 = (struct invStruct *)malloc(sizeof(invStruct));
item2 = (struct invStruct *)malloc(sizeof(invStruct));
item3 = (struct invStruct *)malloc(sizeof(invStruct));
```

Putting Data in Structure Variables

A new operator, the *dot operator,* lets you put data in a structure variable's individual members. Here is the format of the dot operator:

structureVariableName.memberName

To the left of the dot is always the name of a structure variable, such as `item1` or `employee[16]`. To the right of the dot operator is always the name of a member from that structure, such as `quantity`, `cost`, or `name`. The dot operator puts data only in named structure variables. If you want to put data in a heap structure pointed to by a structure pointer variable, you must use the *structure pointer* operator, `->`.

The following program defines an array of three structure variables using the `invStruct` structure tag shown earlier. (The structure is assumed to be stored in INV.H to keep the example short.) The user is asked to fill the structure variables, and then the program prints them. In the next couple of chapters, you'll see how to output the structure variables to a disk file for long-term storage.

using structure variable + dot operator

```c
/* First, include the file with the structure declaration */
#include "c:\inv.h"
#include <stdio.h>
main()
{ int ctr;
  struct invStruct items[3];  /* Array of three
                                  structure variables */
  for (ctr = 0; ctr < 3; ctr++)
    { printf("What is the manufacturer of item #%d?\n",
             (ctr + 1));
      gets(items[ctr].manuf);
      puts("What is the model? ");
      gets(items[ctr].model);
      puts("How many megabytes of disk space? ");
      scanf(" %d", &items[ctr].diskSpace);
      puts("How many megabytes of memory space? ");
      scanf(" %d", &items[ctr].memSpace);
      puts("How many are there? ");
      scanf(" %d", &items[ctr].quantity);
      puts("How much does the item cost? ");
      scanf(" %f", &items[ctr].cost);
      puts("How much does the item retail for? ");
      scanf(" %f", &items[ctr].price);
      getchar();  /* Clears input of last newline
                     pressed for next round of input */
    }  /* Now, prints the data */
  printf("\n\nHere is the inventory: \n");
  for (ctr = 0; ctr < 3; ctr++)
    { printf("#%d: Manufacturer: %s", (ctr + 1),
             items[ctr].manuf);
      printf("\nModel: %s", items[ctr].model);
      printf("\nDisk: %d megabytes\t", items[ctr].diskSpace);
      printf("Memory: %d megabytes\t", items[ctr].memSpace);
      printf("Quantity: %d units\n", items[ctr].quantity);
      printf("Cost: $%.2f\t", items[ctr].cost);
      printf("Selling price: $%.2f\n\n", items[ctr].price);
    }
  return 0;
}
```

member name
-> variable

If you were to store the structures on the heap, you couldn't use the dot operator, because the dot operator requires a variable name. Use -> to store data in heap structures. -> requires a pointer on the left and a member name on the right. Here is an equivalent program to the previous one, except the heap and -> are used instead of structure variables and the dot operator.

```
/* First, include the file with the structure declaration */
#include "c:\inv.h"
#include <stdio.h>
#include <stdlib.h>
main()
{ int ctr;
  struct invStruct * items[3];  /* Array of three
                                   structure pointers */
  for (ctr = 0; ctr < 3; ctr++)
    { items[ctr]=(struct invStruct*)malloc(sizeof(struct
      invStruct));
      printf("What is the manufacturer of item #%d?\n",
           (ctr + 1));
      /* items[ctr] is now a pointer, not a variable */
      gets(items[ctr]->manuf);
      puts("What is the model? ");
      gets(items[ctr]->model);
      puts("How many megabytes of disk space? ");
      scanf(" %d", &items[ctr]->diskSpace);
      puts("How many megabytes of memory space? ");
      scanf(" %d", &items[ctr]->memSpace);
      puts("How many are there? ");
      scanf(" %d", &items[ctr]->quantity);
      puts("How much does the item cost? ");
      scanf(" %f", &items[ctr]->cost);
      puts("How much does the item retail for? ");
      scanf(" %f", &items[ctr]->price);
      getchar();  /* Clears input of last newline
                     pressed for next round of input */
    }  /* Now, prints the data */
  printf("\n\nHere is the inventory: \n");
  for (ctr = 0; ctr < 3; ctr++)
    { printf("#%d: Manufacturer: %s", (ctr + 1),
           items[ctr]->manuf);
      printf("\nModel: %s", items[ctr]->model);
      printf("\nDisk: %d megabytes\t", items[ctr]->diskSpace);
      printf("Memory: %d megabytes\t", items[ctr]->memSpace);
      printf("Quantity: %d units\n", items[ctr]->quantity);
      printf("Cost: $%.2f\t", items[ctr]->cost);
      printf("Selling price: $%.2f\n\n", items[ctr]->price);
    }
  return 0;
}
```

Rewards

✖ Define structures when you want to group items of different data types.

✖ Declare a structure before defining a structure variable.

✖ Use the dot operator to access individual data members within a structure variable.

✖ Use the -> (the *structure pointer* operator) to access individual data members within a structure pointed to by a pointer variable.

Pitfalls

✖ Don't use member names as variables. Member names exist only so you can work with an individual part of a structure.

✖ Don't forget to add a semicolon at the end of all structure definitions.

✖ Don't intermix the dot operator and the structure pointer operator. Remember that a structure variable must appear before the dot operator, and a structure *pointer* variable must appear before the -> operator.

In Review

This chapter's goal was to teach you about structures. A *structure* is an aggregate variable data type. Whereas an array must hold values that are all the same data type, a structure can hold several values of different data types.

Before using a structure variable, you must tell C exactly what the structure looks like with a `struct` statement. The `struct` statement lets C know how many members are in the structure and the data types of each member. A structure variable is like a group of more than one variable of different data types.

Code Example

```
struct telStr {
  char lastName[15];
  char initial;
  char firstname[15];
  int areaCode;
  long int phoneNum;
  char address[25];
  char city[10];
  char state[3];   /* Leaves 1 for the null zero! */
  char zip[6];
};
main()
{
  int i;
  struct telStr friends[50];
```

Code Analysis

This code might be the start of a program that tracks telephone numbers and addresses of your friends. The code first describes a structure that has nine members. The members are made up of character arrays, a character member, an integer member, and a long integer member.

The program that begins in `main()` defines an array of 50 structure variables. (An `int` variable is also defined just to show you that structures are defined in the same location as other variables.) Each of the 50 structure variables has the `telStr` layout.

Part 5

Form Follows Functions

28

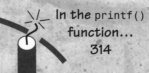

BOTTOM-LESS PIT

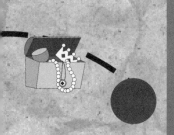

Can My Programs Save Stuff on Disk?

With Sequential Files

None of the programs you've seen so far have been able to store data for very long. Think about this for a moment: If you defined an integer variable, put a 14 in it and then turned off the computer (believe me now and try it later), that variable would no longer have 14 in it! If you turned your computer back on and tried to find the value in the variable, you couldn't find it—no way.

This chapter explains how to save data to your disk. Once the data is on your disk, it will be there until you change or erase it. Data on your disk is just like music on a tape. You can turn off the tape deck and the tape will hold the music until you change it. There is no good reason why a user should enter data, such as historical sales records, more than once.

> **NOTE**
> Files are critical to computer data programs. How useful would a word processor be without files?

Disk Files

Disks hold data in *files*. You already understand the concept of files if you've saved a C program to a disk file. Files can hold either programs or data, as shown in Figure 28.1. Your programs must be loaded from disk into memory before you can run them. You also must load data from the disk file into variables before you can work with the data. The variables also hold data before the data goes to a disk file.

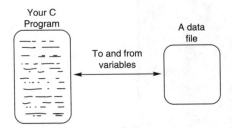

FIGURE 28.1.
Your program file can process data files.

There are two types of files: *sequential-access* and *random-access*. Their types determine how you can access them. If you work with a sequential-access file, you have to read or write the file in the order of the data. In a random-access file, you can jump around, reading and writing any place in the file.

Clue: A sequential file is like a cassette tape, and a random-access file is like a record or a CD. You have to play songs in sequence on a tape (or fast-forward through them in order), whereas you can skip around in the music on a record or a CD.

All disk files have names that conform to the same naming rules as program names. Before you can use a disk file, whether it be to create, read, or change the data in the file, you must *open* the file.

file pointer

Clue: As with a filing cabinet, you can't use a disk file without opening the file. Instead of pulling out a drawer, your computer attaches something called a *file pointer* to the file and makes sure that the disk is properly set up to hold the file you specify.

Opening a File

To open a file, you must use the fopen() function, whose description is included along with printf()'s in STDIO.H. Before seeing fopen(), you have to understand the concept of a file pointer.

fopen() function

NOTE

The concept of a file pointer is easy to understand. A regular pointer simply holds the address of data in a variable. A file pointer simply holds the disk location of the disk file you're working with.

---

*ptr_diskfile

FILE   **fp*   *disk location of the disk file working with*

There is a special statement you must specify to define a file pointer. As with any variable, you can name file pointers anything you want. Suppose you want to open an employee file. Before the `fopen()`, you must define a file pointer variable. If you called the file pointer `fptr`, here is how you would define a file pointer:

```
FILE * fptr;   /* Defines a file pointer named fptr */
```

> **WARNING**
>
> Most C programmers define their file pointers before `main()`. This makes the file pointer *global,* which is a fancy term meaning that the entire program can use the file. (Most other kinds of variables are *local,* not global.) Because part of the file pointer statement is in uppercase, `FILE` is defined someplace with `#define`. `FILE` is defined in STDIO.H, which is the primary reason you should include the STDIO.H header file when your program uses the disk for data.

Once you define a file pointer, you can connect that pointer to a file with `fopen()`. Once you specify `fopen()`, you can use the file throughout the rest of the program. Here is the way to open a file named `C:\EMPS.DAT`. (If you don't have a C: drive, change the `C:` in these examples to a different drive letter.)

```
#include <stdio.h>
FILE *fptr;   /* Define a file pointer */
main()
{
  fptr = fopen("C:\\EMPS.DAT", "w");
  /* Rest of program follows */
  fclose(fptr);  /* Always close the file */
```

For the rest of the program, you'll access the EMPS.DAT file via the file pointer, not via the filename. Using a file pointer variable is easier and less error-prone than typing the filename and complete pathname to the file every time you must access the file.

(handwritten margin note: before main - global, after main - local)

fopen()
fclose()

WARNING

Close your filing cabinet drawers when you're done with your files or you'll hit your head! Close all open files after you're through with them or you could lose some data. `fclose()` is the opposite of `fopen()`. In its parentheses, `fclose()` requires a file pointer of the file you want to close.

WARNING

If the file pointer equals 0, you'll know that an error happened (such as a disk drive door being open). C returns a 0 from `fclose()` if an error occurs when you open a file. For example, if you attempt to open a file on a disk drive that doesn't exist, `fclose()` returns an error.

The `"w"` (the second argument in the previous code's `fopen()`) means *write*. The second argument of `fopen()` must be one of the string *mode* values found in Table 28.1.

Table 28.1. The basic `fopen()` mode strings.

Mode	Description
`"w"`	*Write* mode that creates a new file whether it exists or not.
`"r"`	*Read* mode that lets you read an existing file. If the file doesn't exist, you get an error.
`"a"`	*Append* mode that lets you add to the end of a file or create the file if it doesn't already exist.

add

Using Sequential Files

There are only three things you'll ever do with a sequential file: create it, read it, and add to it (write to it). To write to a file, you can use `fprintf()`. `fprintf()` is easy because it's just a `printf()` with a file pointer at the beginning of its parentheses. The following program creates a file and writes some data to it using `fprintf()`:

```c
#include <stdio.h>
#include <stdlib.h>
FILE * fptr;
main()
{
  int age = 45;  /* Simple variables to write */
  float salary = 9670.50;
  fptr = fopen("C:\\MYDATA.DAT", "w"); /* Opens for output */
  if (fptr == 0)
    { printf("An error occurred while opening the file.\n");
      exit (1);
    }
  fprintf(fptr, "Here is some stuff:\n");
  fprintf(fptr, "I am %d years old.\n", age);
  fprintf(fptr, "I make $%.2f dollars every three months!/n",
          salary);
  fclose(fptr);  /* ALWAYS close your files */
  return 0;
}
```

If you were to run this program and look at the contents of the file named MYDATA.DAT (using the DOS TYPE command, a text editor, or the C program described next), you would see this:

```
Here is some stuff:
I am 45 years old.
I make $9670.50 dollars every three months!
```

Use `fgets()` to read the contents of the file. `fgets()` is nothing more than a `gets()` that you can direct to a disk file. `fgets()` reads lines from a file into character arrays (or allocated heap memory pointed to with a character pointer).

Clue: Think of the *f* at the beginning of `fputs()` and `fgets()` as standing for *file*. `puts()` and `gets()` go to the screen and keyboard respectively; `fputs()` and `fgets()` write and read their data from files.

Unlike `gets()`, `fgets()` requires that you specify a maximum length for the array you're reading into. You might read past the end of the file (producing an error) if you're not careful, so be sure to check for the location of the end of file.

`fgets()` reads one line at a time. If you specify more characters to read in the `fgets()` than actually reside on the file's line you're reading, `fgets()` will stop reading the line of data as long as the file's lines end with a newline character. The previous program that created the MYDATA.DAT file always wrote \n at the end of each line so that subsequent `fgets()` functions would be able to read the file line-by-line.

The following program shows you how to read a file that contains string data and check for end-of-file (with the `feof()` function) along the way:

```c
#include <stdio.h>
FILE * fptr;
main()
{
  char fileLine[81];  /* Will hold the output */
  fptr = fopen("C:\\MYDATA.DAT", "r");  /* Opens for input */
  if (fptr != 0)
    { while (!feof(fptr))  /* Probably the only good
                              use for ! */
      { fgets(fileLine, 81, fptr);  /* Gets no more
                                       than 81 chars */
        if (!feof(fptr))
          { puts(fileLine); }
      }
    }
  else
    { printf("\nError opening file.\n"); }

fclose(fptr);  /* ALWAYS close your files */
return 0;
}
```

feof() returns a true condition if you just read the last line from the file. The feof() really isn't needed in the previous program because we know exactly what the MYDATA.DAT contains (we just created the file in an earlier program). There are three lines in the file, and three fgets() would suffice. Nevertheless, you should generally use feof() when reading from disk files. You often don't know exactly how much data the file contains because other people using other programs may have added data to the file.

SKIP THIS, IT'S TECHNICAL

In the fprintf() function, the file pointer goes at the beginning of the function. In the fgets() function, the file pointer goes at the *end.* There's nothing like consistency!

Clue: There is also an fscanf() you can use to read individual numeric values from a data file if you wrote the values with a corresponding fprintf().

You can add to a file by opening the file in append mode and outputting data to it. The following program adds the line That's all! to the end of the MYDATA.DAT data file:

```c
#include <stdio.h>
FILE * fptr;
main()
{
  fptr = fopen("C:\\MYDATA.DAT", "a"); /* Opens for append */
  if (fptr == 0)
    { printf("An error occurred while opening the file.\n");
      exit (1);
    }
  fprintf(fptr, "\nThat's all!\n");  /* Adds the line */
  fclose(fptr);  /* ALWAYS close your files */
  return 0;
}
```

Here is what MYDATA.DAT now contains (notice the extra line):

```
Here is some stuff:
I am 45 years old.
I make $9670.50 dollars every three months!
That's all!
```

Clue: To write to a printer instead of the screen, open the DOS printer device named LPT1: or LPT2: and use that device name as the first argument of fprintf().

Rewards

- ✖ Store long-term data in data files.
- ✖ Open a file with fopen() before you use the file.
- ✖ Always close a file with fclose() when you're done.

Pitfalls

- ✖ Don't read from a file without checking for feof(), because you might have previously read the last line in the file.
- ✖ Don't use the filename once you open a file. Use the file pointer that you connected to the file with fopen().
- ✖ Don't forget that the file pointer goes at the *beginning* of fprintf() and that fputs() requires a file pointer at the *end* of its argument list.

In Review

The goal of this chapter was to show you how to create, read, and write sequential files. Your C program must open a file before data can be written to, or read from, the file. When your program is done with a file, the program should close the file.

When reading from a file, you must check for the end-of-file condition to ensure that you don't try to read past the end of the file. The feof() function is a built-in C function that you use to check for the end of the file.

Code Example

```
#include <stdio.h>
FILE * tvFile;
main()
{
  char name[] = "Gerald";
  char show[] = "Sign Field";
  int age = 18;
  tvFile = fopen("C:\\SHOWS.DAT", "w");   /* Opens for
                                             output */
  if (tvFile)  /* Same as tvFile != 0) */
    { fprintf(tvFile, "My name is %s.\n", name);
      fprintf(tvFile, "My favorite TV show is %s.\n", show);
      fprintf(tvFile, "I am %d years old.", age);
      fclose(tvFile);
    }
  else
    { printf("There's a problem with opening the file.\n"); }
  return 0;
}
```

Code Analysis

This code describes a complete program that stores several messages in a sequential file. First the file pointer is defined, and then some data is stored in variables.

The file is then opened. If there was not an error during the open process, three messages are written to the disk before the file is closed.

This program is simple, yet it forms the beginning of a more complete database program you might want to write. Instead of assigning data to the variables directly, you might want to ask the user for the values and store the data entered by the user.

29

Values are in
uppercase.
323

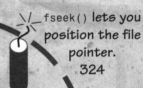

fseek() lets you
position the file
pointer.
324

Use fseek() for
random-access files.
323

The access
mode is a
string.
321

BOTTOM-
LESS PIT

Close a file when
you're done with it.
326

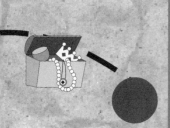

Is There Another Way to Save Files?

Use Random Files

This chapter shows you how to skip around in a file, reading and writing data as you go. The preceding chapter introduced methods you can use to write, read, or append data to a file. The problem is that once you open a sequential file for reading, you can *only* read it.

There might be times when you want to read a customer structure from disk and change the customer's balance. You certainly wouldn't want to have to create a new file just so you could write that one change. Instead, you would want to read the customer information into a variable, change it, and then write it back to disk exactly where it first resided. As Figure 29.1 shows, random files let you skip around in the file, reading and writing at any point you access.

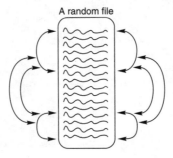

A random file

FIGURE 29.1.
Random files let you read and write data in any order.

The physical layout of a file doesn't define the type of file (whether random or sequential). You can create a file sequentially and then read and change it randomly. To C, a file is just a stream of bytes, and the way you access it isn't linked to any format of the file.

Opening Random Files

To read or write a file randomly, you must open the file randomly. Table 29.1 lists the modes that access random files. As you can see, the cornerstone of random-access files is the use of the plus sign combined with the access modes you learned about in the previous chapter.

> **NOTE**
>
> As with sequential files, the access mode is a string that appears as the last argument of `fopen()`. You will close open random files with `fclose()`, just as you do with sequential files.

Table 29.1. The random-access `fopen()` modes.

Mode	Description
`"r+"`	Opens an existing file for both reading and writing.
`"w+"`	Opens a new file for writing and reading.
`"a+"`	Opens a file in append mode (the file pointer points to the end of the file) but lets you move back through the file, reading and writing as you go.

All three modes let you read and write to the file. The access mode you choose depends on what you want to do *first* to the file. If the file exists and you want to access the file randomly, use the r+ mode. If you want to create the file, use w+. (If the file already exists, C overwrites the existing version.) If you want to add to the end of a file, but optionally "back up" and read and write existing data, use a+.

Here is a sample `fopen()` statement that opens an existing file for writing and reading:

```
fptr = fopen("C:\\LETTERS.DAT", "w+");   /* Opens for
                                            write, then read */
```

As with sequential files, the `fptr` variable must be a file pointer variable. The double backslash is needed if you specify a pathname. Remember that `fopen()` returns a zero if the open fails.

> **NOTE**
>
> You can specify a long pathname if you want to. For instance, the filename might look something like this:
>
> `"C:\\ANDY\\WORK\\CORRESP\\LETTERS.DAT"`
>
> Also, you can store the filename in a character array and use the character array name in place of an actual string literal for the filename. You can use either uppercase or lowercase letters for the filename.

Fun Fact

Credit card companies save purchase records in random files.

Moving Around in a File

Use the `fseek()` function to move around in a file. After you open a file, C initializes the file pointer to point to the next place in the file you can read or write. `fseek()` moves the file pointer so that you can read and write at places that would normally not be pointed at using sequential access. Here is the format of `fseek()`:

```
fseek(filePtr, longVal, origin);
```

The *filePtr* is the file pointer used in the `fopen()` function that used a random-access mode. The *longVal* is a `long int` variable or literal that can be either positive or negative. The *longVal* is the number of bytes to skip forward or backward in the file. The *origin* is always one of the values shown in Table 29.2. *origin* tells `fseek()` from where to start seeking.

Table 29.2. `origin` values that can appear in `fseek()`.

origin	Description
SEEK_SET	Beginning of file
SEEK_CUR	Current position in file
SEEK_END	End of file

The *origin* value tells C the position *from where* you want to access the random file next. Once you position the file pointer with fseek(), you can use file input and output functions to write and read to and from the file. If you position the file pointer at the end of the file (using SEEK_END), and then write data, new data will go to the end of the file. If you position the file pointer over existing data (using SEEK_SET and SEEK_CUR), and then write new data, the new data will replace the existing data.

> **WARNING**
>
> Use fseek() for random-access files only. Sequential files can be accessed only in the order of the data.

Clue: Table 29.2's values are in uppercase, which implies that they're defined somewhere. They're defined in STDIO.H using #define directives.

The following program opens a file for random-access mode, writes the letters A through Z to the file, and then rereads those letters backwards. The file doesn't have to be reopened before the reading begins because of the random-access mode "w+".

```
#include <stdio.h>
#include <stdlib.h>
FILE * fptr;
main()
{
  char letter;
  int i;
  fptr = fopen("C:\\LETTERS.DAT", "w+");   /* Opens for
                                      write, then read */
  if (fptr == 0)
    { printf("An error occurred while opening the file.\n");
      exit(1);
    }
  for (letter = 'A'; letter <= 'Z'; letter++)
    { fputc(letter, fptr);
    }
```

```
    puts("Just wrote the letters A through Z");
    /* Now reads the file backwards */
    fseek(fptr, -1, SEEK_END);  /* Minus 1 byte from the end */
    printf("Here is the file backwards:\n");
    for (i = 26; i > 0; i--)
      { letter = fgetc(fptr);
        fseek(fptr, -2, SEEK_CUR);  /* Reads a letter, then
                                       backs up 2 */
        printf("The next letter is %c\n", letter);
      }
    fclose(fptr);
    return 0;
}
```

Clue: As you can see, fputc() is a great function for outputting individual characters to a file. fgetc() reads individual characters from a file. fputc() and fgetc() are to putc() and getc() what fputs() and fgets() are to puts() and gets().

SKIP THIS, IT'S TECHNICAL

So far, you might not see a purpose for random-access files. Random access, however, offers you the advantage of writing data to a file and then rereading the same data without closing and opening the file. Also, fseek() lets you position the file pointer any number of bytes from the beginning, middle, or end of the file.

Assuming that the file of letters still resides on the disk from the last program, this next program asks the user which position he or she wants to change. The program then positions the file pointer with fseek() and writes an * at that point before fseek()ing to the beginning of the file and printing it again.

```
#include <stdio.h>
#include <stdlib.h>
FILE * fptr;
main()
{
```

```
   char letter;
   int i;
   fptr = fopen("C:\\LETTERS.DAT", "r+");   /* Opens for read,
                                               then write */
   if (fptr == 0)
     { printf("An error occurred while opening the file.\n");
       exit(1);
     }
   printf("What is the position you want to change? ");
   scanf(" %d", &i);
   /* Seeks to that location from the beginning of the file */
   fseek(fptr, (i - 1), SEEK_SET);   /* Subtracts 1 because
                                        first position is 0 */
   /* Writes '*' over that position */
   fputc('*', fptr);
   /* Now prints the file */
   fseek(fptr, 0, SEEK_SET);   /* Back to the beginning */
   printf("Here is the file now:\n");
   for (i = 0; i < 26; i++)
     { letter = fgetc(fptr);
       printf("The next letter is %c\n", letter);
     }
   fclose(fptr);
   return 0;
}
```

The program prints the contents of the file after the * is written at the position indicated by the user. Here is a sample session:

```
What is the position you want to change? 4
Here is the file now:
The next letter is A
The next letter is B
The next letter is C
The next letter is *
The next letter is E
The next letter is F
The next letter is G
The next letter is H
The next letter is I
The next letter is J
   :
   :
```

As you can see, the fourth position of the alphabetical file, the letter D, now contains an asterisk. The rest of the file remains unchanged.

Rewards

✖ Use a plus sign in the `fopen()` mode string if you need to change data in a file.

✖ Remember that `fseek()` moves a file pointer all around a random file so that you can read or write from the beginning, middle, or end.

Pitfalls

✖ Don't forget to close a file when you are done with it.

✖ Don't attempt to work with a file if the `fopen()` fails (by returning a zero).

In Review

The goal of this chapter was to explain how random-access files work. Once you open a file in random-access mode, you can read and write to that file in any order you need to. The fseek() function is the built-in function that skips around the file from position to position.

Being able to change the contents of a file is important when you want to update file data. Often you will want to change a person's address, change an inventory item's quantity, and so on without rewriting the entire file as you would have to if you used sequential file processing.

Code Example

```c
#include <stdio.h>
#include <stdlib.h>
  struct std {
    char id[4];   /* 3-character ID plus a null zero */
    float avg;
  };
FILE *gradePtr;
main()
{
  struct std students;   /* Student records */
  gradePtr = fopen("C:\\GRADES.DAT", "w+");
  if (gradePtr == 0)
    { printf("An error occurred while opening the file.\n");
      exit(1);
    }
  do {
    printf("What is the next student's 3-character ID?\n");
    printf("Enter Q to quit entering students): ");
    gets(students.id);
    if (students.id[0] != 'Q')
      { printf("What is the student's average? ");
        scanf(" %f", &students.avg);
        getchar();   /* Gets rid of the Enter keypress */
        fprintf(gradePtr, "%s%.1f\n", students.id,
                students.avg);
      }
    } while (students.id[0] != 'Q');
  fclose(gradePtr);
  return 0;
}
```

Code Analysis

This code contains a complete program that writes structure data to a random-access file. The program could have just as easily written to a sequential file, but the fprintf() ensures that each structure written to the disk has the same format and length—a three-character string followed by a floating-point value.

You can easily write the code to read or change any record in the file using this fseek():

```
fseek(gradePtr, recNo * sizeof(struct std), SEEK_SET);
```

in which recNo is a record number that the user wants to change.

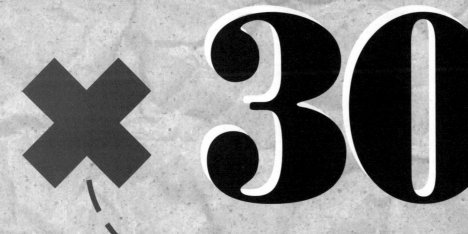

30

The variable g2 is global.
337

Separate functions let you focus on code.
332

If you use only local variables.
338

Each function acts as a building block.
333

BOTTOM-LESS PIT

Don't start out using global variables.
339

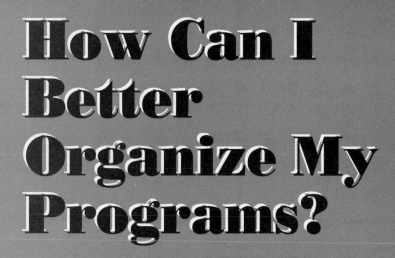

How Can I Better Organize My Programs?

Using Functions

In This Chapter

Typical computer programs are not the 20-to-30-line variety that you see in textbooks. In the "real world," computer programs are much longer; but long programs contain lots of code that would get in the way while learning new concepts. That is why, until this point, you've seen fairly short programs that contain all their code in main().

If you were to put an entire long program in main(), you would spend a lot of time to find anything specific if you later needed to change it. This chapter is the first of three chapters that explore ways to partition your programs into sections via multiple functions. Categorizing your code by breaking it into sections makes programs easier to write and also easier to maintain.

> **SKIP THIS, IT'S TECHNICAL**
>
> People have to write, change, and fix code. The clearer you make the code by writing lots of functions that do individual tasks, the faster you can get home from your programming job and relax! As you'll see, separate functions let you focus on code that needs changing.

Form Follows C Functions

As you might know, C programs aren't like BASIC programs. C was designed to force you to think in a modular style through the use of functions. A BASIC program is often just one very long program that isn't broken into separate routines. (Some of the newer versions of BASIC, such as QBasic, now offer almost the same functionality that C offers.) A C program isn't just one long program. It's made up of many routines named, as you know, *functions*. One of the program's functions (the one always required and usually listed first) is named main().

If your program does very much, break it into several functions. Each function should do one primary task. For instance, if you were writing a C program to get a list of numbers from the keyboard, sort them, and then print them to the screen, you *could* write all of this in one big function—all in main()—as the following program outline shows:

```
main()
{
   /* This is not a working program, just an outline */
      :
   /* C code to retrieve a list of numbers */
      :
   /* C code to sort the numbers */
      :
   /* C code to print the sorted list on-screen */
      :
   return 0;
}
```

This program does *not* offer a good format for the tasks you want accomplished because it's too sequential. All the code appears in main(), even though there are several distinct tasks that need to be done. This program might not require many lines of code, but it's much better to get in the habit of breaking every program into distinct tasks.

Don't use main() to do everything. In fact, you should use main() to do very little except call each of the other functions. A better way to organize this program would be to write separate functions for each task that the program is to do.

Fun Fact

Breaking programs into smaller functions is called *structured programming*.

> **NOTE**
> Of course, every function shouldn't be a single line, but make sure that each function acts as a building block and performs only a single task.

Here is a better outline for the program just described:

```
main()
{
   getNums();    /* Calls a function that gets the numbers */
   sortNums();   /* Sorts the numbers */
   printNums();  /* Prints the numbers on-screen */
   return 0;     /* Quits the program */
}
/* A second function */
getNums()
{  :
   /* C code to retrieve a list of numbers */
   return;
```

```
}
/* A third function */
sortNums()
{   :
  /* C code to sort the numbers */
  return;
}
/* A fourth function */
printNums()
{   :
  /* C code to print the sorted list on-screen */
  return;
}
```

> **NOTE**
>
> Even though this program outline is longer than the previous one, this one's better organized, and therefore, easier to maintain. The only thing that main() does is control the other functions by showing an overview of how they're called.

Each separate function does its thing and then returns to main(), where main() calls the next function until there are no more functions. main() then returns to DOS. main() acts almost like a table of contents for the program. With adequate comments, main() lets you know exactly what functions contain code you need to change.

Clue: A good rule of thumb is that a function should not take more lines than will fit on a single screen. If the function is longer than that, you're probably making it do too much. In high school, didn't you *hate* to read literature books with l-o-n-g chapters? You'll also dislike working on programs with long functions.

Any function can call any other function. For example, if you wanted printNums() to print a title with your name and the date at the top of the page, you might have printNums() call another function named printTitle(). printTitle() would then return to printNums() when it finishes. Here is the outline of such a code:

```
main()
{
  getNums();     /* Calls a function that gets the numbers */
  sortNums();    /* Sorts the numbers */
  printNums();   /* Prints a title AND the numbers on-screen */
  return 0;      /* Quits the program */
}
/* A second function */
getNums()
{   :
  /* C code to retrieve a list of numbers */
  return;
}
/* A third function */
sortNums()
{   :
  /* C code to sort the numbers */
  return;
}
/* A fourth function */
printNums()
{   :
  /* C code to print the sorted list on-screen */
  printTitle();
  return;
}
/* A fifth function called from printNums() */
printTitle()
{
  /* C code to print a title */
  return;  /* Returns to printNums(), not to main() */
}
```

NOTE

Look at all the functions in the Blackjack game in Appendix B. The program is only a few pages long, but it contains several functions. Look through the code and see if you can find a function that calls another function located elsewhere in the program.

The entire electronics industry has learned something from the programming world. Most electronic components today, such as televisions, computers, and radios, contain lots of boards that can be removed, updated, and replaced, without affecting the rest of the system. In a similar way, you'll be able to change certain workings of your programs: if you write well-structured programs by using functions, you can then change only the functions that need changing without having to mess with a lot of unrelated code.

Local or Global?

The program outline explained in the preceding section needs more code to work. Before being able to add code, you need to take a closer look at variable definitions. In C, all variables can be either *local* or *global*. All the variables you have seen so far have been local. Most of the time, a local variable is safer than a global variable because a local variable offers itself on a *need-to-know access*. That is, if a function needs a variable, it can have access to another function's local variables through a variable-passing process described in the next chapter.

If a function doesn't need to access another function's local variable, it can't have access. Any function can read, change, and zero out global variables, so they don't offer as much safety.

The following rules describe the difference between local and global variables:

* A variable is global if and only if you define the variable (such as `int i;`) before a function name.
* A variable is local if and only if you define it after an opening brace. A function always begins with opening braces. Some statements, such as `while`, also have opening braces, and you can define local variables within those braces as well.

Clue: An opening and closing brace enclose what is known as a *block*.

Given these rules, it should be obvious that `i1` and `i2` are local variables and that `g1` and `g2` are global variables in the following program:

```c
#include <stdio.h>
int g1 = 10;
main()
{
  float l1;
  l1 = 9.0;
  printf("%d %f\n", g1, l1); /* Prints global g1 and local */
  prAgain();                  /* l1, calls next function,   */
  return 0;                   /* and returns to DOS         */
}
float g2 = 9.0;  /* A global variable */
/* Next is a separate function */
prAgain()
{
  int l2 = 5;
  printf("%d %f %d\n", l2, g2, g1);  /* Can't print l1! */
  return;
}
```

SKIP THIS, IT'S TECHNICAL

You probably don't yet understand the `return 0;` statement. To make matters worse, `return` by itself is used at the end of the `prAgain()` function. You'll find a detailed description for return in the next two chapters.

Clue: The variable g2 is global because it's defined before a function (prAgain()).

Local variables are usable *only* within their own block of code. Therefore, l1 could never be printed or changed in `prAgain()` because l1 is local to `main()`. Conversely, l2 could never be used in `main()` because l2 is visible only to `prAgain()`. The variable g1 is visible to the entire program. g2 is visible only from its point of definition *down*.

Clue: All global variables are known from their points of definition *down* in the source file. Don't define a global variable in the middle of a program (as is done in the preceding program) because its definition can be too hard to find during debugging sessions. You should limit (or eliminate) the use of globals. If you use them at all, define all of them before main() where they are easy to find (such as if you need to change them or look at their defined data types).

WARNING

There is a problem with the program outline shown earlier. If you use only local variables (and you should always try to), the variable values input in getNums() can be neither sorted in sortNums() nor printed in printNums()! Stay tuned, because the next chapter shows you the solution.

SKIP THIS, IT'S TECHNICAL

If you compile the previous program and receive a compiler warning about a call to a function without a prototype, ignore the error for now. Your questions will be answered in Chapter 32, "How Can I Perfect My Functions?"

Rewards

* Define local variables after a block's opening brace. Define global variables before a function begins.

* Local variables are safer than global variables, so use local variables as much as possible.

* Break your programs into lots of functions to ease maintenance and speed development time.

Pitfalls

✖ Don't define global variables in the middle of a program. They're too hard to locate if you do.

✖ Don't start out using global variables. As your program grows, you may occasionally see the need for a global variable and add one then. (The next chapter explains more about using local variables in place of globals.)

In Review

The goal of this chapter was to teach you the building-block approach to writing C programs. Long programs can become unwieldy unless you break them into several separate functions. One long `main()` function is analogous to a long book without chapter divisions. Break your long programs into separate functions and have each function perform a single, separate task in the program.

Once you divide your programs into several functions, you have to consider how variables are used throughout the code. Local variables are defined inside a function and are usable only in that function. The opposite of a local variable is a global variable, whose value is usable in all functions after its definition. Global variables are frowned upon. Local variables are safer because you can limit their access to only those functions that need to use them. In the next chapter, you'll learn how to share local variables between functions.

Code Example

```c
#include <stdio.h>
char name[] = "Mary";    /* Global */
main()
{
  int age = 25;  /* Local variable */
  /* The following printf() can use name
     because name is global */
  printf("%s is %d years old.\n", name, age);
  nextFun();  /* Calls second function */
  return 0;   /* and returns to DOS    */
}

float weight = 119.0;  /* A global variable */
/********************************************************/
nextFun()
{
  /* The next printf() CANNOT print age because
     age is local and usable only in main() */
  printf("%s is %d years old and weighs %.0f pounds.\n",
         name, age, weight);
  return;  /* Goes back and finishes main() */
}
```

Code Analysis

This program contains three variables, two of which are global (name and weight) and one that is local to main() (age). The first function, main(), is put on hold when it calls nextFun(). When nextFun() concludes, the last line in main() is free to finish.

The nextFun() function can't use the value of age because age is local to main() and therefore usable only in main().

This program contains a comment full of asterisks before the nextFun() function. Programmers often use such separating comments to distinguish one function from another. When looking through the code, you can more easily find the function you're looking for.

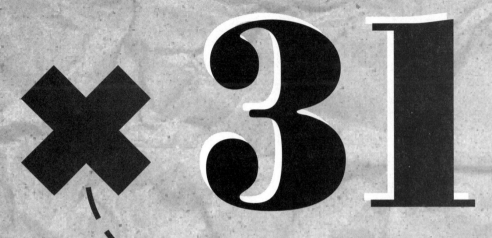

31

Those empty paren-
theses have a use.
345

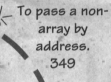

To pass a non-
array by
address.
349

Passing by value
protects a variable.
347

This passing
values stuff is
important.
345

BOTTOM-
LESS PIT

Don't pass an array
variable by value.
351

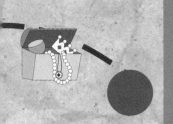

How Do Functions Share Data?

By Passing Variables

The preceding chapter left some questions unanswered. If multiple functions are good (they are), and if local variables are good (they are), then you must have a way to share local variables between functions that need to share them (there is a way). You don't want *all* functions to have access to *all* variables, because not every function needs access to every variable. If full variable access between functions is needed, you might as well use global variables.

To share data from function to function, you must *pass* variables from function to function. When one function passes a variable to another function, only those two functions have access to the variable (assuming the variable is local). This chapter explains how to pass variables between functions.

Passing Arguments

When you pass a variable from one function to another, you are *passing an argument* from the first function to the next. You can pass more than one variable at a time. The receiving function *receives the parameters* from the function that sent the variables.

> **WARNING**
>
> The words *variable, argument,* and *parameter* are sometimes used interchangeably when passing and receiving values. The name is not as important as understanding what is happening. Figure 31.1 helps explain these terms.

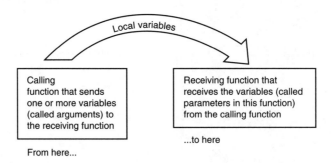

FIGURE 31.1.
Getting the terms correct.

Methods of Passing Arguments

There are two ways to pass arguments from a function to another function: *by value* and *by address*. Both of these methods pass arguments *to* a receiving function from a calling function. There is also a way to *return* a value from a function back to the calling function (see the next chapter).

Clue: All this passing of values talk focuses on the parentheses that follow function names. That's right, those empty parentheses have a use after all! The variables you want to pass go inside the parentheses of the function call, and also in the receiving function, as you'll see in the next section.

NOTE

Yes, this passing values stuff is important! It's easy, though, as you'll see.

Passing by Value

Sometimes *passing by value* is called *passing by copy*. You'll hear these terms used interchangeably because they mean the same thing. Passing by value means that the *value* of the variable is passed to the receiving function, not the variable itself. Here is a program that passes a value from main() to half():

```
#include <stdio.h>
main()
{
  int i;
  printf("Please enter a number... ");
  scanf(" %d", &i);
  /* Now, passes the variable to a function */
  half(i);  /* i is passed by value */
  printf("In main(), i is still %d.\n", i);
  return 0;  /* Goes back to DOS */
}
```

```
/***********************************************/
half(int i)  /* Receives value of i */
{
  i = i / 2;  /* Halves i */
  printf("Your value halved is %d.\n", i);
  return;  /* Returns to main() */
}
```

Here is the program's output:

```
Please enter a number... 12
Your value halved is 6.
In main(), i is still 12.
```

Study this first line of the `half()` function:

```
half(int i)  /* Receives value of i */
```

Notice that you must put the data type (`int`) inside the receiving function's parameter list. As Figure 31.2 shows, the contents of `i` are passed to `half()`. The `i` in `main()` is never changed *because only a copy of its value is passed.*

```
main( )
{
    int i;
    /* Prompt and input code go here*/
    half(i);      value of i
    return 0;
}

                    half(int i)
                    {
                        i = i / 2
                        printf( /*Rest of printf()*/
                        return;
                    }
```

FIGURE 31.2.

The value of `i` *is passed, not the variable* `i`.

If you passed more than one variable separated by commas, all would have to have their data types listed as well, even if they were all the same type. Here is a function that receives three variables: a floating-point, a character array, and an integer:

```
aFun(float x, char name[15], int age)    /* Receives three
arguments */
```

WARNING

Passing by value protects a variable. If the receiving function changes a passed-by-value variable, the calling function's variable is left unchanged. Therefore, passing by value is always safe because the receiving function can't change the passing function's variables—only use them.

NOTE

If the previous program's receiving function called its parameter i2, the program would still work the way it does now. The i2 would be local to half(), whereas the i in main() would be local to main(). The i2s would be local to the half() function and distinct from main().

C uses the passing by value method for all non-array variables. Therefore, if you pass any variable that is not an array to a function, only a copy of that variable's value is passed. The variable will be left unchanged in the calling function no matter what the called function does with the value.

Passing by Address

When you pass an array to another function, the array is passed by address. Instead of a copy of the array being passed, the memory address of the array is passed. The receiving function then places its receiving parameter array *over* the address passed. The bottom line is that the receiving function works with the same address as the calling function. If the receiving function changes one of the variables in the parameter list, *the calling function's argument changes as well.*

The following program passes an array to a function. The function puts x throughout the array and then main() prints the array. Notice that main() prints all xs because the function changed the argument.

```
#include <stdio.h>
#include <string.h>
main()
{
  char name[15] = "Chris Williams";
  change(name);
  printf("Back in main(), the name is now %s.\n", name);
  return 0;
}
/*******************************************************/
change(char name[15])
{
  /* Change the string stored at the
     address pointed to by name */
  strcpy(name, "xxxxxxxxxxxxxxx");
  return;
 }
```

This program produces the following output:

```
Back in main(), the name is now xxxxxxxxxxxxxxx.
```

If you want to override the passing of non-arrays by value, you can force C to pass regular non-array variables by address. However, doing so looks really crazy! Here is a program, similar to the first one you saw in this chapter, that produces a different output:

```
#include <stdio.h>
main()
{
  int i;
  printf("Please enter a number... ");
  scanf(" %d", &i);
  /* Now, passes the variable to a function */
  half(&i);  /* i is passed by address */
  printf("In main(), i is now %d.\n", i);
  return 0;  /* Goes back to DOS */
}
/*********************************************/
half(int *i)  /* Receives address of i */
{
  *i = *i / 2;  /* Halves i */
  printf("Your value halved is %d.\n", *i);
  return;  /* Returns to main() */
}
```

Here is the output from the program:

```
Please enter a number... 12
Your value halved is 6.
In main(), i is now 6.
```

SKIP THIS, IT'S TECHNICAL

It looks strange, but if you want to pass a non-array by address, precede it in the passing function with an & (address-of) symbol and then put a * (dereferencing) symbol in front of the variable *everywhere it appears* in the receiving function. If you think you're now passing a pointer to a function, you're exactly right.

Clue: Now scanf() is not so unfamiliar. Remember that you put an & before non-array variables but not before array variables that you pass to scanf(). When you call scanf(), you must pass it the address of variables so that scanf() can change the variables. Because strings are arrays, when you get a string from the keyboard, you don't put an address-of operator before the array name.

Here is a program that passes an integer i by value, a floating-point x by address, and an integer array by address (as all arrays should be passed):

```
#include <stdio.h>
/* You'll understand the next statement
   after the next chapter! */
changeSome(int i, float *newX, int iAry[4]);

main()
{
  int i = 10;
  float x = 20.5;
  int iAry[] = {10, 20, 30, 40, 50};
  puts("Here are main()'s variables before the function:");
  printf("i is %d\n", i);
  printf("x is %.1f\n", x);
  printf("iAry[0] is %d\n", iAry[0]);
  printf("iAry[1] is %d\n", iAry[1]);
```

```
      printf("iAry[2] is %d\n", iAry[2]);
      printf("iAry[3] is %d\n", iAry[3]);
      printf("iAry[4] is %d\n", iAry[4]);
      /* Without the &, x would pass by value */
      changeSome(i, &x, iAry);
      puts("\nmain()'s variables after the function:");
      printf("i is %d\n", i);
      printf("x is %.1f\n", x);
      printf("iAry[0] is %d\n", iAry[0]);
      printf("iAry[1] is %d\n", iAry[1]);
      printf("iAry[2] is %d\n", iAry[2]);
      printf("iAry[3] is %d\n", iAry[3]);
      printf("iAry[4] is %d\n", iAry[4]);
      return;
   }
   /**************************************************/
   changeSome(int i, float *newX, int iAry[4])
   {
      /* Change all parameters, but only the last
         two remain changed once main() returns */
      i = 47;
      *newX = 97.6;   /* Same location as x */
      iAry[0] = 100;
      iAry[1] = 200;
      iAry[2] = 300;
      iAry[3] = 400;
      iAry[4] = 500;
      return;
   }
```

Here is the output from the program:

```
Here are main()'s variables before the function:
i is 10
x is 20.5
iAry[0] is 10
iAry[1] is 20
iAry[2] is 30
iAry[3] is 40
iAry[4] is 50

main()'s variables after the function:
i is 10
x is 97.6
iAry[0] is 100
iAry[1] is 200
iAry[2] is 300
iAry[3] is 400
iAry[4] is 500
```

The next chapter finishes with the passing of values between functions by showing you how to return a value from one function to another. Also, you will finally understand the true use of STDIO.H.

Rewards

- ✖ Pass local variables from one function to another if you want the functions to share local variables.
- ✖ Pass variables by value if you want their values protected from the called function.
- ✖ Pass variables by address if you want their values changed by the called function.
- ✖ Place an & before non-array variables you want to pass by address. Leave off the & if you want to pass arrays.

Pitfalls

- ✖ Don't pass an array variable by value. There is no way to do that in C.

In Review

The goal of this chapter was to show you how to share local variables between functions. When one function needs access to a local variable defined in another function, you must pass that variable. The parentheses after function names contain the variables you're passing and receiving.

Normally you pass non-array variables *by value,* which means that the receiving function can use them but not affect their values in the calling function. Arrays are passed *by address,* which means that if the receiving function changes them, the array variables are also changed in the calling function. You can pass non-array variables by address by preceding them with the address-of operator, &, and receiving them with the dereference operator, *.

Code Example

```c
#include <stdio.h>
main()
{
  int i, j, k;
  printf("I'll add three variables. \n");
  printf("Please enter the first number: ");
  scanf(" %d", &i);
  printf("Please enter the second number: ");
  scanf(" %d", &j);
  printf("Please enter the third number: ");
  scanf(" %d", &k);
  addThem(i, j, k);  /* Passes variables by value */
  return 0;  /* Goes back to DOS */
}
/**************************************************/
addThem(int i, int j, int k)
{
  int total;  /* Local to this function */
  total = i + j + k;
  printf("\nThe total of the three variables is %d.\n",
         total);
  return 0;  /* Returns to main() */
}
```

Code Analysis

This program accepts three variables in main() and then prints their total in the addThem() function. The variables are passed by value to addThem(). When a function receives variables, as done here, you must put the data type in front of each of them. The following is *not* allowed for the first line of addThem():

```
addThem(int i, j, k)   /* Invalid. int is required
                          three times */
```

The local variable total holds the sum of the three passed variables. After the total is printed, control is returned to main(). The 0 that you see following the return statements in this book's programs will finally be explained in the next chapter.

32

This program uses the long int data type.
358

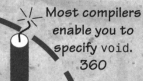

Most compilers enable you to specify void.
360

gets() actually returns a character pointer.
357

Prototypes aren't required, but they are strongly recommended.
360

BOTTOM-LESS PIT

Don't return a noninteger without a prototype.
363

How Can I Perfect My Functions?

Using Return Values and Prototypes

This chapter is not the end of your C learning. This chapter is only the beginning. Sounds deep, doesn't it? This chapter completes the multiple-function picture by showing you how to return values from the called function to the calling function. Also, function *prototypes* are explained.

The bottom line is this: You will now understand why most programs in this book contain this line:

```
return 0;
```

and you will understand the true purpose of header files.

Returning Values

So far you've seen how to send variables *to* functions. You're now ready to learn how to return a value. When a function is to return a value, use the `return` statement to return the value. Often, C programmers put parentheses after the `return` statement, with the return value inside those parentheses, such as `return (answer);`.

> **NOTE**
>
> If a function doesn't return a value, a `return` statement isn't needed because the function will return to the calling function automatically. Nevertheless, if you need to return a value, a `return` statement is required.

Although you can pass several arguments to functions, you can return *only one value* to the calling function! Figure 32.1 explains what is going on. There are no exceptions to this rule.

Although a single return value might seem limiting, it really is not. Consider the built-in `sqrt()` function. You might remember from Chapter 20, "Can C Do My Math Homework?", that `sqrt()` returns the square root of whatever value is passed to it. `sqrt()` doesn't return several values, only one. As a matter of fact, none of the built-in functions returns more than a single value, and neither can yours.

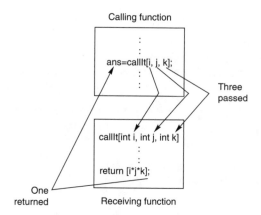

FIGURE 32.1.

You can pass more than one value but return only one.

WARNING

The gets() function seems as if it returns more than one value because it returns a character string array. Remember, though, that an array name is nothing more than a pointer to the array's first position. Therefore, gets() actually returns a character pointer that points to the beginning of the string entered by the user.

The following program contains a function that receives three integer values: a, b, and c. The function named fMul3() multiplies those three values by each other and then returns the answer.

```
#include <stdio.h>
long int fMul3(int var1, int var2, int var3);
main()
{
  int a, b, c;
  long int answer;
  printf("What is the first number to multiply? ");
  scanf(" %d", &a);
  printf("What is the second number to multiply? ");
  scanf(" %d", &b);
  printf("What is the third number to multiply? ");
  scanf(" %d", &c);
```

```
    answer = fMul3(a, b, c);   /* Passes three variables and
                                    returns the answer */
    printf("\nThose three values multiplied by each other "
           "equal %ld.", answer);
    /* It's okay to continue a string literal over two lines */
    return 0;
}
/*******************************************************/
long int fMul3(int var1, int var2, int var3)
{
    int locAnswer;
    locAnswer = var1 * var2 * var3;
    return (locAnswer);
}
```

Clue: This program uses the `long int` data type because the three integers might produce a large value when multiplied by each other.

Here is a sample output from this program:

```
What is the first number to multiply? 3
What is the second number to multiply? 4
What is the third number to multiply? 5

Those three values multiplied by each other equal 60.
```

NOTE

Notice that `main()` assigned the `fMul3()` return value to `answer`. `main()` had to do something with the value that was returned from `fMul3()`.

You can put an expression after `return` as well as variables. This:

```
sales = quantity * price;
return (sales);
```

is identical to this:

```
return (quantity * price);
```

The *Return* Data Type

At the beginning of the `fMul3()` function, you see `long int`. `long int` is the data type of the returned value `locAnswer`. You *must* put the return data type before any function name that returns a value. If the function returned a `float`, `float` would have to precede the function name.

If you don't specify a return data type, C assumes `int`. Therefore, C expects that every function without a return data type specified explicitly will return `int`. *Both* of these functions' first lines mean exactly the same thing to C:

```
int myFun(int a, float x, char c)
```

and

```
myFun(int a, float x, char c)   /* int is assumed */
```

Clue: Guess what? Even `main()` is assumed to return an `int` value unless you specify an overriding return data type. *That* is why you've seen `return 0;` at the end of most of these programs! Because `main()` has no specified return data type, `int` is assumed, and the `return 0;` ensures that an `int` is returned to DOS. DOS, by the way, just ignores the return data type unless you want to use the advanced DOS `errorlevel` command to receive the 0.

If your function doesn't return a value or if your function isn't passed a value, you can insert the keyword `void` for either the return data type or the parameter list or both. Therefore, the first line of a function that neither gets any value nor returns any value might look like this:

```
void doSomething(void)   /* Neither is passed nor returns */
```

SKIP THIS, IT'S TECHNICAL

`main()` can't be of type `void` if you use strict ANSI C. It must be of type `int`. (Most compilers, however, even those that promote themselves as ANSI C-compatible, enable you to specify `void` as `main()`'s return type.)

One Last Step: Prototype

There is one last step to making a function work properly. If a function returns any value other than `int`, you should *prototype* that function. Actually, you should prototype functions that return integers as well.

The word *prototype* means a model of something else. A prototype of a function is just a model of the actual function. At first, a C prototype seems like a total waste of time.

The reason functions that return `int` values don't need prototypes is because `int` is the default prototyped return value unless you specify a different return value. Therefore, these two prototypes *both* model the same function:

```
int aFunc(int x, float y);   /* 2 passed, one integer returned */
```

and

```
aFunc(int x, float y);   /* 2 passed, one integer returned */
```

NOTE

Prototypes aren't required if you don't return a value or if you return an integer value, but they are *strongly recommended.* Once you prototype, C ensures that you don't pass a `float` value to a function that expects to receive a `char`. Without the prototype, C would try to convert the `float` to a `char`, and a bad value would be passed as a result.

To prototype a function, place an exact duplicate of the function's first line somewhere before `main()`. The prototype for `fMul3()` appears right before `main()` in the program you saw earlier. The line is *not* a function call because it appears before `main()`. The line is not a function's actual first line because of the semicolon that follows all prototypes. The line is a function prototype. If your program calls 20 functions, you should have 20 prototypes.

Prototype every function in your programs—every function called by your code and even the built-in functions such as `printf()`. "Huh?" might be a good question at this point. You might wonder how you can prototype `printf()` when you didn't write it to begin with. The file STDIO.H contains a prototype for `printf()`, `scanf()`, `getchar()`, and many other input and output functions! The prototype for `strcpy()` appears in STRING.H. You should find out the name of the header file when you learn a new built-in function so that you can `#include` it and make sure that each function is prototyped.

SKIP THIS, IT'S TECHNICAL

You do not need to prototype `main()`. `main()` needs no prototype as long as you place `main()` as the first function in the program. `main()` is known as a *self-prototyping* function because no other functions call `main()` before `main()` appears in the code.

The following program does not work correctly because the `float` return type is not prototyped correctly. Remember, C assumes that an `int` is returned (even if you return a different data type) unless you override the return type in the prototype.

```c
#include <stdio.h>
compNet(float atomWeight, float factor);  /* Bad prototype */
main()
{
  float atomWeight, factor, netWeight;
  printf("What is the atomic weight? ");
  scanf(" %f", &atomWeight);
  printf("What is the factor? ");
  scanf(" %f", &factor);
  netWeight = compNet(atomWeight, factor);
```

```
      printf("The net weight is %.4f\n", netWeight);
      return 0;
}
/*********************************************************/
/* The function definition below doesn't work because the
   prototype does not indicate that a float is returned  */
compNet(float atomWeight, float factor)
{
   return ((atomWeight - factor) * .8);
}
```

This shows the incorrect output:

```
What is the atomic weight? .0125
What is the factor? .98
The net weight is 0.0000
```

To fix the problem, you have to change the prototype to this:

```
float compNet(float atomWeight, float factor);
```

and the `compNet()`'s definition line (its first line) to match the prototype like this:

```
float compNet(float atomWeight, float factor)
```

Wrapping Things Up

Never pass or return a global variable if you use one. Global variables don't have to be passed. Also, the parameter lists in the calling function, receiving function, and prototype should match in both numbers and data types. (The names of the values don't have to match.)

You now know everything there is to know about passing parameters and returning values. Put on your official programmer's thinking cap and start your C compiler!

Rewards

✖ Place the return data type before a function name that returns a value.

✖ The return value appears after a `return` statement.

✖ In the calling function, do something with the return value. Print it or assign it to something. Calling a function that returns a value is useless if you do nothing with the return value.

✖ Use void as the return data type or in the parameter list if you neither return nor pass values to a function.

Pitfalls

✖ Don't return more than one value from a function.

✖ Don't return a noninteger without a prototype. Better yet, prototype *all* functions except main( ).

In Review

The goal of this chapter was to round out your knowledge of functions by explaining prototypes and return values. When your program contains lots of functions, prototype those functions somewhere before `main()`. The prototypes tell C what to expect. After you prototype, you can pass and return variables of any data type. (You can return `int`s only if you don't prototype.)

The prototype ensures that you don't inadvertently pass the wrong data types to functions. For example, if the prototype states that you'll pass two `float`s to a function, but you accidentally pass two `int`s, C will complain. C won't complain if you don't prototype, and you might get wrong results because of it.

Now that you know how to return values, you can write functions that mirror those that are built in, such as `sqrt()` and `rand()`. When you call a function, that function returns a value based on the function's code. A function can return a maximum of one value, just like functions that are built in.

Code Example

```c
#include <stdio.h>
float divideIt(float numFromMain);   /* Prototype */
main()
{
  float myNum, half;
  printf("Please type a number: ");
  scanf(" %f", &myNum);
  half = divideIt(myNum);
  printf("Your number divided by two is %.1f.\n", half);
  return 0;
}
/************************************************************/
float divideIt(float numFromMain)
{
  float halfNum;
  halfNum = numFromMain / 2.0;   /* Divides main()'s number */
  return (halfNum);   /* Sends the halved value back */
}
```

Code Analysis

This program shows how to prototype and call a function that returns one-half the value passed to it. The prototype lets C know that the function named divideIt() receives and returns a floating-point value. Because divideIt()'s local variable can't be used in main(), its value is returned to main() and captured in main()'s variable named half.

It would be more efficient to divide the value by 2 in main(), but this example better demonstrates the concepts in this chapter. Here is a sample output from the program so you can see how it works:

```
Please type a number: 45.6
Your number divided by two is 22.8.
```

A

Where Do I Go from Here?

This appendix lists some books that you might want to read now that you know C. All these books are from Sams Publishing.

Teach Yourself C in 21 Days

With this best-selling book, users can achieve C success now! Each lesson can be completed in two to three hours or less. Shaded syntax boxes, Q & A sections, and "Do/Don't" sections reinforce the important topics of C. (Beginning to Intermediate)

Advanced C

Here's the next step for programmers who want to improve their C programming skills. This book gives efficiency tips and techniques for debugging C programs and improving their speed, memory usage, and readability. (Intermediate to Advanced)

Moving from C to C++

This book is an invaluable guide for C programmers who want to learn how to move from C to C++. It shows how one application written in C is converted to C++ with more efficient code. It includes tips and techniques for making the transition from C to C++ and shows the "why" of object-oriented programming before teaching the specifics. (Beginning to Intermediate)

C++ Programming 101

Readers take an active approach to learning C++ in this step-by-step tutorial/workbook. Special features such as Find the Bug, Try This, Think About..., Finish the Program, and Still Confused? give the reader a thorough understanding of the language. (Beginning)

Turbo C++ Programming 101

Readers take an active approach to learning Turbo C++ in this step-by-step tutorial/workbook. Special features such as Find the Bug, Try This, Think About..., Finish the Program, and Still Confused? give the reader a thorough understanding of the language.
(Beginning)

Advanced C++

This comprehensive guide is the next step for programmers who have achieved proficiency with the basics of C++ and want to learn about advanced topics.
(Intermediate to Advanced)

B

Playing Around with C Blackjack

Programming is not all work and no play, and the following Blackjack game proves it! The game provides a long example that you can study as you master C. Although the game has been kept extremely simple, a lot happens in this program.

As with all well-written programs, this one is commented thoroughly. In fact, if you have read each chapter of this book, you will understand the programming of Blackjack. One of the reasons the program is kept simple is to keep it compiler-independent. For example, there is no screen-clearing routine. The comments in the function named `dispTitle()` explain what you might want to do to add a fancier screen-clearing routine than the generic one provided. Also, you might want to find out how your C compiler produces colors on-screen so that you can add pizazz to the game's display.

Clue: Once you master enough of C to understand the program's inner workings, you'll want to explore graphics capabilities and actually draw the cards.

Numbers appear to the left of many code lines. These are the numbers of the chapters that discuss the concepts used in the lines. If a line confuses you, refer to the appropriate chapter.

```
1  /* Filename: BLAKJACK.C

3  This program plays a game of Blackjack with you. The
   computer is the dealer and you are the victim-er, I mean
   player. The dealer gets a card that you can see. The dealer
   then asks if you want another card by asking "Hit" or
   "Stand." If you choose to hit, the dealer gives you another
   card. If you choose to stand, the dealer draws or stands,
   and the game is played out according to the cards you and
   the dealer have. As with real Blackjack, the dealer stands
   on 17. The winner is announced only after both the player's
   and the dealer's hands are finished. */

   /*****************************************************************
   ANSI C standard header files appear next */
7  #include <stdio.h>
   #include <time.h>
```

```
#include <ctype.h>
#include <stdlib.h>

/***************************************************************
Defined constants appear next */
#define BELL '\a'
#define DEALER 0
#define PLAYER 1

/* Must keep two sets of totals for dealer and for player. The
first set counts Aces as 1 and the second counts Aces as
11. Unlike "real world" Blackjack, this program doesn't
allow some Aces to be 1 while others Aces are 11 in the
same hand. */
#define ACELOW 0
#define ACEHIGH 1
/* Only one global variable is used in this entire program.
The variable holds 0, which means false initially. Once the
user enters his or her name in initCardsScreen(), this
variable is set to 1 (for true), so the name is never asked
for again the rest of the program. */
int askedForName = 0;  /* False initially */
/***************************************************************
This program's specific prototypes */
void dispTitle(void);
void initCardsScreen(int cards[52], int playerPoints[2],
int dealerPoints[2], int total[2],
int * numCards);
int  dealCard(int * numCards, int cards[52]);
void dispCard(int cardDrawn, int points[2]);
void totalIt(int points[2], int total[2], int who);
void dealerGetsCard(int *numCards, int cards[52],
int dealerPoints[2]);
void playerGetsCard(int *numCards, int cards[52],
int playerPoints[2]);
char getAns(char mesg[]);
void findWinner(int total[2]);

/***************************************************************
C's program execution always begins at main() here */
main()
{
int numCards;  /* Equals 52 at beginning of each game */
int cards[52], playerPoints[2], dealerPoints[2], total[2];
char ans;  /* For user's Hit/Stand or Yes/No response */
do { initCardsScreen(cards, playerPoints, dealerPoints,
total, &numCards);
```

The left-margin numbers alongside the listing are:
7, 7, 5, 32, 2, 5, 21, 14, 24

```
31  dealerGetsCard(&numCards, cards, dealerPoints);
 4  printf("\n");  /* Prints a blank line */
31  playerGetsCard(&numCards, cards, playerPoints);
    playerGetsCard(&numCards, cards, playerPoints);
14  do {
31  ans = getAns("Hit or stand (H/S)? ");
11  if (ans == 'H')
31  {  playerGetsCard(&numCards, cards,
    playerPoints);
    }
    } while (ans != 'S');
31  totalIt(playerPoints, total, PLAYER);
    /* Player's total */
14  do {
31  dealerGetsCard(&numCards, cards, dealerPoints);
    } while (dealerPoints[ACEHIGH] < 17);
    /* 17: Dealer stops */
    totalIt(dealerPoints, total, DEALER);
    /* Dealer's total */
    findWinner(total);
    ans = getAns("\nPlay again (Y/N)? ");
    } while (ans == 'Y');
32  return;
    }


 3  /*************************************************************
    This function initializes the face values of the deck of
    cards by putting four sets of 1-13 in the 52-card array. Also
    clears the screen and displays a title. */
30  void initCardsScreen(int cards[52], int playerPoints[2],
    int dealerPoints[2], int total[2],
    int *numCards)
    {
 5  int sub, val = 1;  /* This function's Work variables */
 6  char firstName[15];  /* Holds user's first name */
21  *numCards = 52;  /* Holds running total of
                         number of cards */
15  for (sub = 0; sub <= 51; sub++)  {  /* Counts from
                                           0 to 51 */
13  val = (val == 14) ? 1 : val;  /* If val is 14,
                                      reset to 1 */
21  cards[sub] = val;
13  val++;  }
15  for (sub = 0; sub <= 1; sub++)  /* Counts from 0 to 1 */
 9  { playerPoints[sub]=dealerPoints[sub]=total[sub]=0; }
31  dispTitle();
11  if (askedForName == 0)  /* Name asked for only once */
```

```
 4  { printf("\nWhat is your first name? ");
 8  scanf(" %s", firstName);
 5  askedForName = 1;  /* Don't ask prompt again */
 4  printf("Ok, %s, get ready for casino action!\n\n",
        firstName);
18  getchar();  /* Discards newline. You can safely */
    }            /* ignore compiler warning here.    */
32  return;
    }


 3  /****************************************************************
    This function gets a card for the player and updates the
    player's points. */
30  void playerGetsCard(int *numCards, int cards[52],
    int playerPoints[2])
    {
 5  int newCard;
31  newCard = dealCard(numCards, cards);
 4  printf("You draw: ");
31  dispCard(newCard, playerPoints);
    }


 3  /****************************************************************
    This function gets a card for the dealer and updates the
    dealer's points. */
30  void dealerGetsCard(int *numCards, int cards[52],
    int dealerPoints[2])
    {
 5  int newCard;
31  newCard = dealCard(numCards, cards);
 4  printf("The dealer draws: ");
31  dispCard(newCard, dealerPoints);
    }


 3  /****************************************************************
    This function gets a card from the deck and stores it in
    either the dealer's or the player's hold of cards. */
    int dealCard(int * numCards, int cards[52])
    {
 5  int cardDrawn, subDraw;
    time_t t;  /* Gets time for a random value */
20  srand(time(&t));  /* Seeds random-number generator */
    subDraw = (rand() % (*numCards));  /* From 0 to numcards */
    cardDrawn = cards[subDraw];
24  cards[subDraw] = cards[*numCards --1];  /* Puts top card */
24  (*numCards)-;                 /* in place of drawn one */
32  return cardDrawn;
    }
```

```
 3  /****************************************************************
    Displays the last-drawn card and updates points with it. */
30  void dispCard(int cardDrawn, int points[2])
    {
17  switch (cardDrawn) {
    case(11) : printf("%s\n", "Jack");
10  points[ACELOW] += 10;
21  points[ACEHIGH] += 10;
16  break;
    case(12) : printf("%s\n", "Queen");
10  points[ACELOW] += 10;
21  points[ACEHIGH] += 10;
16  break;
    case(13) : printf("%s\n", "King");
10  points[ACELOW] += 10;
21  points[ACEHIGH] += 10;
16  break;
    default :  points[ACELOW] += cardDrawn;
11  if (cardDrawn == 1)
    { printf("%s\n", "Ace");
10    points[ACEHIGH] += 11;
    }
    else
10  {   points[ACEHIGH] += cardDrawn;
 4      printf("%d\n", cardDrawn); }
    }
32  return;
    }


 3  /****************************************************************
    Figures the total for player or dealer to see who won. This
    function takes into account the fact that Ace is either 1
    or 11. */
28  void totalIt(int points[2], int total[2], int who)
    {
 3  /* The following routine first looks to see if the total
    points counting Aces as 1 is equal to the total points
    counting Aces as 11. If so, or if the total points
    counting Aces as 11 is more than 21, the program uses
    the total with Aces as 1 only. */
11  if ((points[ACELOW] == points[ACEHIGH]) ||
    (points[ACEHIGH] > 21))
21  { total[who] = points[ACELOW]; }   /* Keeps all Aces
                                           as 1 */

    else
21  { total[who] = points[ACEHIGH]; }  /* Keeps all Aces
                                           as 11 */
```

```
11 if (who == PLAYER)   /* Determines the message printed */
 4 { printf("You have a total of %d\n\n", total[PLAYER]); }
   else
   { printf("The house stands with a total of %d\n\n",
               total[DEALER]); }
32 return;
   }


 3 /****************************************************************
   Prints the winning player.   */
   void findWinner(int total[2])
   {
11 if (total[DEALER] == 21)
 4 { printf("The house wins.\n");
32   return;}
12 if ((total[DEALER] > 21) && (total[PLAYER] > 21))
 4 { printf("%s", "Nobody wins.\n");
32   return; }
12 if ((total[DEALER]>=total[PLAYER])&&(total[DEALER]<21))
 4 { printf("The house wins.\n");
32   return; }
12 if ((total[PLAYER] > 21) && (total[DEALER] < 21))
 4 { printf("The house wins.\n");
32   return; }
 4 printf("%s%c", "You win!\n", BELL);
32   return;
   }


 3 /****************************************************************
   Gets the user's uppercase, single-character response. */
30 char getAns(char mesg[])
   {
 5 char ans;
 4 printf("%s", mesg);  /* Prints the prompt message passed */
18 ans = getchar();
   getchar();  /* Discards newline. You can safely */
               /* ignore compiler warning here.    */
19 return toupper(ans);
   }


 3 /****************************************************************
   Clears everything off the screen. */
30 void dispTitle(void)
   {
 5 int i = 0;
14 while (i < 25)     /* Clears screen by printing 25 blank */
 4 { printf("\n");    /* lines to "push off" stuff that     */
```

```
   i++; }            /* might be left over on the screen    */
                     /* before this program               */
 4 printf("\n\n*Step right up to the Blackjack tables*\n\n");
32 return;
   }
```

C

The ASCII Table

Dec X_{10}	Hex X_{16}	Binary X_2	ASCII Character
000	00	0000 0000	null
001	01	0000 0001	☺
002	02	0000 0010	☻
003	03	0000 0011	♥
004	04	0000 0100	♦
005	05	0000 0101	♣
006	06	0000 0110	♠
007	07	0000 0111	●
008	08	0000 1000	■
009	09	0000 1001	○
010	0A	0000 1010	■
011	0B	0000 1011	♂
012	0C	0000 1100	♀
013	0D	0000 1101	♪
014	0E	0000 1110	♪♪
015	0F	0000 1111	☼
016	10	0001 0000	►
017	11	0001 0001	◄
018	12	0001 0010	↕
019	13	0001 0011	‼
020	14	0001 0100	¶
021	15	0001 0101	§
022	16	0001 0110	▬
023	17	0001 0111	↨
024	18	0001 1000	↑
025	19	0001 1001	↓

Dec X_{10}	Hex X_{16}	Binary X_2	ASCII Character
026	1A	0001 1010	→
027	1B	0001 1011	←
028	1C	0001 1100	FS
029	1D	0001 1101	GS
030	1E	0001 1110	RS
031	1F	0001 1111	US
032	20	0010 0000	SP
033	21	0010 0001	!
034	22	0010 0010	"
035	23	0010 0011	#
036	24	0010 0100	$
037	25	0010 0101	%
038	26	0010 0110	&
039	27	0010 0111	'
040	28	0010 1000	(
041	29	0010 1001	)
042	2A	0010 1010	*
043	2B	0010 1011	+
044	2C	0010 1100	,
045	2D	0010 1101	-
046	2E	0010 1110	.
047	2F	0010 1111	/
048	30	0011 0000	0
049	31	0011 0001	1
050	32	0011 0010	2
051	33	0011 0011	3
052	34	0011 0100	4

Dec X_{10}	Hex X_{16}	Binary X_2	ASCII Character
053	35	0011 0101	5
054	36	0011 0110	6
055	37	0011 0111	7
056	38	0011 1000	8
057	39	0011 1001	9
058	3A	0011 1010	:
059	3B	0011 1011	;
060	3C	0011 1100	<
061	3D	0011 1101	=
062	3E	0011 1110	>
063	3F	0011 1111	?
064	40	0100 0000	@
065	41	0100 0001	A
066	42	0100 0010	B
067	43	0100 0011	C
068	44	0100 0100	D
069	45	0100 0101	E
070	46	0100 0110	F
071	47	0100 0111	G
072	48	0100 1000	H
073	49	0100 1001	I
074	4A	0100 1010	J
075	4B	0100 1011	K
076	4C	0100 1100	L
077	4D	0100 1101	M
078	4E	0100 1110	N
079	4F	0100 1111	O
080	50	0101 0000	P

Dec X_{10}	Hex X_{16}	Binary X_2	ASCII Character
081	51	0101 0001	Q
082	52	0101 0010	R
083	53	0101 0011	S
084	54	0101 0100	T
085	55	0101 0101	U
086	56	0101 0110	V
087	57	0101 0111	W
088	58	0101 1000	X
089	59	0101 1001	Y
090	5A	0101 1010	Z
091	5B	0101 1011	[
092	5C	0101 1100	\
093	5D	0101 1101	]
094	5E	0101 1110	^
095	5F	0101 1111	—
096	60	0110 0000	`
097	61	0110 0001	a
098	62	0110 0010	b
099	63	0110 0011	c
100	64	0110 0100	d
101	65	0110 0101	e
102	66	0110 0110	f
103	67	0110 0111	g
104	68	0110 1000	h
105	69	0110 1001	i
106	6A	0110 1010	j
107	6B	0110 1011	k
108	6C	0110 1100	l

Dec X_{10}	Hex X_{16}	Binary X_2	ASCII Character
109	6D	0110 1101	m
110	6E	0110 1110	n
111	6F	0110 1111	o
112	70	0111 0000	p
113	71	0111 0001	q
114	72	0111 0010	r
115	73	0111 0011	s
116	74	0111 0100	t
117	75	0111 0101	u
118	76	0111 0110	v
119	77	0111 0111	w
120	78	0111 1000	x
121	79	0111 1001	y
122	7A	0111 1010	z
123	7B	0111 1011	{
124	7C	0111 1100	¦
125	7D	0111 1101	}
126	7E	0111 1110	~
127	7F	0111 1111	DEL
128	80	1000 0000	Ç
129	81	1000 0001	ü
130	82	1000 0010	é
131	83	1000 0011	â
132	84	1000 0100	ä
133	85	1000 0101	à
134	86	1000 0110	å
135	87	1000 0111	ç
136	88	1000 1000	ê

Dec X_{10}	Hex X_{16}	Binary X_2	ASCII Character
137	89	1000 1001	ë
138	8A	1000 1010	è
139	8B	1000 1011	ï
140	8C	1000 1100	î
141	8D	1000 1101	ì
142	8E	1000 1110	Ä
143	8F	1000 1111	Å
144	90	1001 0000	É
145	91	1001 0001	æ
146	92	1001 0010	Æ
147	93	1001 0011	ô
148	94	1001 0100	ö
149	95	1001 0101	ò
150	96	1001 0110	û
151	97	1001 0111	ù
152	98	1001 1000	ÿ
153	99	1001 1001	Ö
154	9A	1001 1010	Ü
155	9B	1001 1011	¢
156	9C	1001 1100	£
157	9D	1001 1101	¥
158	9E	1001 1110	P$_t$
159	9F	1001 1111	ƒ
160	A0	1010 0000	á
161	A1	1010 0001	í
162	A2	1010 0010	ó
163	A3	1010 0011	ú
164	A4	1010 0100	ñ

Dec X_{10}	Hex X_{16}	Binary X_2	ASCII Character
165	A5	1010 0101	Ñ
166	A6	1010 0110	ª
167	A7	1010 0111	º
168	A8	1010 1000	¿
169	A9	1010 1001	⌐
170	AA	1010 1010	¬
171	AB	1010 1011	½
172	AC	1010 1100	¼
173	AD	1010 1101	¡
174	AE	1010 1110	«
175	AF	10101111	
176	B0	1011 0000	
177	B1	1011 0001	
178	B2	1011 0010	
179	B3	1011 0011	│
180	B4	1011 0100	┤
181	B5	1011 0101	╡
182	B6	1011 0110	╢
183	B7	1011 0111	╖
184	B8	1011 1000	╕
185	B9	1011 1001	╣
186	BA	1011 1010	║
187	BB	1011 1011	╗
188	BC	1011 1100	╝
189	BD	1011 1101	╜
190	BE	1011 1110	╛
191	BF	1011 1111	┐
192	C0	1100 0000	└

Dec X_{10}	Hex X_{16}	Binary X_2	ASCII Character
193	C1	1100 0001	⊥
194	C2	1100 0010	⊤
195	C3	1100 0011	├
196	C4	1100 0100	—
197	C5	1100 0101	+
198	C6	1100 0110	
199	C7	1100 0111	╟
200	C8	1100 1000	╚
201	C9	1100 1001	╔
202	CA	1100 1010	╩
203	CB	1100 1011	╦
204	CC	1100 1100	╠
205	CD	1100 1101	=
206	CE	1100 1110	╬
207	CF	1100 1111	╧
208	D0	1101 0000	╨
209	D1	1101 0001	╤
210	D2	1101 0010	╥
211	D3	1101 0011	╙
212	D4	1101 0100	╘
213	D5	1101 0101	╒
214	D6	1101 0110	╓
215	D7	1101 0111	╫
216	D8	1101 1000	╪
217	D9	1101 1001	┘
218	DA	1101 1010	┌
219	DB	1101 1011	█
220	DC	1101 1100	▄
221	DD	1101 1101	▌

Dec X_{10}	Hex X_{16}	Binary X_2	ASCII Character
222	DE	1101 1110	▮
223	DF	1101 1111	■
224	E0	1110 0000	α
225	E1	1110 0001	β
226	E2	1110 0010	Γ
227	E3	1110 0011	π
228	E4	1110 0100	Σ
229	E5	1110 0101	σ
230	E6	1110 0110	μ
231	E7	1110 0111	τ
232	E8	1110 1000	Φ
233	E9	1110 1001	θ
234	EA	1110 1010	Ω
235	EB	1110 1011	δ
236	EC	1110 1100	∞
237	ED	1110 1101	ø
238	EE	1110 1110	∈
239	EF	1110 1111	∩
240	F0	1110 0000	≡
241	F1	1111 0001	±
242	F2	1111 0010	≥
243	F3	1111 0011	≤
244	F4	1111 0100	⌠
245	F5	1111 0101	⌡
246	F6	1111 0110	÷
247	F7	1111 0111	≈
248	F8	1111 1000	°
249	F9	1111 1001	•

Dec X_{10}	Hex X_{16}	Binary X_2	ASCII Character
250	FA	1111 1010	.
251	FB	1111 1011	√
252	FC	1111 1100	η
253	FD	1111 1101	2
254	FE	1111 1110	■
255	FF	1111 1111	

Index

Symbols

GO AHEAD. PLUG YOURSELF INTO
PRENTICE HALL COMPUTER PUBLISHING.
Introducing the PHCP Forum on CompuServe®

Yes, it's true. Now, you can have CompuServe access to the same professional, friendly folks who have made computers easier for years. On the PHCP Forum, you'll find additional information on the topics covered by every PHCP imprint—including Que, Sams Publishing, New Riders Publishing, Alpha Books, Brady Books, Hayden Books, and Adobe Press. In addition, you'll be able to receive technical support and disk updates for the software produced by Que Software and Paramount Interactive, a division of the Paramount Technology Group. It's a great way to supplement the best information in the business.

WHAT CAN YOU DO ON THE PHCP FORUM?

Play an important role in the publishing process—and make our books better while you make your work easier:

- Leave messages and ask questions about PHCP books and software—you're guaranteed a response within 24 hours

- Download helpful tips and software to help you get the most out of your computer

- Contact authors of your favorite PHCP books through electronic mail

- Present your own book ideas

- Keep up to date on all the latest books available from each of PHCP's exciting imprints

JOIN NOW AND GET A FREE COMPUSERVE STARTER KIT!

To receive your free CompuServe Introductory Membership, call toll-free, **1-800-848-8199** and ask for representative **#597**. The Starter Kit Includes:

- Personal ID number and password

- $15 credit on the system

- Subscription to CompuServe Magazine

HERE'S HOW TO PLUG INTO PHCP:

Once on the CompuServe System, type any of these phrases to access the PHCP Forum:

GO PHCP　　　　　　**GO BRADY**
GO QUEBOOKS　　　 **GO HAYDEN**
GO SAMS　　　　　　 **GO QUESOFT**
GO NEWRIDERS　　　 **GO PARAMOUNTINTER**
GO ALPHA

Once you're on the CompuServe Information Service, be sure to take advantage of all of CompuServe's resources. CompuServe is home to more than 1,700 products and services—plus it has over 1.5 million members worldwide. You'll find valuable online reference materials, travel and investor services, electronic mail, weather updates, leisure-time games and hassle-free shopping (no jam-packed parking lots or crowded stores).

Seek out the hundreds of other forums that populate CompuServe. Covering diverse topics such as pet care, rock music, cooking, and political issues, you're sure to find others with the sames concerns as you—and expand your knowledge at the same time.

CIBC

1 800 387 5627

1 800 387 5627